Requiem for Reconstruction

THE JOHN HOPE FRANKLIN SERIES IN AFRICAN AMERICAN HISTORY AND CULTURE

Waldo E. Martin Jr. and Patricia Sullivan, *editors*

The best scholarship in African American history and culture compels us to expand our sense of who we are as a nation and forces us to engage seriously the experiences of all Americans who have shaped the development of this country. By publishing pathbreaking books informed by several disciplines, the John Hope Franklin Series in African American History and Culture seeks to illuminate America's multicultural past and the ways in which it has informed the nation's democratic experiment.

A complete list of books published in the John Hope Franklin Series in African American History and Culture is available at https://uncpress.org/series/the-john-hope-franklin-series-in-african-american-history-and-culture.

ROBERT D. BLAND

Requiem for Reconstruction
Black Countermemory and the Legacy of the Lowcountry's Lost Political Generation

The University of North Carolina Press *Chapel Hill*

© 2026 The University of North Carolina Press
All rights reserved
Set in Arno by codeMantra
Manufactured in the United States of America

Cover art: *Left*: Robert Smalls, ca. 1875. Brady-Handy Photograph Collection, Prints and Photographs Division, Library of Congress. *Right*: William J. Whipper, 1882. New York Public Library. *Background*: Seascape of Hilton Head Island © Adobe Stock/Peter Lakomy.

Library of Congress Cataloging-in-Publication Data
Names: Bland, Robert D. author
Title: Requiem for Reconstruction : Black countermemory and the legacy of the Lowcountry's lost political generation / Robert D. Bland.
Other titles: John Hope Franklin series in African American history and culture
Description: Chapel Hill : University of North Carolina Press, [2026] | Series: The John Hope Franklin series in African American history and culture | Includes bibliographical references and index.
Identifiers: LCCN 2025032996 | ISBN 9781469691862 cloth alk. paper | ISBN 9781469691879 paperback alk. paper | ISBN 9781469688756 epub | ISBN 9781469691886 pdf
Subjects: LCSH: Smalls, Robert, 1839–1915 | Republican Party (S.C.)—History—19th century | African Americans—South Carolina—History—19th century | African Americans—Political Activity—South Carolina | Reconstruction (U.S. history, 1865–1877)—South Carolina | Collective memory—South Carolina | South Carolina—Politics and government—19th century | BISAC: SOCIAL SCIENCE / Ethnic Studies / American / African American & Black Studies | SOCIAL SCIENCE / Race & Ethnic Relations
Classification: LCC E185.93.S7 B53 2026 | DDC 975.7/041—dc23/eng/20250904
LC record available at https://lccn.loc.gov/2025032996

For product safety concerns under the European Union's General Product Safety Regulation (EU GPSR), please contact gpsr@mare-nostrum.co.uk or write to the University of North Carolina Press and Mare Nostrum Group B.V., Mauritskade 21D, 1091 GC Amsterdam, The Netherlands.

To the memory of my grandfathers and grandmothers

Robert Edward Bland (1921–1997)
David Leon Henderson (1925–2009)
Ruth Elizabeth Bumbry Bland (1924–2016)
Mabel Black Henderson (1926–2017)

Contents

List of Illustrations ix

Introduction 1

Part I
The Making of the Lowcountry's Rival Political World

CHAPTER ONE
A Great Movement in South Carolina: The Black Port Royal Experiment and the Origins of Postbellum Racial Destiny 21

CHAPTER TWO
A Multiple-Front Memory War: Redemption and Remembering Reconstruction-Era Violence 42

CHAPTER THREE
The Rise of the Black Seventh: Racial Gerrymandering, Rival Geography, and the Struggle over the Republican Party's Destiny in South Carolina 64

Part II
The Postbellum Public Sphere and the Production of Black Countermemory

CHAPTER FOUR
Reconstruction's Last Congressman: The Gilded Age Black Public Sphere and the Battle over Robert Smalls's Legacy 81

CHAPTER FIVE
More Good from Nazareth: The Lowcountry's Long Reconstruction, Disfranchisement, and Archiving Countermemory at the Century's End 107

Part III
The Afterlife of the Reconstruction Generation

CHAPTER SIX
The Jim Crow Generation: Black Teachers, the Industrial School Movement, and the Educational Battle over Reconstruction's Legacy in the Segregated South 135

CHAPTER SEVEN
Requiem for Reconstruction: The Great Migration, Interwar African American History, and the Afterlife of the Reconstruction Generation 157

Epilogue 183

Acknowledgments 189

Notes 193

Bibliography 215

Index 241

Illustrations

FIGURES

Portrait of Judge W. J. Whipper 2
Miss Frances Anne Rollin 23
Freedmen's Bureau in Beaufort 29
Advertisement for Whipper, Elliott, and Allen 35
"The Late Rev. B. F. Randolph" 43
"In Memoriam: B. F. Randolph" 46
Illustration of 1877 Emancipation Day in Charleston 50
Handbill for the 1876 mass meeting on the Hamburg Massacre 54
Chromolithograph of major Black leaders, including Robert Smalls 92
Lithograph of Robert Smalls 93
Metropolitan AME Church 95
Antoinette Norvell's history class 134
USCT veterans in Beaufort, South Carolina 147
Penn School teachers' group 151
Hastings Gantt 154
Women viewing the Gantt Cottage 155
Robert Smalls's obituary 158
"The Last of the 'Old Guard'" 161
"From Slavery to Reconstruction" 179
Paradise Room in Small's Paradise 180
Robert Smalls High School marching band 186
Archivist Sara Dunlap Jackson 187

MAPS

Southeast United States 11
1872 presidential election results in South Carolina by county 47

1876 presidential election results in South Carolina by county 57

South Carolina counties, 1871–1877 59

South Carolina counties, 1878–1907 59

1880 presidential election results in South Carolina by county 67

1882 South Carolina gubernatorial election results by county 69

"The Congressional Districts of South Carolina, as 'Gerrymandered' by the Democracy in 1882" 74

1892 presidential election results in South Carolina by county 121

1900 presidential election results in South Carolina by county 143

1912 presidential election results in South Carolina by county 162

Requiem for Reconstruction

Introduction

They can't bulldoze us here, for we're too strong, but all the rest of the State they will manipulate.
—Robert Smalls

I have long felt that the last opportunity to collect data concerning this interesting period in our history is while this present generation lives. The next generation will have no interest in it.
—Helen James Chisholm

No requiem, save the night wind, has been sung over their dead bodies.
—Ida B. Wells

On January 23, 1883, a group of Black citizens convened for the Bethel Literary and Historical Society's weekly meeting at the Metropolitan African Methodist Episcopal (AME) Church in Washington, DC. Despite the bitter cold, the church's auxiliary building, Bethel Hall, was packed, and the attendees filled the meeting space to hear and participate in the city's most prestigious lyceum. That night's keynote lecture was on the subject of "Reconstruction." The lecturer, William J. Whipper, was the nephew of one of the country's most prominent Black abolitionists, a veteran of the United States Colored Troops, and a former agent for the Freedmen's Bureau in the South Carolina Lowcountry. After the Civil War, he helped found the state's first chapter of the Republican Party, served as a delegate at the 1868 constitutional convention, and held an elected position in the South Carolina General Assembly in the 1870s. Denied an appointment to South Carolina's circuit court by the state's moderate Republican governor, Whipper had become demonized in the white press, North and South. In the Black world and Black press, however, he remained popular and now split time between the Lowcountry county of Beaufort, where he was a probate judge, and Washington, DC, where his wife Frances Anne Rollin Whipper held an appointed clerical position in the Department of the Interior.[1]

In what was likely one of the lyceum's most controversial speeches of the year, Whipper argued that Reconstruction had been a failure and laid the blame directly on the leaders of South Carolina's Republican Party. Lambasting members of his own party for being "venal, corrupt, and immoral," Whipper's attack on South Carolina's Republicans angered many in the crowd. "One

Judge William J. Whipper, 1882. Schomburg Center for Research in Black Culture, New York Public Library, New York.

would judge that South Carolina was the only State that was reconstructed," remarked one of the nation's most prominent Black newspapers.[2]

Another speaker noted that Whipper had faced accusations about his own moral character during Reconstruction. "Men whose personal records are so vulnerable should be kept in the political graves to which Mr. Hayes [President Rutherford B. Hayes] had consigned them," exclaimed prominent Washington businessman J. P. Waddleton, "and not try to parade themselves as political martyrs."[3]

While a full account of that Tuesday night's debate has not been preserved, John W. Cromwell, one of the founders of the Bethel Literary and Historical Society, would later recall that Whipper put forth a "conservative position" and argued that Reconstruction's collapse should be attributed "to bad legislation enacted by the Republicans." While some members of the audience agreed with his position on the era's legacy, many rejected his claims about this imagined failure—because they had been his political colleagues. By the early 1880s, many of the South's former Republican leaders now lived in Washington, and several of South Carolina's previous luminaries were in attendance for Whipper's speech. Among them were Francis Lewis Cardozo, a Charlestonian who had been South Carolina's secretary of state, and Richard T. Greener, who had briefly been a professor at the University of South Carolina during the Reconstruction era and now served as dean of the Howard University Law School. Most important, the Civil War hero and current South Carolina congressman Robert Smalls offered a response filled with "anger and conviction." Both men began their political careers in the Reconstruction-era Lowcountry, and they had been longtime political rivals. Now one of the last Black men still serving in Congress, Smalls had embodied, in his life and political career, the counterargument to the claim that Reconstruction had failed.[4]

The seemingly serendipitous clash between two Lowcountry officeholders in one of Black America's most august intellectual spaces was not happenstance. More than any other site in late nineteenth-century Black America, the Lowcountry had come to represent the zenith of the previous generation's political ambition. The site of a larger "rehearsal for Reconstruction," the Lowcountry not only attracted a wide-ranging cohort of antislavery Northerners hoping to lay the foundation of a postslavery world but also served as a beacon for Black Americans seeking to capture the broadest political promise of the new era. And, for a rising generation of Black writers, journalists, and amateur historians, the legacy of the Reconstruction-era Lowcountry was freighted with both the promise and peril of the race's future. In this way, the debate about Reconstruction, between two Reconstruction-era Lowcountry politicians, in a room meant to embody the pinnacle of their generation's intellectual aspirations, highlights an emergent cultural architecture that now united the once disparate nodes of late nineteenth-century Black America.[5]

Requiem for Reconstruction retraces the cultural history of the political world that William Whipper, Robert Smalls, and countless others established during the Civil War, struggled to preserve during the Gilded Age, and continued to commemorate during the nadir of the Jim Crow era. Connecting the local political battles in the postbellum South to the ongoing national struggle over sectional reconciliation and Reconstruction's place in national collective memory, this book highlights how the Lowcountry remained a pivotal site of Black countermemory in the half century that followed the removal of federal troops from the region. In so doing, this book argues that the broad cohort of Black Americans in the orbit of the late nineteenth century's Republican Party used the Lowcountry's Reconstruction-era political history to produce and preserve a rival memory of Reconstruction. These historical practices not only provided a foundational pillar for late nineteenth-century ideas of racial destiny but also structured an emergent intellectual spirit that would eventually give shape to the modern discipline of African American history.

At the center of my book is a cohort that shaped and defended this countermemory—a group that I call the "Reconstruction generation." A broad and diverse assembly of Black Americans, this generation experienced Reconstruction as the formative political moment of their youth and spent the rest of their lives preserving the era's legacy. They were largely born between 1840 and 1860, so while its oldest Southern-born members would have a deep understanding of life in bondage, most of the generation would spend their adult lives in freedom. This generation included the first group of Black Americans to attend school in South and graduate from the region's newly formed Black colleges as well as the nation's elite universities. Educational attainment and academic ambition would become the defining feature of this generation's leaders, animating their arguments about the proper direction of the race's future, organizing debates about postbellum schools and their curricula, and shaping who would have power over the production of the Black past.[6]

Most important, they were the first generation of Black Americans to experience widespread enfranchisement. By either bondage, restrictive state law, or lack of a viable political geography that would support Black officeholding, nearly all Black Americans were barred from both the ballot box and political office before Reconstruction. In the aftermath of the 1867 Reconstruction Act, which mandated the creation of new state constitutions that guaranteed universal manhood suffrage for readmission into the Union, and the ratification of the Fifteenth Amendment, new political geographies emerged across the South that would elect Black officeholders.[7]

Recognizing this transformative generational shift as it was happening, Black Northerners of means and ambition flocked to the South. The group of teachers, missionaries, soldiers, Freedmen's Bureau agents, journalists, and lawyers who traveled to the South during the Civil War era were at the vanguard of the Reconstruction generation. While spread across the region, Black Northerners saw the Lowcountry as the epicenter of their generation's most important social movement. The wartime Lowcountry served as the opening chapter of a broader postbellum cultural milieu; it became a Black political mecca, the likes of which had never been seen in the United States. Put another way, the generation who traveled south had a tangible sense that they were entering a new era in Black history that would profoundly alter the destiny of the race.

However, as the Republican Party was violently overthrown in the South and abandoned by politicians and cultural elites in the North, the Reconstruction generation was slowly erased from national memory. Initially hypervisible, both as heroic figures in the public sphere that orbited the Republican Party and as villains in much of the white South, the Black voters and officeholders who had been central in shaping the political story of Reconstruction were now treated as discordant notes that could not be blended with the new harmony of sectional reconciliation. By the end of the century, the Reconstruction generation not only faded from nineteenth-century American political life but also found themselves being written out of both academic and popular accounts of the Civil War era. In a sense, this cohort, as a political generation, became "lost."

More specifically, the Reconstruction generation would become lost in three ways. First, this political generation ceased to exist as an electoral bloc during their own lifetime. Experiencing a series of legal and extralegal attacks in the decades that followed the end of federal occupation of the South, Black voters in the South were formally disfranchised by the wave of new state constitutions passed at the turn of the century; two decades later, the remaining federally appointed Black officeholders in the region would be removed by Woodrow Wilson's segregationist administration. Second, the Reconstruction generation's legacy was silenced in the nation's collective memory by the architects of the Lost Cause. In what became the dominant accounting of the Civil War era, academic historians, Southern civic organizations, and Northern elites in the public sphere erased the complex and wide-ranging accounts of the Black Northerners and freedpeople who built the postbellum South's new political world. The story of the Reconstruction generation was flattened into a myth of "Negro domination." Finally, this cohort, like the post–World War I Lost Generation in Western Europe, experienced the psychic and spiritual toll of seeing their central political project shattered.[8]

Here, the "requiem" in this book's title seeks to capture the funereal dimension of the Reconstruction generation's cultural afterlife. More than simply embodying the chimerical dream of multiracial democracy, Reconstruction's defeat left its former architects with a deep sense of tragedy that shaped the cadence of their memorial practices. David Blight has observed that early debates on Reconstruction had the "tones of a requiem." At the 1889 National Colored Press Convention in Washington, DC, *Richmond Planet* editor John Mitchell Jr. drew on this elegiac framework in his keynote speech at the convention, in which he cited Ida B. Wells's praise for the *Richmond Planet*'s efforts to list the victims of Southern lynching. Wells had lamented, "No requiem, save the night wind, had been sung over their dead bodies. No memorial service to bemoan their sad and horrible fate had before been held in their memory, and no record of the time and place of their taking off, save this [the *Richmond Planet*'s list], is extant; and like many a brave Union soldier their bodies lie in many an unknown and unhonored spot."[9]

Wells's lament for a missing requiem and the various ways that the rising generation of journalists and their national newspaper networks amplified her message highlight an emergent cultural architecture of postbellum Black countermemory. For the Reconstruction generation, remembering the recent Black past required a new set of historical practices, including new archives to preserve Black accounts of postbellum Southern political history, new forms of grassroots political culture to allow for the practice of Black countermemory in local communities, and new networks in the national Black press to share updates on the fate of Republican Party politics in the South. Ultimately, the Reconstruction generation would need to develop a deeper interpretive framework for understanding the relationship between the Civil War era and the world that they now occupied. Over the next half century, Wells and the generation of writers, scholars, and activists who followed in her footsteps would transform their requiem into the modern intellectual foundation of African American history.[10]

Race, Reunion, and the Legacy of Reconstruction

In examining the Reconstruction generation's long struggle to produce and preserve a Black countermemory, this book enters a broader historiographical debate about the shape of sectional reconciliation. An extended cultural process that pushed far beyond the immediate moment of national reunion during the 1860s and 1870s, sectional reconciliation served as a long debate over the meaning of the Civil War, the legacy of Reconstruction, and how the nation would recount the postbellum past in national and collective memory. Inextricably linked to late nineteenth-century anxieties about gendered and racial hierarchy, historians of sectional reconciliation have debated the extent to which the cultural project of sectional reconciliation was seized by a Southern elite seeking to elevate the myth of the Lost Cause into the national collective memory. In this retelling, Northern intellectuals and cultural elites embraced the white Southern accounting of Reconstruction's failure, which, in turn, pushed continued federal defense of Black Southern civil and political rights outside the window of viable policymaking—and thus opening the door for disfranchisement, segregation, and the rise of the one-bloc Solid South.[11]

Black efforts to preserve a countermemory of Reconstruction occurred as the South was beginning to win the larger cultural struggle over sectional reconciliation. As Southern civic organizations reshaped the region's commemorative landscape and dotted the region's public squares and town centers with monuments to major and minor Confederate figures, Black Americans waged their own battle over the meaning of the Civil War. More than challenging the white supremacy embedded in the dominant stories of sectional reconciliation, Black memory producers and their white allies tried to reclaim the mantle of the Union cause broadly, and the world-historical importance of emancipation more specifically. Across the South, Black communities continued to celebrate the Union cause during events like Emancipation Day, Decoration Day, and Juneteenth. Additionally, Black veterans, officeholders, and journalists participated in a national Unionism, joining Grand Army of the Republic (GAR) encampments, making claims to federal pensions, and defending the legacy of the party of Lincoln in the public sphere. These defenses of the Union cause produced their own commemorative landscape, provided a counterbalance to the nascent vision of the Lost Cause.[12]

As the country moved toward national reunion and sectional reconciliation, Black leaders began deploying a new countermemory of the era to highlight the violence embedded in the abandonment of Reconstruction. In an 1875 Independence Day speech in DC's Anacostia neighborhood, Frederick Douglass posed the rhetorical question, "If war among the whites brought peace and liberty to the blacks, what will peace among the whites bring?" In an 1884 essay for the *A.M.E. Church Review*, writer and poet Frances Ellen Watkins Harper described sectional reconciliation as a deeply uneven process. "Behind the facts of the present, is the history of the past. The present facts are a divided North and a solid South, a defeated Democracy grasping again the reins of Government, stronger in its representative basis than when it went out of power." In his 1903 examination of the Freedmen's Bureau, W. E. B. Du Bois framed Reconstruction's defeat as the "heavy heritage of this generation." In the arc of their respective interpretations of national reunion and sectional reconciliation, Harper, Wells, and Du Bois highlight the rise of a specific Black countermemory of the Reconstruction era.[13]

During their exile in the political wilderness, the Reconstruction generation's rival vision of the postbellum past matured and the sites where this countermemory was produced began to increase. This vision diverged even further from a triumphant Unionism. In lyceums, literary societies, local celebrations, and the pages of the Black press, former political leaders became amateur historians, developing both a broader interpretation of the recent past and a set of practices for archiving and preserving their account of their unfinished revolution. Over time, the late nineteenth-century literary and historical societies like the one where William Whipper and Robert Smalls debated the meaning of Reconstruction gave rise to more formal organizations for researching and archiving the Black past. Twentieth-century organizations like the American Negro Academy, the Negro Society for Historical Research, and the Association for the Study of Negro Life and History could trace their immediate roots to the Gilded Age institutions designed to discuss the race's recent past and future destiny.[14]

The dominant theme of this countermemory portrayed the Reconstruction era as a pivotal break from a past rooted in bondage and the beginning of the long march toward a new "racial destiny." Coalescing around an idea that historian Michele Mitchell has connected with a deeply gendered vision of postbellum racial uplift, a new generation of leaders saw the larger destiny of the race as hopeful and filled with the possibility of regeneration and renewal. A framework that corresponds to what political scientists call "linked fate," racial destiny highlights the postbellum origins of a collective Black electoral bloc and the later intellectual debates about the how the bloc should pursue its political goals in the aftermath of Reconstruction's collapse. More recently, Henry Louis Gates Jr. has traced the origins of the idea of the "New Negro," a vision of Black cultural rebirth traditionally associated with the Harlem Renaissance, to an earlier set of debates in the Reconstruction-era Black public sphere. "We can think of the concept of the New Negro as a metaphorical form of 'Reconstruction,'" Gates argues. "Not as official government program . . . but an attempt almost two decades after the fact, to transform the image of the upper classes of [the] race." Confronting a hydra-headed, and distinctly modern, form of anti-Blackness, postbellum Black leaders turned to the "kingdom of culture" to combat vicious racism in popular culture, the larger public sphere, and American intellectual life.[15]

The ongoing debate among Black leaders over Reconstruction and its legacy also adds much needed texture to how historians understand the shifting political mood within the postbellum Black public sphere. Formally united by the new national press network, racial destiny was also connected by a more invisible emotional bond. The affective dimension of the Reconstruction generation's countermemory becomes evident when seen through the lens of what literary scholar Raymond Williams has called a "structure of feeling." The emergent portrait of a generation's worldview, a structure of feeling highlights nascent challenges to the dominant social order that remain outside of the cultural mainstream. Reflecting an alternative accounting of what sectional reconciliation cost the nation, Black Americans' countermemory of Reconstruction crystallized their initial hopes toward the promise of Reconstruction, as well as their later sorrows over its unmaking. Organized by a deeply felt sense of what Reconstruction meant, the producers of late nineteenth-century African American history often embedded a saturnine maker's mark within their accounts of the postbellum past. This deep sense of political loss would become part of the larger cultural fabric of the Black public sphere during the Gilded Age.[16]

Inextricable from the rise of new class divisions within the Black community, the generational struggle over Reconstruction's countermemory offers a valuable lens into the cultural politics of the "talented tenth." The aspirations of the antebellum Black elite shaped the contours of the wartime social movement in the Lowcountry and the ambitions of a new postbellum elite reshaped the legacy of the Reconstruction era in the decades that followed the removal of federal troops from the South. In their efforts to establish new educational and social institutions, serve on the front lines of the Freedmen's Bureau, and, most important, hold major political offices and shape policy for the first time in the nation's history, the cohort of Northern-born Black men and women who traveled to the South during Reconstruction viewed themselves as at the vanguard of a new chapter in the race's larger destiny. Largely defined by academic accomplishment and educational credentials, the leaders of the Reconstruction generation used the pages of the Black press and intellectual spaces like Bethel Hall, alongside a host of other cultural outlets, to produce a vision of the past that reflected their own vision of racial destiny. This specific form of elite capture was contested by freedpeople and Southern-born Black leaders—most notably Robert Smalls—but ultimately the ideas and institutions of this elite dominated the countermemory of Reconstruction.[17]

In this generational struggle over cultural capital, gender was among the most important battlegrounds. Initially, Black women played a critical role in shaping Reconstruction's countermemory. Women in the Reconstruction generation traveled to the Lowcountry to participate in the Port Royal Experiment as teachers, missionaries, and writers; at the apex of Reconstruction, these women would shape the era's broader political culture, exercising influence over the political practices of their husbands, sons, and brothers, as well as continuing to shape the debates around postbellum politics in the public sphere. As Elsa Barkley Brown has demonstrated, this maps onto a larger pattern of Black women initially having equal footing in an expansive and inclusive Reconstruction-era Black public sphere. While men would begin to dominate the leadership positions across Jim Crow–era associational life, Black women continue to be at the vanguard of the memory work that made possible the documentation, archiving, and, later, retrieval of the Reconstruction generation's history. Black women were present at every stage of the production of Reconstruction's countermemory, even as the place they once held in the Reconstruction-era Black public sphere began to shrink.[18]

Some historians question the usefulness of countermemory as a framework for understanding African American intellectual history. For these scholars, countermemory reduces Black historical thinking to a site of secondary motion—a vision of the past that is only legible when it challenges white racism. As Thavolia Glymph, Hilary Green, and others have demonstrated, a grassroots memory of the Civil War emerged in Southern Black communities long before the architects of the Lost Cause captured the collective memory of the war and its meaning in American life.[19]

Taking these concerns seriously, *Requiem for Reconstruction* argues that the production of Reconstruction's countermemory was a generational project rooted in the cultural politics of the late nineteenth-century Black public sphere. At the same moment that sectional reconciliation had reached its crescendo, African American leaders began crafting a rival Reconstruction story in rooms like Bethel Hall. Here, it is important to note that the century's penultimate decade not only marked the rise of the Lost Cause as a cultural force in national life but also saw the concurrent ascent of racial destiny in Black America. In this milieu, the disagreements in the Black public sphere over how to remember the previous political era had an almost existential tinge. Caught between the valley of white supremacy and the mountaintop of racial destiny, the producers of Reconstruction's countermemory synthesized those twin intellectual challenges and created a story of the Civil War era that spoke to the deepest concerns of the Black Gilded Age.

At the same time, not all Black Americans saw themselves reflected in this first draft of African American history. The struggle within the Black public sphere over Reconstruction's memory was shaped by an uneven access to the levers of social and cultural power. And, as Michel-Rolph Trouillot has demonstrated, the production of the past—even a rival, radical past—always contains the danger of reproducing a "cycle of silences" within the facts it records, the archives it assembles, the narratives it retrieves from this archival material, and, most importantly, in the claims toward retrospective significance that freight history with social, cultural, and political meaning.[20]

The South Carolina Lowcountry served as the primary site for the Reconstruction generation's countermemory. A prominent and well-trod site in Civil War–era scholarship, the Lowcountry has long been understood to be at the center of wartime Reconstruction and the long struggle to make postemancipation Black freedom meaningful. One of the first places in the

Greater Lowcountry. Detail of a map of the Southeast United States by Archibald Fullarton, ca. 1870.

South where the planter class was expelled during the war, the Lowcountry became a hub for experiments in establishing free labor ideology, saw some of the first efforts to organize regiments of the formerly enslaved into the US military, was used as a platform where the Union army broadcast the official enactment of the Emancipation Proclamation, and experimented with some of the most radical efforts in wartime land redistribution. The Lowcountry was also home to one of the first national cemeteries in the Deep South and a cornerstone in Union memory of the war—highlighting the highest-frequency promise of emancipation.[21]

An important site for the memories of the Union cause and emancipation, the Lowcountry was also the center of an ongoing debate over Black America's political future. The region attracted a series of in-migrations, including Gullah-speaking freedpeople from the greater Lowcountry, Black Northerners who viewed the Sea Islands as the most important battleground in the struggle for racial destiny, and Black South Carolinians fleeing the state's Upcountry during Redemption to seek safety. Understanding at a deeply felt level what Reconstruction had meant, these new arrivals sought to hold the Lowcountry accountable to their freedom dreams. In this way, the Lowcountry belongs to a larger cultural geography that mirrors what Pierre Nora has described as "lieux de mémoire"—sites of memory that served as "places of refuge," "sanctuaries of spontaneous devotion and silent pilgrimage," and spaces that embodied the "living heart of memory." More than a mausoleum for a broad and undifferentiated Northern unionism, the Lowcountry's commemorative landscape remained a living mecca for Black countermemory well into the twentieth century. Part of a larger story that Manisha Sinha has framed as the brief epoch's "long waning," the persistence of the Lowcountry's Republican political world challenges a traditional periodization of Reconstruction and demands a more complex portrait of the era's ending.[22]

Often portrayed as a site of excess and corruption in the white press, the Lowcountry would become a cultural battleground over the meaning of Reconstruction. For national Black leaders, it was place that captured the promise of postemancipation racial destiny. Hoping to preserve the region's usable past, journalists in the Black press continued to update their readers on the political events, economic progress, and cultural life of the Lowcountry in the decades that followed the initial North-South reunion.[23]

In doing so, a new journalistic "beat" emerged in the Reconstruction-era Black press: Southern political reporting. Providing the growing Black public sphere with in-depth coverage of the region and its progress, the newspapers that covered the postbellum Republican Party in the South played an indispensable role in shaping the larger story of the race's destiny. In particular, the Lowcountry's political world consumed the imagination of a growing Black *national* reading public, which, in turn, reshaped the way Black Americans imagined themselves as a national community with a shared destiny.[24]

Beginning in the centers of Black Northern life, Black political reporting eventually took root in the South. As a new generation of Southern journalists reimagined the contours of the Black public sphere, the contours of the racial destiny debate were reshaped. Southern stories on the efficacy of the Republican Party, the rise of political violence, and the slow lurch toward disfranchisement all mattered in the emerging story of Black America's political future. Every election in the region became a referendum on the Black future; every officeholder became an avatar of Black aspiration; every report of wanton violence served as a stark reminder of this political project's precarious future. In the pages of the Gilded Age Black press, racial destiny went from an abstract vision of uplift to a specific and ongoing story of postbellum progress that could be observed, measured, and then debated.[25]

While the Lowcountry played an outsized role in shaping the Black countermemory of Reconstruction, it was far from the only Black geography that captured national attention. Other sites of postbellum Black political power—like Eastern North Carolina, the Mississippi Delta, the Alabama Black Belt, as well as Southern cities like New Orleans, Memphis, and Richmond—possessed many of the same political elements as the Lowcountry, continued to either elect or appoint Republican officials, and maintained a broader network of newspapers, schools, churches, and Black civic institutions that furthered countermemory practices. In her expansive examination of the postbellum Black South, Thulani Davis depicts a nascent "emancipation circuit" where Black activism and Black political thought—and likely Black countermemory—circulated across the greater South during the Civil War and Reconstruction.[26]

In this way, *Requiem for Reconstruction* offers a profound reevaluation of the relationship between the nation's second founding and the rise of the discipline of African American history. Confronting the broader anxieties over the legacy of their generational political project, the cohort who traveled to places like the Lowcountry during the war, participated in Southern politics, and reported their experiences to the Black press increasingly believed that a broad defense of the Black past was needed—and that the capstone of that historical project had to be a defense of Reconstruction. Sparking a "golden age" of Black historical writing, the late nineteenth century saw the publication of the first book-length monographs on African American history by Black scholars. These self-made historians were marked by the ambitions and anxieties of their generation's cultural world and produced accounts of the past that reflected their era's faith in racial destiny.[27]

When we pay attention to how the Reconstruction generation grappled with postbellum political history, new dimensions of the modern Black public sphere begin to appear. While many members of the Reconstruction generation possessed a deep familiarity with the antebellum world of colored conventions, Black church networks, and the Black press, Reconstruction radically altered the scale and scope of the nation's imagined Black public. A largely Northern project before the Civil War, the new networks of communication between South and North during Reconstruction helped to dramatically expand the circulation and vision of the Black public sphere. The exponential increase in the number of schools and colleges in the South greatly expanded the base of readers for the Black press. In addition, emancipation and Reconstruction transformed the South into a new theater for journalistic coverage and consumption, first for accounts of the Black teachers and missionaries taking part in wartime Reconstruction, and later in the coverage of the wave of officeholders who embodied the highest promise of the postbellum racial destiny. The postbellum Black public sphere was not only larger and more deeply invested in debates about political representation and political power than its precursor but also served as the new foundation for a new set of debates about multiracial democracy and the nation's political future.[28]

Put another way, within the late nineteenth-century Black public sphere, the cohort that had once attempted to establish a new political order in the postbellum South now sought to preserve the legacy of their generational dream. In these historical accounts that were produced in the Reconstruction era, debated during the Gilded Age, and archived during the first decades of Jim Crow, the Reconstruction generation provided the documentary foundation for later Black scholars like Carter G. Woodson, Alrutheus Ambush Taylor, and W. E. B. Du Bois to write the first histories that captured the full story of the now-maligned era. Long hidden in plain sight, the Reconstruction generation's scattered archive of political history provides a lost map of the late nineteenth century's Black freedom struggle.[29]

Chapter Outline

Requiem for Reconstruction follows how the Reconstruction generation experienced the rise and fall of the Republican political world in the greater Lowcountry and examines how the cadence of this story became foundational in a Black countermemory of the postbellum past. The book explores this history over the course of seven chapters organized into three sections.

Part I, "The Making of the Lowcountry's Rival Political World," explores the rise of the Lowcountry as a Reconstruction-era political mecca. Chapter 1, "A Great Movement in South Carolina: The Black Port Royal Experiment and the Origins of Postbellum Racial Destiny," explores the rise of Beaufort County as a Black political geography and the role the larger Lowcountry played in shaping the trajectory of Reconstruction. A beacon for both Black Northerners affiliated with the abolitionist movement and freedpeople seeking a more expansive vision of freedom, Beaufort County became a thriving hub of postbellum Black political life. By the 1870s, however, cleavages along the lines of education, previous condition of servitude, and region of birth divided Beaufort County's Republican Party and led to intense factional and political rivalries. Casting the county as a hotbed for the excesses of radical Reconstruction, Northern travel writers, Southern journalists, and the moderate wing of the state's Republican Party sought to blame the Lowcountry for the party's 1876 defeat at the hands of Wade Hampton.

Chapter 2, "A Multiple-Front Memory War: Redemption and Remembering Reconstruction-Era Violence," examines the ways Black residents of the Lowcountry challenged efforts by white terrorist groups to erase the legacy of Reconstruction and inscribe the story of Redemption onto the landscape in the years that followed their 1876 campaign. As South Carolina became the site of a long campaign to "redeem" the state government for white supremacy, both the Democratic and Republican Parties reimagined their long-term strategies for political success in the state. As the Democratic Party, and its paramilitary wing, the Red Shirts, continued to mobilize political violence to accomplish its goals, Black Lowcountry residents contested these efforts in their own grassroots self-defense efforts, producing a countermemory of violence that would be central to their memory of the era's larger political history.

Chapter 3, "The Rise of the Black Seventh: Racial Gerrymandering, Rival Geography, and the Struggle over the Republican Party's Destiny in South Carolina," explores the way movement and racial boundary-making simultaneously shrank Black political power in South Carolina and created a new, hypervisible site of political power and memory production. In the aftermath of the Democratic Party's redemption of the state for white supremacy, Beaufort County continued to serve as a bastion of Republican Party politics. As the state's Upcountry became plagued with anti-Black violence, and growing numbers of Black South Carolinians looked to the Trans-Mississippi West or Liberia, the Lowcountry's leaders used the recent legacy of Reconstruction to encourage migrants to make their home in the Lowcountry. Most important, as the state's white leaders tried to redraw county lines and redistrict the state's congressional map, the newly gerrymandered Seventh Congressional District became the most visible "Black district" in the country and would continue to embody the promise of Reconstruction-era racial destiny.

Part II, "The Postbellum Public Sphere and the Production of Black Countermemory," explores the relationship between the Lowcountry's political world, the nascent national Black public sphere, and the emergent historical practices at the center of postbellum countermemory. Chapter 4, "Reconstruction's Last Congressman: The Gilded Age Black Public Sphere and the Battle over Robert Smalls's Legacy," highlights the rise and fall of Robert Smalls and the Lowcountry political machine that he commanded during the 1880s. One of the most famous Black Americans of the late nineteenth century, Smalls stood atop a finely tuned political machine, which he used dole out patronage and punish his enemies. many in the Black press believed that Smalls, in his rule over one of the last places where Black voters and politicians would retain access to political power, blocked the political rise of the Reconstruction generation's vanguard. When rampant Election Day irregularities and voter fraud cost Smalls his congressional seat in 1886, some of Smalls's enemies in the local and state Republican Party used the moment to call for a generational changing of the guard.

Chapter 5, "'More Good from Nazareth': The Lowcountry's Long Reconstruction, Disfranchisement, and Archiving Countermemory at the Century's End," explores the fall of South Carolina's "Black district." Still able to send Black politicians to the US Congress and hold massive Decoration Day celebrations that attracted revelers from across the region, Lowcountry leaders and their allies still held out hope that the national Republican Party would remember the highest-frequency version of the Reconstruction generation's political project. While the Lowcountry's local party became increasingly divided, and a more virulently white-supremacist faction of the Democratic Party was on the rise, South Carolina's Republican Party still sent Black politicians to Congress and worked with moderate Democratic leaders to share local offices. A razor-thin 1894 election victory allowed the state's Democratic Party to call a constitutional convention that effectively disfranchised the state's remaining Black voters and eliminated the old Black district. However, despite this final collapse of the Lowcountry's formal political order, Black Republican leaders from Beaufort challenged the antidemocratic measures on the floor of the 1895 constitutional convention and in the pages of the Black press, thereby helping to disseminate a new countermemory of Reconstruction that would spread throughout the Black public sphere during the early twentieth century.

Part III, "The Afterlife of the Reconstruction Generation," examines the legacy of the Lowcountry's political generation in the early twentieth-century Black world. Chapter 6, "The Jim Crow Generation: Black Teachers, the Industrial School Movement, and the Educational Battle over Reconstruction's Legacy in the Segregated South," highlights the role of the Lowcountry's Black industrial schools in redefining the memory of Reconstruction. While focusing on the Penn School, an institution founded in 1862 by Northern, abolitionist-minded teachers, the chapter explores the larger rise of industrial education in the Lowcountry and Sea Islands. As many of the white educational leaders who had been part of the Port Royal Experiment began to die, they were replaced by new educational leaders who wanted to bring what they perceived to be the cutting edge of Black Southern education to the Lowcountry. In their efforts to replace academic curricula with agricultural and mechanical skills training, the new generation of educators replaced teachers who had witnessed and supported Republican rule and often infused their lessons with radical politics. In effect, the industrial school movement sought to erase the legacy of Reconstruction. These efforts were contested by residents of the Sea Islands who remembered Reconstruction and sought to preserve the region's radical history.

Chapter 7, "Requiem for Reconstruction: The Great Migration, Interwar African American History, and the Afterlife of the Reconstruction Generation," examines the efforts to remember the legacy of the Reconstruction generation and produce an accurate historical accounting of their lost world among the cohort of Black scholars, journalists, and readers who were creating and consuming interwar African American history. In the midst of the Great Migration, leaders in the Black press, as well as members of the nascent profession of African American history, sought out the surviving members of the Reconstruction generation and used their accounts to write new histories of the post–Civil War era, reimagine a broader useable past for the interwar cultural moment, and begin imagining a new political future in Northern Black communities where they could once again exist as voters and officeholders.

Part I

The Making of the Lowcountry's Rival Political World

CHAPTER ONE

A Great Movement in South Carolina
The Black Port Royal Experiment and the Origins of Postbellum Racial Destiny

At the dawn of Reconstruction, Frances Anne Rollin returned to the Lowcountry to join her generation's great social movement. Born on November 19, 1845, Rollin, the eldest daughter from one of Charleston's most notable free Black families, moved to Philadelphia shortly before the onset of the Civil War to attend the prestigious Institute for Colored Youth. She not only learned from some of the nation's most decorated Black educators and "pioneers of high culture" but also found herself in the epicenter of the Black abolitionist world. She would befriend Charlotte Forten, granddaughter of one of the city's most influential Black leaders; share classes with John Wesley Cromwell, the future president of the Bethel Literary and Historical Society; and count the famed educators Sarah Mapps Douglass and Octavius Catto as teachers and mentors. When Union soldiers began their occupation of the Sea Islands just south of Charleston, a wave of Rollin's Northern friends and classmates joined the larger march of antislavery activists who saw the region as next stage in the long war against the South's slave power.[1]

In 1867, when Rollin returned to the Lowcountry, these Black abolitionists had already laid the foundation of a new postslavery world with the region's freedpeople. Charlotte Forten joined the Port Royal Experiment and served as a teacher on St. Helena Island, one of the Lowcountry's major Sea Islands; Mary Still, the sister of Underground Railroad leader William Still, joined a larger group of Black missionaries who sought to bring racial uplift by spreading the gospel in the region; Harriet Tubman, then living in upstate New York, traveled south to assist the Union's war effort in the Lowcountry by serving as a nurse, spy, and leader of a raid that liberated more than 750 people along the Combahee River. Martin Delany, the nation's leading Black nationalist, had been stationed in Charleston as a major in the 104th United States Colored Troops and remained in the Lowcountry as a Freedmen's Bureau agent because he saw the region's Black majority as a proving ground for the race's larger destiny. "As before the whole South depended upon you," he cautioned a group of freedpeople on Hilton Head Island, "now the whole country will depend upon you."[2]

Rollin would find herself at the epicenter of this new generation's social movement. Initially a teacher in the Lowcountry's Freedmen's Bureau, Rollin entered the national spotlight when she successfully sued a white ferry conductor for denying her a first-class seat, becoming the first Black person to win a civil rights case in South Carolina. In 1868, she would return North—this time to Boston—to find a publisher for her biography of Martin Delaney, now a friend and benefactor. She quickly became a fixture in the city's abolitionist world, where William Lloyd Garrison, Wendell Phillips, and Thomas Wentworth Higginson would become mentors. She would also socialize in the city's Black elite world; Richard T. Greener, the first Black Harvard graduate and a future Reconstruction-era leader, would become a friend and failed suitor.[3]

Her 1868 book, *Life and Public Services of Martin R. Delany, Sub-assistant Commissioner Bureau Relief of Refugees, Freedmen, and of Abandoned Lands, and Late Major 104th U.S. Colored Troops*, not only provided a deep chronicle of Delaney's heroic place in African American history but also framed the work of the Freedmen's Bureau in South Carolina as a turning point in the larger story of the race's destiny. "He made the genius, habits, and peculiarities of the people he was over his constant study," Rollin exalted, "which, together with his unbounded popularity with them, eminently fitted him for the position." While she wrote with significant critical and objective distance, going so far sign her work "Frank A. Rollin" to hide her gender, it was clear that the daughter of Charleston's Brown Fellowship elite and student of the Northern Black abolitionist world saw her own personal history blend with the Lowcountry's generation-marking moment. "As the war cloud fades out from our sky," she wrote, "we are enabled to look more soberly upon the stupendous revolution, its causes and teachings, and to consider the men and new measures developed through its agency, the material with which the country is to be reconstructed."[4]

For Rollin, the desire to "look more soberly upon the stupendous revolution" was born out of her experience participating in it. Coming of age during the destruction of slavery, Rollin and her Northern generational peers, many of whom were children of the Black abolitionist movement, remade the Black world on South Carolina's seacoast. Historian Martha Jones has argued that highly educated Black women like Frances Rollin "were drawn to Beaufort, South Carolina, where they saw the future being defined by the fate of these new communities of freedpeople." This feeling of being at the vanguard of a new chapter in the race's destiny gave Rollin and her peers a sense of intellectual stewardship for their movement—a need to document Reconstruction's history and counteract the inevitable misrepresentations of their political project. "Begirt with loyal hearts and strong arms, the mission of our revolution

Miss Frances Anne Rollin, undated. Leigh R. Whipper Papers, Schomburg Center for Research in Black Culture, New York Public Library, New York.

shall embrace centuries in its march, securing the future stability of our country," she proclaimed.⁵

This chapter examines the world that Black Northerners, free-born Black Southerners, and freedpeople built together after the Civil War. With the onset of wartime Reconstruction, the Lowcountry quickly became the center of the nineteenth-century Black freedom struggle. Once the foundation of a Black-majority slave society—and home to one of the largest free Black communities in the South—the region would be transformed into a mecca for a wide swath of Black Americans seeking postbellum freedom. At times holding competing, if not contradicting, ideas over the final shape of this political project, Black Northerners, free-born Black Southerners, and freedpeople shared an understanding that they, as a generation, shared a collective responsibility for a new racial destiny.⁶

In so doing, this chapter traces a long social history of the Black abolitionist movement. The Black Northerners who descended upon the region during the 1860s had seen their parents and grandparents build a broad, interstate political struggle through the Black press, colored conventions, vigilance committees, and the extensive network of the Underground Railroad. For the children of this earlier crusade, a group I call the Black Port Royal Experiment, wartime Reconstruction not only offered an opening for new social and political opportunities but also served as a proving ground for their generational dream of collective racial destiny. Like their white Northern peers who traveled to the region as missionaries, educators, and free labor idealogues, the participants in the Black Port Royal Experiment also saw the tentative freedom of the Lowcountry's formerly enslaved population as something that needed paternalistic shaping. Often envisioning themselves as a nascent elite, the "representative" men and women who came to the Lowcountry during the 1860s often espoused classical notions of republican virtue and natural aristocracy that swam against the democratic tide of the era—a tide being led by the region's freedpeople.[7]

Despite the similarities to their white counterparts, the leaders of the Black Port Royal Experiment reflected a sharp break from the mainstream of Northern antislavery politics. Similar to the observation of poet and novelist Frances Ellen Watkins Harper that women were increasingly "all bound up together" across lines of class and race in the postbellum United States, Reconstruction-era Black Americans were in the process of making a new vision of collective destiny that would need to reach across divides of education, class, gender, and previous condition of servitude. This process felt especially pronounced in the Lowcountry. As Reconstruction in the Palmetto State progressed and a new state constitution guaranteeing universal manhood suffrage was created, the larger Black world looked to South Carolina as the next chapter in the race's future. Deeply aware that the political events in South Carolina came to embody the larger story of Reconstruction, Black journalists covered events there with a watchful eye and a sense of history's burden. Building political alliances across the traditional divides, the Lowcountry's postbellum political leaders envisioned a radically expansive Black public, a vision that also reimagined the outer edges of what the nation's nascent multiracial democracy could entail.[8]

The Port Royal Experiment and the Rival Geography of Wartime Reconstruction

The Civil War radically changed the racial geography of the greater Lowcountry. The site of one of the nation's largest and longest-enduring slave societies, the colonial and antebellum Lowcountry was anchored by a powerful planter class that created much of the intellectual architecture for secession. This white minority–Black majority power structure would collapse in the aftermath of the November 1861 Battle of Port Royal. As the former planter class fled the region, the Lowcountry's racial geography would shift in both profound and subtle ways. In the months that followed federal occupation, enslaved refugees flocked to the Lowcountry—giving rise to one of the war's largest contraband camps. In the midst of this wartime upheaval, enslaved people inscribed a new "rival geography" across the Union-occupied landscape. In a type of placemaking first described by Stephanie Camp, bondspeople's rival sense of the Southern landscape had previously offered important—albeit brief—opportunities to remake freedom on their own terms. Now, with the opening of the war, a more sustained vision of a rival geography was possible. The pivotal stories of Civil War–era African American history, including the first experiments with free labor, the efforts to enlist enslaved men, the formal declaration of the Emancipation Proclamation, and the thwarted attempt at land redistribution were all connected to the Lowcountry's specific rival geography. While the spirit of this rival geography persisted into Reconstruction, the rise of the Freedmen's Bureau would bring an end to the most radical vision of wartime freedom and introduce a more formal structure to the Lowcountry's postbellum Black geography.[9]

Before the war, the Lowcountry's slave society embodied one of the most pronounced antebellum worlds of both the planter class and those in bondage. The region's planter class, while increasingly overshadowed by the growing wealth in the Mississippi River Valley, was still among the wealthiest groups in the nation. The cities of Charleston and Savannah were social and cultural hubs that anchored elite society of the greater seaboard South. The ostentatious displays of wealth and power in these coastal centers came from the valuable long staple cotton on the region's Sea Islands and the inland empire of rice. The region's particular absentee plantation system gave rise to a majority Black world where a flexible task system provided the region's enslaved population more autonomy than the heavily supervised gang labor system that emerged in the Cotton Belt. In the deep inequality of the antebellum Lowcountry's Black and white worlds, rival bodies of knowledge emerged: among the white elites, a deep antidemocratic first principle that would ultimately lead to secession; among the enslaved, a mastery over a set of small worlds within and adjacent to the plantation where African cultural retention, robust kinship networks, and underground economies could flourish.[10]

The arrival of Union gunboats brought about the collapse of the enslavers' hierarchical society but left uncertain how the enslaved would reimagine the region's shifting wartime landscape. On November 7, 1861, at the Battle of Port Royal, Union forces quickly defeated Confederates, forcing the region's white elites to flee to the state's interior. In the process of occupying the region, the federal government unintentionally created a beacon for Black freedom. In the four months between the fall of the slaveholding class and the arrival of the Northern missionaries charged with leading the Port Royal Experiment, the Black population on Port Royal Island would increase by 3,000 people. One section of Botany Bay Island that was protected by Union war vessels went from 1,000 Black South Carolinians to 2,300 in just a few days. The Northern press reported on "stampedes" of enslaved refugees entering Union lines in the occupied regions of the South. Entering an overstretched and overcapacity network of contraband camps, enslaved people in South Carolina continued to seek refuge in the Lowcountry's liminal world at the edge of freedom and slavery.[11]

The prospect of the region's becoming a site of unconstrained Black freedom vexed military officials and Northern Republican leaders. As Amy Murrell Taylor has shown, the war created a regionwide humanitarian crisis that the Union army was woefully unprepared to handle. While the military's initial contraband policy served as a blunt instrument for addressing the stream of Black refugees to Union-occupied regions of the South, the crisis would ultimately require more deliberate congressional intervention in the form of the Confiscation Acts of 1861 and 1862. In some cases, this rival geographic thinking on the part of the enslaved pushed military emancipation at a speed faster than national leadership was ready to embrace. As leader of the Department of the South, Gen. David Hunter ran into headwinds from Congress and President Lincoln, first, when he forcefully enlisted Black men in the Lowcountry into a Union army regiment and again on April 25, 1862, when he issued General Order Number 11, declaring all persons held in bondage in Georgia, Florida, and South Carolina "forever free." Responding to the specific movements of enslaved refugees in the greater Lowcountry, Hunter's military orders highlight not only the way bottom-up forces shaped the course of emancipation but also the specific geographic thinking among the enslaved that brought new centers of demographic gravity to the Union-occupied portions of the Lowcountry.[12]

The Lowcountry's Black rival geography also reshaped the wartime Reconstruction and civilian intervention in the region. The site of the much-vaunted Port Royal Experiment, the Lowcountry became a proving ground for how antislavery white Northerners confronted the making of a free labor South. The motley crew of entrepreneurs, missionaries, and teachers reflected the broad, and at times contentious, spectrum of antislavery activism in the North. While some of these leaders held hierarchical ideas of race and civilization and could only envision the region's Black population as unrefined clay in need of molding, a sizable contingent of white Northerners in the region quickly became aware that the region's bondspeople brought fully formed ideas of freedom and the racial future. Heather Andrea Williams has shown that the utopian views of the white Northerners "answered, rather than generated" the Black desire for schools and education—a desire to fulfill a new racial destiny. "They are learning to read and write—some are learning lawyer, some are learning doctor, and some learn minister," one resident of the Lowcountry observed about the educational world emerging during wartime Reconstruction. Northern-born white teacher Laura Towne, who in 1862 would establish the first school for freed children in the South, confirms this preexisting desire for education and saw the Lowcountry's Black refugees transforming the Union-occupied region into a hub for education. "The old folks and the school-children troop to see us," she remarked.[13]

The Emancipation Proclamation brought the Lowcountry's wartime rival geography into the national light. At an assembly organized by Gen. Rufus Saxton, nearly 7,000 Black residents of the Lowcountry looked on as the document was read for the first time. Immediately freeing the nearly 20,000 refugees in the Union-occupied Lowcountry, the Emancipation Proclamation provided legal protection for the world Black refugees began constructing after the Battle of Port Royal. Also opening the door for Black enlistment in the Union military, the proclamation made the Lowcountry the epicenter of the Black military experience. Northern white abolitionist Thomas Wentworth Higginson, who led the First South Carolina Volunteers—later the Thirty-Third United States Colored Troops (USCT), saw a deep poetry in the events that were unfolding in the Lowcountry. "As the scene of the only effort on the Atlantic coast to arm the negro, our camp attracted a continuous stream of visitors, military and civil," Higginson wrote. "A battalion of black soldiers, a spectacle since so common, seemed then the most daring of innovations, and the whole demeanor of this particular regiment was watched with microscopic security by friends and foes." The site of the famed Battle of Fort Wagner, Harriett Tubman's daring raid along the Combahee River, as well as smaller skirmishes like the Battle of Honey Hill, the Lowcountry provided the nation with an important window on the Black military experience.[14]

No figure more fully embodied the intertwining stories of emancipation and the Black military experience than Robert Smalls. Born into slavery in 1839, Smalls spent his young adult life as a longshoreman, sailmaker, and wheelman in Charleston harbor. With the fall of Fort Sumter, the still-enslaved Smalls was forced into being a military transport pilot of the CSS *Planter* on the region's various waterways. This knowledge of the Lowcountry's aquatic world allowed him to undertake one of the war's most daring feats. On May 12, 1862, Smalls, with his wife, Hannah, and their blended family in tow, navigated the vessel through a series of checkpoints, each of which required knowledge of specific Confederate naval signals. Upon delivering the *Planter* to the Union, Smalls not only gained freedom for himself and his family but also became immortalized as a war hero. His exploit would be broadcast across the Northern press, and Smalls would make several trips to major cities to raise funds for the formerly enslaved and advocate for enlisting Black men into the Union military. While never receiving an official commission to the rank of pilot in the Navy, Smalls would continue to man the *Planter* over the course of the war, providing crucial support for Gen. William Tecumseh Sherman's army during the March to the Sea.[15]

Sherman's December 1864 arrival in Savannah opened the window on one of the most radical visions of rival geography and Black freedom—land redistribution. Initially conducted under the auspices of the Treasury Department in the form of tax sales of abandoned land in the Lowcountry, land acquisition represented the most expansive possible racial destiny for the region's freedpeople. In the aftermath of his army's march from Atlanta to Savannah, General Sherman heeded the call of Black preacher and community leader Garrison Frazier on how to tackle his army's growing orbit of freed refugees. "The way we can best take care of ourselves is to have land, and turn it and till it by our own labor," Frazier told a January mass meeting in Savannah. Sherman's Field Order Number 15 would redistribute 400,000 acres of land across the Lowcountry into forty-acre parcels for heads of household. By the end of the 1860s, the rural counties of the Lowcountry possessed one of the highest Black land ownership rates in the country—a pattern that would persist until the Great Migration. "They came out of slavery with their attachment for locality and the desire for land-ownership fully developed," one Black Northerner observed. "They were ready to become property-holders." While Field Order Number 15 was reversed by President Andrew Johnson, Black residents of the Lowcountry continued to view landownership as the most meaningful embodiment of postbellum freedom.[16]

As the war ended, the government realized that the patchwork and uneven process of emancipation would require more structure and a deeper federal commitment. In March 1865, Congress created the Bureau of Refugees, Freedmen, and Abandoned Lands—the largest investment made in civilian social welfare up to that point in history. Designed to guide the South's transition from slavery to free labor, the Freedmen's Bureau operated schools,

Freedpeople in front of the Freedman's Bureau in Beaufort, South Carolina, undated. Miriam and Ira D. Wallach, Division of Art, Prints and Photographs: Photography Collection, New York Public Library, New York.

adjudicated legal disputes over labor contracts and marriage documents, facilitated the auction of tax-delinquent land, and provided healthcare for the sick and indigent. To do so, the bureau employed hundreds of agents to canvas the South and represent the US government's investment in freedpeople's postbellum progress—a miniscule number considering the scope of its ambitions and scale of its regional project. While the Freedmen's Bureau reflected a real investment in postbellum Southern communities, often serving as a bulwark against recalcitrant white supremacist forces in the region, the organization often conflicted with the rival worldmaking practices of the South's freedpeople.[17]

When confronted with the perceived excesses of Black freedom, the bureau did not hesitate to enforce its own vision of an ordered free labor society. "Do not think of leaving the plantations where you belong.... If you try to go to Charleston, or any other city you will find no work to do, and nothing to eat," warned one Freedmen's Bureau agent. "Stay where you are, in your own homes, even if you are suffering." Most infamously, Freedmen's Bureau agents in the South Carolina and Georgia Lowcountry were tasked with informing the region's freedpeople that President Johnson had reversed Field Order 15, dashing the dream of widespread land redistribution. An ambitious and vitally important institution, the Freedmen's Bureau often espoused a view of postbellum progress that tamped down the broader ambitions of the Lowcountry's freedpeople. A world shaped by upheaval, movement, and migration, the Lowcountry's wartime rival geography appeared disordered from afar. As Reconstruction began, Northerners, both Black and white, would attempt to provide a new order that aligned with their own vision of race and progress.[18]

Black Northerners, Racial Destiny, and the Remaking of the Postbellum Lowcountry's Political Order

Black Northerners saw the onset of wartime Reconstruction as turning point in the nineteenth century's long movement for abolition and civil rights. As soon as the white missionaries began discussing the establishment of an antislavery outpost in the South Carolina Sea Islands, leaders in the Black press began to field calls for a Black Port Royal Experiment.

"I have received important communications from a number of prominent colored gentlemen of the North, relative to sending colored teachers into this Department, and would take occasion to say that I shall, as soon as possible, answer them through the columns of the *Anglo-African* and *Recorder*," remarked the *Christian Recorder*'s editor. Black teachers, especially Black women teachers, proved to be the most durable shock troops of this movement. By the end of the decade, the percentage of Black teachers and missionaries in the South as part of the American Missionary Association more than tripled. More than 50 percent of the Presbyterian Committee on Freedmen's teaching staff was Black.[19]

Many of the members of the Black Port Royal Experiment were veterans of the antebellum abolitionist movement. Charlotte Forten was the granddaughter of the prominent Philadelphia abolitionist James Forten. USCT veteran and Freedmen's Bureau agent William James Whipper was named for his uncle, another key fixture of Philadelphia's Black abolitionist world. In 1864, Mary Still, the sister of William Still, the Underground Railroad's most important "conductor," left Pennsylvania to join the Lowcountry's growing freedom struggle. She partnered with Jane Lynch, a Northern-born teacher who was also inspired by the movement fervor that was emanating from Philadelphia's AME Church world. "Miss Mary Still and Miss Jennie Lynch have proved themselves almost indispensable among the freedmen," remarked Jonathan Jasper Wright, another Black Pennsylvanian who now lived in the Lowcountry. In August 1865, Mary Still and Jane Lynch joined with Sarah Bram, another Northern-born Black teacher, and Hannah Smalls, a freedwomen married to the war hero Robert Smalls, to organize a fair that would aid the region's freedpeople during the difficult postwar harvest season. Writing on behalf of the "Beaufort Ladies Committee," Jane Lynch and Sarah Bram used the *Anglo-African* to highlight the work of their "Great Movement in the South." Seeing their project as more than a rehearsal for Reconstruction, the missionaries, teachers, and soldiers who had once been affiliated with the abolitionist movement descended upon the Lowcountry after the Civil War with the belief that they stood at the vanguard of the next chapter of the long struggle for Black freedom.[20]

After the war, the Freedmen's Bureau also served as an uneven instrument for Black leaders pursuing racial destiny in the South. A second wave of Black Northerners would travel to the Lowcountry to work for the bureau. Jonathan Wright, the first Black Pennsylvanian to pass the bar, would become a legal advisor for the bureau. Frances Rollin returned to Charleston to teach at a school run by the Freedmen's Bureau. Most famously, Martin Delany would join the bureau—viewing it as a potential vehicle to deliver his own vision of racial destiny. While speaking before a group of freedpeople on Hilton Head Island, Delany created a minor political crisis within the institution when he espoused these views. "Believe not in these Schoolteachers, Emissaries Ministers and agents, because they never tell you the truth," he warned his audience. He cautioned the newly freed group that "as before the whole South depended upon you, now the whole country will depend upon you." In many ways, Frances Rollin's later biography of Delany served as an effort to reframe the specific moment in history for former abolitionists, Black and white, and put Delany's postwar efforts in the context of a larger movement. At least fifteen Black Freedmen's Bureau agents would go on to become elected officials in South Carolina, suggesting that the bureau was an especially important pathway for Northern Black aspiration.[21]

The postbellum activists' continued interest in the Lowcountry signaled that the region remained a site of racial destiny, and a second boom in its Black population followed the war. In the two decades after emancipation, Charleston's Black population grew from 17,000 to 27,000; By 1870, Black Savannah had grown from 8,400 to just over 13,000. Possessing historic churches, organizations that supported mutual aid and associational life, and a wide range of professions that allowed both free-born and formerly enslaved people to accumulate economic resources, industrial skills, and autonomy, the major port cities in the Lowcountry were able to quickly establish the political architecture needed to support the postbellum Republican Party.[22]

While lacking the population density and the networks of historic institutions that anchored antebellum free Black life in Charleston and Savannah, the rural Lowcountry would soon rival the urban centers in political and cultural importance. Charleston County's Black population grew from 41,000 in 1860 to over 60,000 in 1870. Beaufort County, which had only one township with over 1,000 people, would have a Black population of nearly 30,000 in 1870. Most important, Black residents would make up over 80 percent of the county's population for the duration of the late nineteenth century. This demographic strength, combined with the early bedrock of wartime Unionism, transformed the former slave society into one of the strongest bastions for Republican Party politics in the state—if not the entire South.[23]

By the end of the war, South Carolina became the Southern epicenter of the African Methodist Episcopal Church. Charleston, which housed Mother Emanuel, the South's oldest AME church, became a natural anchor for missionary work in the state. Waves of Black missionaries affiliated with the African Methodist Episcopal Church traveled to the region during the war to midwife the nascent postslavery world. The largest Black institution in the nation on the eve of the war, delegates at the AME Church's 1863 Annual Conference voted to send ministers and missionaries to the South after witnessing the enactment of the Emancipation Proclamation and the creation of the United States Colored Troops. Altogether, twenty-seven AME missionaries would fan across the South during the Reconstruction era. By 1866, the number of members of the AME Church had increased from 20,000 to 73,000.[24]

In addition to the organization's grassroots missionary work, the AME Church's newspaper, the *Christian Recorder*, played a central role in both shaping the nascent vision of postemancipation racial destiny and stitching together a new circulatory system of Black thought through the Lowcountry's Black world. Elisha Weaver, the *Christian Recorder*'s Civil War–era editor, dramatically increased the periodicals publishing schedule and expanded the paper to a national scale. "I hope the brethren will not fail to use all the energy possible to sustain such a noble paper," remarked a member of the USCT. "It goes forth as a messenger, delivering tidings of joy and intelligence.... It visits the family at home and the soldier in the field.... Is it not a marvel that such a paper should be found in this land of oppression, where every thing has worked against us?"[25]

The postbellum Black press stitched together a new Black public sphere across the North and South—and more particularly between Northern Black elites and the Lowcountry. In his examination of *Christian Recorder* subscribers, literary scholar Eric Garner has highlighted that South Carolina's thirty-six paid subscribers was not only the highest number in the South but was second only to Philadelphia, the epicenter of the AME world. Those missionaries regularly wrote to the *Christian Recorder*, framing the stakes of their fieldwork in the Palmetto State in the stark terms of moral duty and racial uplift. Richard Harvey Cain, who served as superintendent of AME missions and presiding minister of Mother Emanuel, approached the work with a paternalist sense of racial elevation. While Cain lamented the freedpeople's moral condition, he also saw the larger arc of racial destiny being reciprocal, and not just top-down uplift. "Viewing them generally," Cain wrote, "I find that there is a disposition to work, and get land, possess property, educate their children; and thus elevate themselves and the race to which they belong." Writing to an imagined audience of Black Northerners, Cain and other missionaries framed the missionary work in South Carolina as an extension of the race's larger collective journey toward its highest destiny. "Christian young men and women, come forth from your cozy corners of luxurious ease—from the circles of refined enjoyment, from every recess of selfish obscurity, and work," exclaimed one missionary working in the South Carolina Sea Islands. "Everyone can do something. . . . Let us arise and claim it."[26]

In the Lowcountry, more than anywhere else, the synthesis of Black Northern political aspiration and freedpeople's democratic desires would produce the most forceful vision of Radical Reconstruction. Partnering with Northern-born politicians Richard Howell Gleaves, Jonathan Wright, and William Whipper to form a school board, Robert Smalls used the pages of the national Black press to appeal for funds for the region's first public school. These individuals would also make history in creating the first chapter of the Republican Party in the South. On March 26, 1867, Smalls, Gleaves, Whipper, and thirty-nine other residents of the county held a meeting that would lead to the formation of the Beaufort County Republican Party. The following month, the *Christian Recorder* reported that it was "the largest political meeting ever held in South Carolina. . . . Every man and woman appeared to understand, as if by inspiration, the great political issues of the day."[27]

The Lowcountry's Black political world deeply influenced the state's larger Black political culture. In 1871, when a group of Black politicians from across the region met for a colored convention in Columbia, the legacy of the antebellum Black political world collided with the current struggle to define the next chapter of racial destiny in the postbellum South. "It is our privilege, in addressing you, to utter the voice of four million of citizens of this great country," remarked Robert Brown Elliott, a Northern-born attorney who now represented the Lowcountry in Congress. "That voice is addressed to those whose human feelings rendered practicable that consummate act that elevated so vast a body at once to the enjoyment of civil and political manhood."[28]

Beyond the hypervisible political conventions and matters of policymaking in the statehouse, the Lowcountry's political leaders played an outsized role in orchestrating the direction of the state Republican Party and the contours of the state's Black political culture. Through the Lowcountry's local chapters of the Republican Party, a grassroots world of mass meetings emerged, giving freedmen and freedwomen an opportunity to hold local and state leaders accountable to their specific political concerns. The Union League, which worked along more clandestine channels, offered freedpeople a deeper level of political education, as well as a secret fraternity within a powerful paramilitary network that organized across the state.[29]

At the zenith of this nascent political culture stood the Rollin sisters' salon in Columbia. Led by Frances Rollin Whipper, alongside her younger sisters Katherine, Charlotte, Marie Louise, and Florence, the Charlestonian family regularly hosted Black and white politicians, lobbyists, and journalists in their regal home near the statehouse, which became the "Republican headquarters" of the state. "Their manners were refined, their conversation unusually clever and their surroundings marked them as ladies of keen taste and rare discernment," remarked one Northern journalist. "But for their color they might move in the highest circles of Washington and New York Society." At once avatars for an exoticized Black elite and persistent myths about color and class distinction, the Rollin sisters were, above all else, architects of a Reconstruction-era Republican Party's inner sanctum, a place where political ideas were debated and political favors traded. "If you want a thorough posting upon political affairs in South Carolina you must call on the Rollins," explained one political insider.[30]

Some of these transformations were part and parcel of a larger shift in postbellum African American political culture. Across the South, freedpeople embraced the Union League, the Republican Party, and the secret and large-scale meetings that accompanied the two organizations. Other political centers also beckoned the ambitious and aspiring political class. New Orleans, Vicksburg, Richmond, and Jacksonville would all attract Black Northern missionaries, many of whom would remain in the region as politicians during Reconstruction. Washington, DC, became the new national hub of Black officeholders, and the Lowcountry's politicians played a critical role in shaping Black Washington's nascent political culture. Historian Kate Masur has observed that Ulysses S. Grant's inauguration served as a turning point in Washington's Black political history, with a noticeable uptick of migration among Northern Black civic and religious leaders during the new president's first months in office. Despite losing its territorial government, and right to self-rule, in 1874, Washington remained "the mecca of the colored pilgrim" during the Reconstruction era.[31]

W. J. Whipper, R. B. Elliott, Macon B. Allen.

WHIPPER, ELLIOT, & ALLEN,

SOLICITORS, COUNSELLORS,

AND

ATTORNEYS AT LAW.

OFFICE No. 91 BROAD STREET,

CHARLESTON S.C.

Will practice in all the Courts of the State, especially those of the Counties of Charleston, Beaufort, Barnwell and Colleton.

☞ Mr. Allen will also practice in the United States Courts in South Carolina.

Newspaper advertisement for the Charleston law firm Whipper, Elliott, and Allen. All three men were born in the North and migrated to South Carolina during Reconstruction. *Weekly Louisianian*, December 22, 1870.

The most pronounced and distinct example of the Lowcountry becoming a Black political mecca was the massive in-migration of Black lawyers. Preceded by an almost invisibly small group on the eve of the Civil War, many of the nation's most prominent Black attorneys traveled to the South to assist the Freedmen's Bureau, craft postbellum state constitutions, and pursue the newfound opportunity to hold political office. In this way, Black lawyers embodied the highest political ambition of their generation. "Black lawyers stepped into the arena of nation building with a fervor of democratic ideas, which were no less expressive than the founders of the nation," argues legal historian W. Lewis Burke.[32]

Over the course of Reconstruction, South Carolina would become the center of the Black legal world. In 1865, Macon B. Allen, the first Black person to both pass a bar exam in the United States and argue before an American jury, moved from Massachusetts to Charleston after the Civil War to practice law. In the former cradle of the former Confederacy, Allen would join William Whipper and Robert Elliott to establish the nation's first Black law firm. That same year, Pennsylvania-born Jonathan Wright moved to Beaufort, where he would practice law, hold political office, and eventually serve on the state supreme court. In 1866, Richard Gleaves also left Philadelphia for Beaufort to practice law and pursue political office. By the 1870s, graduates of Howard University's new law school regularly traveled to South Carolina to establish their legal careers. Likely mentored by the law school's dean, Richard T. Greener, who earned a juris doctorate from the University of South Carolina's law school during Reconstruction while also serving on that university's faculty, nearly fifty Black attorneys were admitted to the bar in South Carolina during the Reconstruction era, outpacing all other states in the South.[33]

The cohort of Black attorneys who traveled to the South during Reconstruction held an outsized place in the imagination of white Southerners. Emphasizing the perceived disorder of "Black Reconstruction," both Northern liberal republicans and Southern white redeemers painted Black Northern attorneys as avatars of corruption. State supreme court justice Jonathan Wright was regularly accused of being "a drunkard." Moderate Republican governor Daniel Chamberlain would refuse to certify William Whipper's appointment to the state supreme court because the Northern-born attorney was reputed to be a high-rolling gambler. During a late nineteenth-century trial in Beaufort, one of the county's leading white prosecutors questioned whether the "'76 lawyer" he faced in the courtroom could read or write. A slur aimed toward those Reconstruction-era Black lawyers who remained in the state after 1876, the caricature of the '76 lawyer served as a broad-brushed attack on Black attorneys as a group. Later framed as incompetent, corrupt, or venal in white Southern memory, Black lawyers embodied the postbellum South's seismic social transformation and would remain a persistent bête noire in the Lost Cause's cultural imagination.[34]

No figure more fully embodied these perceived dangers than Aaron Alpeoria Bradley. A Southern-born attorney who fled to the North before the war and returned to the Lowcountry during Reconstruction to practice law and pursue political office, Bradley represented the most radical vision of the new political order. In the Georgia Lowcountry, Bradley would build a robust and hard-edged political machine that stood up against the region's white landowning elites and advocated for policy reforms like ending the state's convict lease system, enforcing an eight-hour workday, and redistributing land held by former slaveowners to freedpeople. Unafraid of the Lowcountry's Bourbon (conservative Democrat) elites, he "led riots against white citizens and police" that stoked white fear that the region's Black majority would be weaponized in a manner not seen since Saint-Domingue. The *Savannah News and Herald* warned its readers that the region's Black majority was now engaged in open rebellion "under the teaching and drill of the villainous Bradley and other white and black emissaries" and that 134 arrest warrants had been issued for "insurrection and rebellion."[35]

In contrast, the Northern Black press portrayed the state's Black attorneys as the vanguard of Reconstruction. In describing the state's first Republican convention, the *Christian Recorder* remarked that Richard Gleaves, the convention's "colored president," not only led the assembly "with great dignity of manner" and a "firm hand" but also "manage[d] to stop the long discussions on points of order," thus preventing the proceedings from getting derailed or mired in minor detail. When the Philadelphia-born attorney Jonathan Wright was appointed by the Freedmen's Bureau to be an agent for the Lowcountry's Sea Islands, the Northern Black press noted that "Mr. Wright will be of great service to the people, on account of his integrity and ability." Speaking before the first class of Howard University Law school graduates, Oliver Otis Howard remarked, "My young friends, I believe you will be true to us who are a sort of pioneers of an epoch in the educational field." Many of that school's first cohort of attorneys would go to South Carolina to help build the state's Republican Party.[36]

The Black Press and Its Coverage of South Carolina Politics

The Reconstruction-era Lowcountry gave rise to the Black press's political reporting. Where antebellum papers like *Freedom's Journal* and the *North Star* covered the Colored Conventions Movement and observed the rise and fall of the Second Party System with a close eye, the emergence of the postbellum South's Republican political party sparked a new chapter in the history of Black journalism. Black Northerners who traveled south regularly reported on the events that were unfolding in the South and the progress that freedpeople were making. "The people here are calculating to defend themselves, as well as stand on their own feet," remarked one Black Northerner. Jane Lynch, part of one of the nation's most prominent AME families, used the press to appeal for more Black Northerners to help build the postbellum world. "Christian young men and women, come forth from your cozy corners of luxurious ease . . . and work." The Northern Black press's coverage of Reconstruction also provided the first instances of Black political gossip. "Let me whisper a secret here," one reporter remarked on the potential political future of Francis Cardozo. "The day is probably not far distant when Mr. Cardoza [sic] may be seated in the United States Senate chamber as a representative of this State."[37]

As Reconstruction took hold in the Lowcountry, Northern Black newspapers covered the region's political events as part of a broader story of the race's postbellum destiny. "All interested in the enlightenment and advancement of the colored people of the South will assist in extending the circulation of the *New National Era*," declared Frederick Douglass's Washington, DC–based periodical. Jane Lynch concluded her reports to the *Christian Recorder* on educational progress in the South Carolina Lowcountry with the valediction "yours for the elevation of the race." One American Missionary Association teacher saw the spark of Providence in the historical moment. "The people are striving to act, and are acting very differently from what they were taught while in a state of slavery," reported Jonathan Wright on what he saw in Beaufort County. "I can truly say that Ethiopia is stretching forth her hands unto God, and that spark of high civilization and intellectuality, which once shed such a brilliant light, that the whole world was attracted by its brightness, is again being enkindled." Framing Reconstruction in the language of Ethiopianism, the aspirational rhetoric that found the race's redemption in the story of the Biblical African kingdom, Wright crystallized the epoch-shifting moment for the Black press's readership.[38]

The preeminent Black newspaper of the 1870s, the *New National Era* covered the Republican Party through a lens often inflected by the politics of South Carolina. Charlestonian Thomas W. Cardozo, brother of politician and school leader Francis Cardozo, covered Mississippi politics for the paper while he lived in the state and held local and state offices. T. McCants Stewart, a Charlestonian who was now attending Howard University, began his long career in journalism writing for the *New National Era*. In 1873, Richard T. Greener briefly served as staff writer for the paper before he made his departure to South Carolina to become a professor at the state's flagship university. The paper's writers and editors had a firm grasp on Reconstruction's connection to the story of racial destiny. A quintessentially Reconstruction-era institution, the *New National Era* captured the fundamentally new and national aspect of the postbellum moment in racial destiny.[39]

No figure would capture the imagination of the postbellum Black public sphere more than Robert Elliott. In the Black national press's coverage of the South Carolina congressman, it found a figure who both embodied Reconstruction generation's North Star. Educated, ambitious, and a powerful orator, Robert Elliott appeared in the *New National Era* more than any other Black politician. Before a crowd in New York's Cooper Union, he recounted the recent history of the "wonderful revolution which had grown out of John Brown's efforts and President Lincoln's devotion." A fixture in Washington's Black elite circles, the South Carolina congressman's lofty vision of racial destiny mirrored the *New National Era*'s high-flown portrait of the era. Asked to deliver the keynote address for the tenth anniversary of the District of Columbia's Emancipation Act of 1862, Elliott captured and crystallized the sentiment that guided his generation: "Behind us lie two hundred and forty-three years of suffering, anguish, and degradation, around us are the gathered fruits of the entire achievements, labors, and triumphs of those who fought for the cause of freedom and humanity; before us lies our mighty future, with all its hopes and aspirations. That future is ours to shape. Let us then lift ourselves to the height of our responsibilities."[40]

While this speech won widespread support, many in the Black press latched onto a warning embedded in the middle of his discussion: "Despite the trite aphorism that 'revolutions never go backward,' is not true, nor is it consonant with the nature of man," lamented Elliott. "Revolutions have gone backward." For Elliott, this reversal of Reconstruction appeared like the specter of a second slavery. "Calamity and disaster, if not identical, certainly quite as overwhelming as any from which we may have escaped." This conservative viewpoint, which placed considerable emphasis on individual and communal responsibility over structural power, was echoed by many of the leaders in the Black press. "A few years of experiment in this condition have passed, and we are called on to witness the spectacle of a fatal relaxation in vigilant watchfulness against the operation of those forces which inevitably drive us backward," described one editor.[41]

This stance became increasingly difficult to hold as a growing disillusionment with the state's Republican Party pervaded the Northern elite press. "To mention South Carolina is to merit the sneers of the commonwealths of the North," lamented the *New National Era*. As white Northern reporters began to crisscross the Reconstruction-era South, a series of lurid reports emphasizing corruption and Black incompetence began to circulate in the nation's elite Northern periodicals and books by Northern white journalists. Most notorious of these accounts was James S. Pike's lurid series of articles on South Carolina's postbellum political world, which he would turn into the 1874 book *The Prostrate State: South Carolina under Negro Government*. A journalist from Maine who had professed support for abolition before the Civil War, Pike had come to despise the South's Reconstruction-era state governments. In his dismal portrait of Reconstruction, Pike presented Black officeholders as evidence that the state's political order was out of alignment. Initially a single exposé for Horace Greeley's *New York Tribune*, the Liberal Republican editor would commission Pike to write several more articles over the course of 1873, stoking popular demand in the North for his later book.[42]

Pike's book, like many of the attacks on Reconstruction by Northerners, was sourced almost entirely from accounts provided by the South's white elites. However, some of the Black leaders who had helped establish the state's new political order in the previous decade now also called into question the direction of South Carolina's Republican Party. The famed abolitionist and former Freedmen's Bureau agent Martin Delany viewed the state's Republican Party's leadership class as the "lowest grade of northern society." He also lamented "the destitution of political knowledge among the newly enfranchised and emancipated people of South Carolina." This whiggish response provoked a fierce rebuke from Frederick Douglass. "It does not seem to me that their degeneracy is so complete as you describe it to be," Douglass argued. "Were you not M. R. Delaney, I should say that the man who wrote thus of the manners of the colored people of South Carolina had taken his place with the old planters." Pleading patience, Douglass remarked that "the colored people of the South are just now, going to school. It is hardly worthwhile to lament that the school is not better than it is."[43]

The respectful but contentious debate in the *New National Era* would serve as a turning point for the former business partners. Frederick Douglass would step down from the *New National Era* to become president of the fledgling Freedman's Savings Bank. Martin Delany, seeing only deficiency and corruption in the traditional Republican Party coalition, would join the Liberal Republican movement, which sought to move the party to the right on economic and racial issues. After the 1874 midterm elections, the *New National Era* would collapse. In the face of major defeats in the House and Senate, as well as a growing chorus of criticism in the national press, the *New National Era* remained committed to the beleaguered and increasingly racially polarized Republican Party in the Palmetto State. "Can the colored leaders of South Carolina have any higher political aspiration than to make their State an honor to their race? If the best class of white people hold aloof, they must be shown that their pride has no justification in any mismanagement of State affairs." Sensing that the fate of the entire party was in jeopardy, Robert Elliott resigned from the House at the peak of his national celebrity to become the Speaker of the South Carolina House of Representatives.[44]

By the dawn of the 1870s, the postbellum Lowcountry had produced the nation's first Black political generation. A region with a long-standing Black majority due to its two-century-old slave society, the Lowcountry and its Black geography had been reshaped by several waves of in-migration. These migrations, first by freedpeople seeking wartime refuge and later by free-born Black Americans who had either been born or educated in the North, organized the national political story of this nascent generation. Together, the free-born and recently freed reshaped old political institutions and built new ones; they led a burgeoning grassroots democratic project and offered a new lodestar for the race's political future. Finally, members of the Reconstruction generation reimagined the Black press as a project that now offered on-the-ground political reporting and editorial analysis on the state of Reconstruction and racial destiny. In turn, this journalistic work would stitch together a national network of Black newspapers that now stretched into the South.

Members of the Reconstruction generation were keenly aware that they were at the forefront of a larger social movement. Those who remained in the region returned to the memory of the Lowcountry's earlier political world in their speeches and political rallies, seeing their generational origin story as the critical lens through which to understand their larger political era. Those who returned to the North, or traveled to the Lowcountry in later decades, confronted revisions of this story—some of which contrasted sharply with those first drafts of radical Reconstruction's history. Most important, the longing for the Lowcountry's lost political world would become a key ingredient in Reconstruction's countermemory. The story that follows is how this generation's political project survived and persisted through the nadir of Redemption and sectional reconciliation, and the various ways that the Reconstruction era's afterlife would shape the production of African American history during the late nineteenth and early twentieth centuries.

CHAPTER TWO

A Multiple-Front Memory War
Redemption and Remembering Reconstruction-Era Violence

Benjamin Franklin Randolph kept a watchful eye on the events unfolding in the wartime South. A free-born and Oberlin-educated Ohioan, he was part of a generation that saw the Civil War open a new portal for the race's future. When the opportunity to serve in the Union army presented itself, he joined the Twenty-Sixth United States Colored Troops, which was organized out of Riker's Island and deployed in Beaufort, South Carolina. At the close of war, he petitioned the Freedmen's Bureau for a post in the South Carolina Lowcountry. "I am desirous of obtaining a position among the freedmen where my qualifications and experience will admit of the most usefulness," he remarked. "I don't ask position or money. But I ask a place where I can be most useful to my race." Serving as assistant superintendent for education in Charleston, he established schools for freedpeople in the city and recruited teachers to the region.[1]

Randolph understood the political bent of the postbellum worldbuilding project and launched himself into his generation's great social movement. After the Freedmen's Bureau closed, he founded a weekly newspaper in the Lowcountry and became a minister for the Methodist Episcopal Church. His peers in Charleston elected him as a delegate to the 1868 South Carolina Constitutional Convention, and from the floor of that body he authored language around some of the document's most radical provisions, including free public education, granting landless men the right to vote, and an equal protection clause that would align with the not-yet-adopted Fourteenth Amendment's own equal protection language. He would even go so far as to advocate for widespread land redistribution from the planter class to the state's freedpeople. In many ways, he embodied the era's most expansive political vision and served as one of the chief architects of what W. E. B. Du Bois would later call "abolition democracy."[2]

As the 1868 fall election drew closer, Randolph threw himself deeper into the political work of Reconstruction. In the immediate aftermath of the constitutional convention, he was elected to the state senate, where he was made chair of the state's Republican Central Committee. In this capacity, he not only traveled to Chicago for the 1868 Republican National Convention but

"The Late Rev. B. F. Randolph, of South Carolina," *Harper's Weekly*, October 25, 1868.

also crisscrossed South Carolina campaigning on behalf of local and national candidates. On October 15, he traveled to Abbeville in the state's Upcountry, where he gave a campaign speech on behalf of the Republican Party and local candidates. The next day, while changing trains, Randolph was gunned down by three white men in broad daylight. Despite many witnesses being present, the assailants escaped on horseback without pursuit. While state and federal authorities were ultimately able to identify the men involved, no one was brought to trial for Randolph's murder.[3]

Benjamin Randolph's assassination would become an indelible moment in the Reconstruction generation's countermemory of the era. Occurring at the height of the most violent period in the history of the postbellum South, Randolph's murder crystallized the stakes of the Reconstruction generation's political project. If the Reconstruction generation's political vision was going to survive the onslaught of Klan violence, they would not only need to challenge paramilitary violence with their own show of force but also think deeply about how the omnipresent violence during what historian Gregory Downs has called "postsurrender wartime" would require a countermemory of the Civil War era that could account for the Union's failure to protect them.[4]

The particularities of Reconstruction-era violence reshaped the Black public sphere in profound ways. Kidada Williams has highlighted how new networks between freedpeople and their Black Northern allies were created to amplify the accounts of Southern violence—a project that not only helped to defeat the first iteration of the Ku Klux Klan but also played a pivotal role in establishing a political consciousness that would serve as the foundation of the modern antilynching movement.[5]

At the apex of 1860s Klan violence, the Lowcountry's Republican world became a haven in the statewide storm of white supremacy. The region's leaders placed a renewed emphasis on military and militia service, with local chapters of the state national guard now occupying a growing role in shaping the social and cultural terrain of memory. Home to the first efforts by freedpeople to remember the fallen Union dead, the Lowcountry continued to serve as a rival geography in the state during the 1860s and 1870s. Emancipation Day and Decoration Day would be transformed into important civic holidays that not only retold the story of the Union cause but also shepherded a new accounting of the recent past. During these celebrations, Lowcountry Republican Party leaders would increasingly embrace their own version of "bloody shirt" politics, using the memory of the martyred dead to remind their allies, and opponents, of the new and uncompromising lines that needed to be drawn in the fight for Reconstruction.[6]

These conflicts were brought into sharp relief during the 1870s as a movement emerged to "redeem" the state of South Carolina from the perceived misrule of the Republican Party. In this kaleidoscopic moment, the redeemers could be both the patrician Wade Hampton, who, at least publicly, eschewed violence and promised compromise with conservative Black leaders, and the paramilitary Red Shirts, who relished the opportunity to engage in a campaign of terror. The Republicans were equally split along the lines of radicals and moderates, Northerners and Southern-born, white and Black, and political elites versus the party's recently emancipated working-class base.

Far from being concentrated in the 1876 campaign, this was a "long Redemption" that began in the early 1870s and continued until the end of the decade. The many violent clashes that shaped this era would give rise to a new grammar of Black memory that the period's survivors would carry forth and deploy for the rest of their political lives. Ultimately, the politicians, voters, and armed freedpeople who fought against Redemption reshaped Black memory practices that survived Reconstruction's valley of the shadow and carried the violent lessons into the century's final decades.

Remembering Klan Violence and Resisting Redemption

By 1868, the Ku Klux Klan had taken deep root in South Carolina's Upcountry. Organized in the immediate aftermath of the Civil War, the Klan found its greatest success in the rural piedmont regions of the South, offering a clandestine paramilitary fraternity to white men who refused to adjust to the South's new social and political order. Where cities and Black-majority regions of the rural South offered the protections of Union occupation, predominantly Black national guard units, and broader communities that could provide collective security, South Carolina's Upcountry racial parity and lack of population density allowed night-riding to flourish. When the Joint Select Committee of the House of Representatives began its inquiry into Klan violence, it drew extensively on the testimony of Black South Carolinians living in Upcountry counties. "They said I must stop that republican paper that . . . was then coming to me from Charleston," remarked one Black Upcountry resident. "It came to my name. They said I must stop it, quit preaching, and put a card in the newspaper renouncing republicanism, and they would not kill me." Testifying to the most violent edge of the Klan's pogrom, Black Upcountry residents gave Congress the evidentiary body needed to create and pass the Enforcement Acts—measures that broke the back of the first Ku Klux Klan.[7]

While Black testimony and a broader collective memory of violence was crucial for building a federal response to Klan violence, it would be through the Reconstruction generation's Lowcountry political world that a specific countermemory of the era would emerge. In the immediate aftermath of Benjamin Randolph's assassination, prominent members of the Lowcountry's political bloc began to deploy Randolph's death to harden the political edges around the Republican coalition. "He seemed to fully comprehend the fact that our State had been very much broken, the fragments scattered, and to gather them up, and properly unite them, master workmen were required," lamented Jonathan Wright. "In every sense of the word, he was a master workman."[8]

Wright hoped that the Randolph's legacy would "be felt by generations yet unborn," a sentiment echoed by many of his Republican colleagues in the legislature. Stephen Swails, a free-born Black New Yorker who had met Randolph in 1864 when both men were stationed in the Lowcountry with different USCT regiments, commented "Senator Randolph is dead, but he still lives in

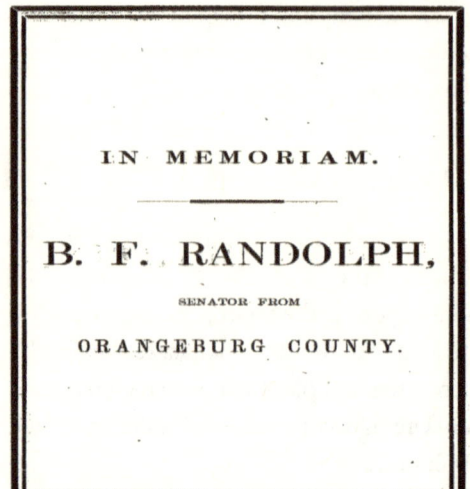

Memorial insert for Benjamin Randolph in the December 1868 issue of the *Journal of the House of Representatives of the General Assembly of South Carolina.*

the memories of the Senators who are now here, and his memory will be ever cherished in the hearts of the people of this State." William Whipper remarked "it is our duty to erect a monument to his memory, not only to mark his resting place, but to commemorate the cause for which he lived and for which he so nobly laid down his life." Charlestonian Charles D. Hayne called for a memoriam page in the upcoming issue of the *Journal of the House of Representatives of the State of South Carolina.*[9]

Most radically, Whipper and Robert Elliott both called on sending the 3,000 men of the Lowcountry's regiment of the National Guard to the Upcountry's Union County. While the thought of sending a Black regiment into the Upcountry was rejected by the party's more pragmatic leaders, Elliott's and Whipper's call for Black-led martial law illustrates a radical vision of Reconstruction that diverged from the more moderate ideal held by most leaders within the Republican Party.[10]

Hyperconscious of claims that it had become the party of "Negro domination" or "Black Reconstruction," South Carolina's Republican Party struggled over the racial makeup of its leadership. White Northerners in Columbia resisted placing Black men in the upper echelons of party executive or elected leadership, fearing this would further delegitimize the party in the eyes of native-born white people. When Randolph was elected chair of the party's executive committee, some white leaders grumbled that he was "totally unfit for that position" and that such a move was inappropriate at this stage in the party's history.[11]

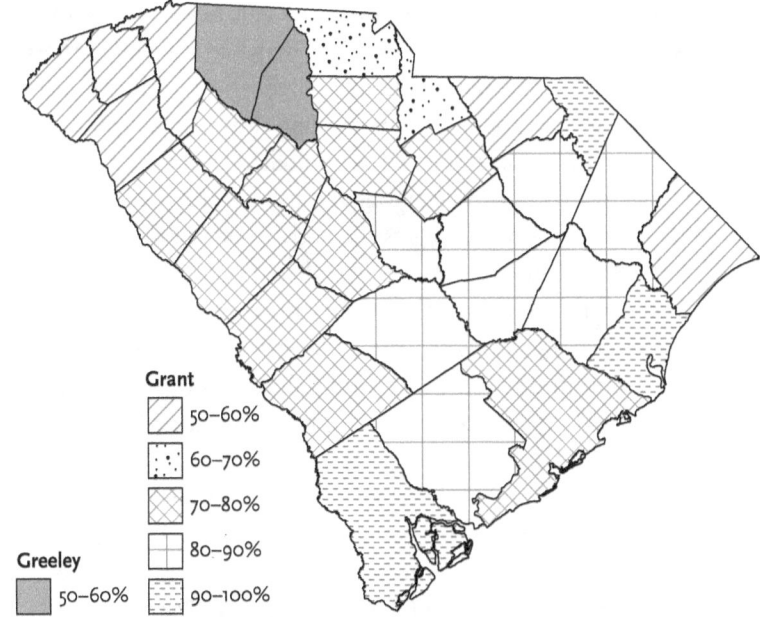

1872 presidential election results in South Carolina by county. The counties with patterns were won by Republican Party candidate Ulysses Grant. The counties with solid colors were won by Democratic Party candidate Horace Greeley.

Over time, the Lowcountry's leaders called for greater Black political power in the state. Highlighting the Black majority in the state legislature's lower house, Black leaders believed that they should not be barred from the party's highest offices. In 1870, Jonathan Wright's election to the state supreme court served as the first test of this promise. In 1872, gubernatorial candidate Franklin Moses would add Robert Gleaves to the ticket, placing the Black Lowcountry leader to receive the highest political position in the state government attained by a member of his race.[12]

Not all of the Reconstruction generation embraced increasing the size of the Black leadership class. In 1872, Martin Delany would begin drifting away from the Republican Party when it was at its apex of political power in the state, believing that its radical leaders were going to alienate white elites in Charleston. Delany, who had previously opposed symbolic efforts to nominate John Mercer Langston or Jonathan Wright for vice president, increasingly saw the South Carolina Republican Party's emphasis on Black officeholding as misguided. "The White race is true to itself," Martin Delany told Wright. "It is useless and doing injustice to both races to conceal the fact, that in giving liberty and equality of rights to the Blacks, they had no desire to see them rule over their own race. Radicalism, as taught by political leaders for selfish motives and personal gain, has led the masses of our untutored race to believe otherwise, and act accordingly." As Nell Irvin Painter has highlighted, Delany's turn away from the Republican Party reflected a preexisting elitism in his vision of racial destiny that became more pronounced as his political influence waned and a more grassroots politics took hold among the state's freedpeople.[13]

More than rhetorical nods to aggression and self-determination, the Lowcountry's Republican leaders increasingly embraced a broader militarization of the region's day-to-day political culture as a part of this larger grassroots turn in Black Southern political culture. The South Carolina National Guard served as a premier position of power and political patronage. "The South Carolina National Guard is altogether a negro organization," lamented one white Charlestonian. Leadership in the state national guard was seen as an ideal platform for the Lowcountry's aspiring Black politicians. Created in 1869 by an act of the state legislature, the National Guard of South Carolina would include more than 1,000 Black South Carolinians—making it the largest and most active state militia during the Reconstruction era. The state militia and its twelve statewide regiments would also serve as another vehicle for Black political leadership. Robert Elliott was appointed as commanding officer of the state national guard. Organized into twelve regional regiments, natives of the Lowcountry dispersed the state to lead units of Black soldiers. Prince Rivers, a former officer in First South Carolina Volunteers who had been born in Beaufort, commanded a regiment of the state militia in Hamburg. Black Charlestonians George McIntyre and Henry Hayne led the state's Fourth Regiment, which organized men in the upper Lowcountry counties of Colleton and Barnwell.[14]

Two of the Lowcountry's most prominent Black politicians would battle for the leadership of Beaufort's Third Regiment during the early 1870s. The largest regiment in the Blackest part of the state, the Third Regiment embodied the rival geography that was emerging in the rural Lowcountry. On August 1, 1870, the leaders of the Third Regiment requested 1,000 rifles and 5,000 cartridges of ammunition, far outpacing the regiments representing larger towns and cities like Charleston and Columbia. First led by William Whipper, who held the rank of brigadier general, the Third Regiment's leadership mantle would be passed to upstart politician Robert Smalls in retribution for Whipper's leadership in a failed impeachment against then-governor Robert Scott. A well-known Civil War hero, Robert Smalls had not yet ascended to regional or statewide power. In the Lowcountry, Richard Gleaves, Jonathan Wright, and William Whipper all held more prestigious political offices or were understood to be more important leaders within the state Republican Party. However, with his appointment to brigadier general of the Lowcountry's Third Regiment, Smalls found the trajectory of his political career radically changed. With "General" now attached to his name, Smalls would have the prestige, and the local patronage network, to defeat Whipper in Beaufort County's 1872 state senate election—thus birthing both his own Lowcountry political machine and the fierce political rivalry that would persist between the two men for the rest of their lives.[15]

Leadership of the Lowcountry's postbellum Black army conferred on its brigadier general a greater sense of social and cultural authority in a world where power was shaped by both ballots and bayonets. In the Georgia Lowcountry, Northern-born Republican leader Tunis Campbell used a 300-person militia to protect his political machine and the sizable community of Black landowning constituents who supported it from surging statewide Klan violence. In South Carolina, state national guard regiments occupied an outsized place in postbellum Black associational life. Bedecked in parade regalia for Emancipation Day and Decoration Day celebrations, companies of the state national guard would often be the highlight of the region's civic holidays. In Charleston's Emancipation Day celebrations, Black militiamen "armed with muskets and bearing all of the paraphernalia of war" served as the focal point of the ceremonies. Crowds would be "thrown into a flutter of excitement as some gorgeous militiaman stepped by with pompous stride on his way to the rendezvous." Military marching bands offered the musical backdrop and children ran alongside the marchers, seeking to emulate the gait of their favorite parading officer.[16]

At Beaufort's 1872 Emancipation Day celebration, six companies of the Third Regiment mustered into the town "from all directions" to participate in the parade. Beaufort, the site of the nation's first public reading of the Emancipation Proclamation, and its regiment of the state militia connected the story of wartime freedom to Reconstruction-era Black self-defense. "There are at present in the 3d regiment from four to five hundred of those who enrolled in the 1st regiment, and who were present under those giant oaks, and rejoiced that the year of jubilee," Robert Smalls remarked. The martial memory on display during these Emancipation Day celebrations was more than a collective effort to retain a rival set of commemorative practices, it was also part of the ongoing work of building a Reconstruction-era Black political world.[17]

The rise of Black militias animated white South Carolinians' deepest anxieties about the new political order. They corresponded with the ratification of the Fifteenth Amendment, and the rise of the first generation of Black politicians

"South Carolina—The Celebration of Emancipation Day, January 8th. In Charleston—Scenes and Incidents of the Parade," *Frank Leslie's Illustrated Newspaper*, February 10, 1877. Charleston Museum Illustrated Newspaper Collection, Charleston Museum, South Carolina.

elected to office in the state. "We have all round us negro national guards armed and equipped by the Legislature and the Governor at our expanse," one white Charlestonian told a Northern journalist. "Grant is determined to frighten us, if he can, by a display of armed force, and then, while we are under the fright, carry the state when time comes for a presidential election." Another white leader saw the Robert Smalls's appointment to lead the Lowcountry regiment as a dangerous omen for the region's white population: "It is needless to say that Smalls is the most bitter personal enemy of the white man in the State, and he would, it is hinted, only be too glad to draw a Winchester rifle on the entire white population of South Carolina." Historian Stephen Kantrowitz argues that Black men in the militia "provoked the same mass mobilization of white men that rumors of slave revolts had prompted." Already aggrieved by increased taxes, perceived corruption, and Black officeholders at the helm of local and state government, white South Carolinians saw the growing number of armed Black men cloaked in the authority of the state as an existential threat to their social and political order.[18]

Republican Party Turmoil, the 1876 Election, and the Rise of Hampton County

As white South Carolinians developed a coherent opposition to Reconstruction, Republicans in the state grew increasingly divided over how to move forward in the increasingly hostile political climate. The national party had soured on the state's executive leadership, and many privately and publicly questioned the efficacy of Black officeholding. "The Republicans of South Carolina must see to it that the State is redeemed by election of only true and honest men to office in the future," wrote Rufus Saxton, the former leader of South Carolina's Freedmen's Bureau. "Unless you do this, your present position is one of great peril, your race is on trial and the Nation's [sic] are watching with breathless interest this great experiment of universal suffrage."[19]

The call for reform led to the 1874 election of the moderate Republican Daniel Chamberlain. A white, Ivy League–educated abolitionist, Chamberlain had led a Black regiment during the Civil War and was part of the 1868 constitutional convention that produced the ambitious new governing document for the state. Chamberlain, however, was more a patrician than a populist. He had been part of the moderate wing of the party that opposed Benjamin Randolph's rise to party leadership and likely was stung by Randolph's election over him as party chair. Campaigning on a return to good government, Chamberlain appealed to the state's Lowcountry white elites not only as a matter of shrewd political calculus but also as a desire to be embraced by fellow patricians. "It was no secret among the whites of South Carolina's upper class that the governor desperately wanted their acceptance," observed historian Thomas Holt. Sensing that a steady and respectable hand was needed on the till, the Northern Black press supported Chamberlain's election over an Independent Republican ticket that had famed abolitionist Martin Delany running for lieutenant governor. "The political cloud is fast rising in this Commonwealth, and the bugle notes of the campaign have been sounded. Reform is the cry from the mountain to the seaboard, echoed alike by Democrat and Republican."[20]

Once in office, Chamberlain waged war on real and perceived corruption within the state Republican Party. When representatives elected former governor Franklin Moses and Lowcountry leader William Whipper to serve on the state Supreme Court, Chamberlain stretched his executive authority and overrode the will of the general assembly and state senate and refused to provide the final approval needed to commission the two men to the high court. In defending his decision, Chamberlain decried, "The civilization of the Puritan and the Cavalier, of the Roundhead and the Huguenot, is in peril." He told a New York reporter that the election of Whipper and Moses sent a "thrill of horror through the state" and compared their placement in the state judiciary to Tammany Hall's William Macy Tweed receiving a judicial position in a New York.[21]

Where Moses had been credibly accused of accepting a $15,000 bribe while serving as governor, Whipper's perceived corruption was much more ambiguous. With no criminal convictions, or accusations, Chamberlain simply claimed that Whipper was "utterly unfit for the office." Sensing that once again the state's white Republicans were drawing a color line within the party, several Republican clubs in the Lowcountry passed resolutions officially condemning Chamberlain's veto of Whipper's election to the state supreme court. Robert Elliott, who was now Speaker of the House of Representatives, made the house vote on Whipper's judgeship a fidelity test within the party and used his significant political capital to turn Black public opinion against Chamberlain.[22]

The party's internal fissures were temporarily patched over when Republicans were forced to confront another violent attack on high-profile members of the Reconstruction generation. On July 4, 1876, a group of Black men in the Ninth Regiment of the State Militia were confronted by a group of local men who found the drilling and parading to be obnoxious. Claiming that the men were not only creating a public nuisance but also providing unsanctioned Black militias with weapons from the state armory, nine men in the Ninth Regiment were brought before trial justice Prince Rivers. Four days later, more than 100 men from surrounding counties circled the courthouse and demanded custody of the Black prisoners. In the ensuing firefight, one of the militiamen was killed. The remaining men were captured and executed by the mob in the nearby woods.[23]

The Hamburg Massacre served as a stark reminder for the state's Republican leaders that the intertwined future of Reconstruction and racial destiny would be decided at the ballot box. "We are driven to believe that the Hamburg massacre was not only an assault upon our right to exercise our privilege as a part of the arms-bearing population of our country, but a part of a deliberate plan, arranged and determined upon by at least the members of the party, who not only constitute a positive quantity in its ranks, but who control its organization," argued a conference of Black politicians that included Robert Elliott, Richard Gleaves, and Jonathan Wright. This sense that the violence in

Hamburg was political in nature was not unfounded speculation. Matthew Butler, a former Confederate general and current Democratic politician, had actively stoked the mob violence—by the fall, he would be a leader in a local chapter of the Red Shirts, a grassroots movement of white gun clubs who committed themselves to redeeming the state on behalf of the Democratic Party and white supremacy. By the end of the year, there were nearly 300 white gun clubs that understood themselves to be paramilitary wings of the state Democratic Party.[24]

Wade Hampton, Chamberlain's Democratic rival, would publicly distance himself from this political violence and speak in the whiggish language of good government on the campaign trail. A Lowcountry aristocrat, former slaveowner, and Confederate general, Hampton embodied the aristocratic world that Daniel Chamberlain desperately sought to court. While speaking of the "horror of Hamburg" in public addresses, he also offered a series of resolutions removed weapons from the state's Black militias and preventing unsanctioned groups from "assembling, drilling, parading, or otherwise engaging in any military exercises." This move appears to have appeased some white elites. "The State arms have been surrendered with alacrity and the colored men who held them are said to be contracting freely for agricultural labor."[25]

This move, however, further polarized the racial and regional divide within the state Republican Party. On July 14, Chamberlain visited Beaufort to shore up his weak support among the Lowcountry's Black Republican base. As Brian Kelly has noted, the Lowcountry counties of Beaufort and Colleton "constituted the epicenter of anti-Chamberlain sentiment in the 1876 campaign." While Chamberlain had placed Beaufort leader Richard Gleaves on his ticket, the governor had never visited the Sea Island Black political center before and anticipated a hostile audience. "I am here to listen to any charges and complaints and to answer them, not in a spirit of defiance, not in a spirit of rebuke, but in a spirit of one who understands that what the people have given me, the people have the right to take away, and for the trust placed in my hands they have the right to call me to account." While he refused to discuss his decision to reject Whipper's judgeship, he made a broad appeal that the Lowcountry's support would be needed to retain Republican political control of the state. "I want the [R]epublican [P]arty of Beaufort County and of South Carolina to stand together and trust that there may be no dissension in the ranks in this county," Chamberlain pleaded.[26]

As mass meetings condemning the violence in Hamburg continued across the state, an alternative to Chamberlain's vision emerged that emphasized the role of Black South Carolinians in shaping the race's larger postbellum destiny.

> **ATTENTION!**
>
> **Colored Citizens Attention!**
>
> There will be a mass meeting of the Colored Citizens on Monday night, July 17th, in front of Market Hall, to express our indignation, and to adopt resolutions setting forth the enormity of General M. C. Butler's outrage in Hamburg So'Ca'. The following gentlemen will address the Meeting.
>
> Rev. R. H. Cain.
> Genl. R. B. Elliott.
> Rev. E Adams.
> Hon. W. J. Whipper

Handbill for the 1876 Charleston mass meeting held by Black South Carolinians in response to the Hamburg Massacre. Broadsides from the Colonial Era to the Present collection, South Caroliniana Library, University of South Carolina, Columbia.

On July 17, a group of Black citizens in Charleston issued an address that they circulated to several Northern papers highlighting the danger of what would happen if the political violence in Hamburg went unchecked. "This unarming of the colored Militia is the precursor of their work of blood and murder which they propose to inaugurate this Fall, in order to carry the election," the petitioners forewarned. Going further, the Black citizens who attended the Charleston mass meeting gave voice to a new generational vision that radically diverged from a more moderate one espoused by state and national Republican leaders. Highlighting that there were tens of thousands of freedmen and freedwomen who knew how to "bear Winchester rifles," "light a torch," or "use the knife," the meeting's attendees sought to make clear that a radical vision of freedom was taking hold among the state's young people.

There are 100,000 boys and girls who have not known the lash of a white master, who have tasted freedom once and forever, and that there is a deep determination never, so help their God, to submit to be shot down by lawless regulators for no crimes committed against society and law. ... The rising generation are as brave and daring as white men; already that spirit is taking deep root in the minds of thousands who have nothing to lose in the contest, and who would rejoice in an opportunity to sacrifice their lives for their liberty.

The region's "rising generation" would not wait patiently as leaders like Governor Chamberlain sought to acquiesce to or to accommodate the state's white elites. For the growing cohort of South Carolinians born after the destruction of slavery, a forward-looking vision of racial destiny mobilized a powerful grassroots defense of Reconstruction.[27]

As the state prepared for the 1876 election, local leaders were forced to provide an accounting for the diminishing economic conditions that hit the region's working-class freedpeople especially hard. Already within the long tail of the Panic of 1873, as well as a broader cash-poor postbellum Southern economy, Black agricultural workers in the Lowcountry had begun to agitate against both local landowning white elites and Republican politicians. In late May, rice workers began to strike along the Combahee River. Demanding higher wages and an end to being paid in paper scrip that was only redeemable at planter-owned stores, rice strikers targeted both scabs and Republican leaders with violence. Armed with "clubs, pistols, swords, and other weapons," the aggrieved rice workers destroyed the property belonging to the planters, including wagons carrying harvested rice. When Robert Smalls, now a US congressman, was called upon by Governor Chamberlain to quell the protests, he was told by his constituents that they would "tie him up and give him one hundred and fifty lashes on his big, fat ass" should the politician try to interfere with their actions. Meeting with more than 300 of the strikers, Smalls declined to have the men charged and ultimately arrived at their point of view, telling the governor that the rice region's emergent system of debt peonage was "worse than the evils of slavery" and needed to be abolished.[28]

Another issue that divided the Reconstruction generation's political leaders from its grassroots base involved the collapse of the Freedmen's Bank. Founded in 1868, the Freedmen's Bank initially reflected the broader optimism within the generation's vision of postbellum racial destiny. "Our bank, with its twenty-five branches, has now become an institution of the colored race, a great lever in their entire elevation, stimulating industry, enterprise and education; indeed, is in itself an educator, almost equal to the schools," reported one prominent Black Northern newspaper. In 1874, when embezzlement and corruption brought about the bank's collapse and closure, the economic institution quickly became synonymous with the federal government's betrayal of freedpeople. Built on the meager savings of soldiers and freed families, the bitter experience with the Freedmen's Bank would remain an era-defining experience for most Black Southerners.[29]

The Freedmen's Bank had branches across the Lowcountry, in Charleston, Savannah, and Beaufort, and its failure remained a live issue for the region's Republican voters during the 1876 election. At the beginning of the year, the federal government started reimbursing the bank's depositors with up to 50 percent of their lost savings, but this rollout was poorly executed and only added more confusion. At local political rallies and mass meetings, the cry "Tell us something about the Freedmen's Bank" was often shouted from the crowd. Lieutenant Governor Richard Gleaves invited Robert Purvis, one of the commissioners of the Freedman's Bank, to Beaufort so that he could directly address local depositors. A story that faded from the national imagination by the century's penultimate decades, the collapse of the Freedmen's Bank would remain a painful memory for the generation that lived through Reconstruction, making future promises from the federal government more difficult to trust.[30]

Bulldozing and Bloody Shirt Memory: The Lowcountry's Long Redemption

Marred by violence, ballot box stuffing, Election Day irregularities, both the Republican and Democratic Parties claimed to have won their statewide elections. With the neither national party receiving the necessary Electoral College votes to secure the White House, a bipartisan commission would be needed to determine the outcome of the 1876 election. In Columbia, both parties made claims on the governor's mansion and the statehouse. With the presidency conceded to Republican Rutherford B. Hayes in exchange for the removal of federal troops from the South, South Carolina Republicans realized that it would be impossible to hold the statehouse in the face of federal abandonment, a weakened state militia, and an energized paramilitary network willing to use extraordinary means to defend their counterrevolution.[31]

Despite their electoral victory, South Carolina's Democratic Party did not feel as though it had fully "redeemed" the state. Sensing that violence would not be enough to secure a new political order, Democratic leaders began redrawing the state's county lines to weaken the Lowcountry's Republican political world. On December 13, 1877, a bill was introduced in the South Carolina House of Representatives to make the portion of Beaufort County west of the

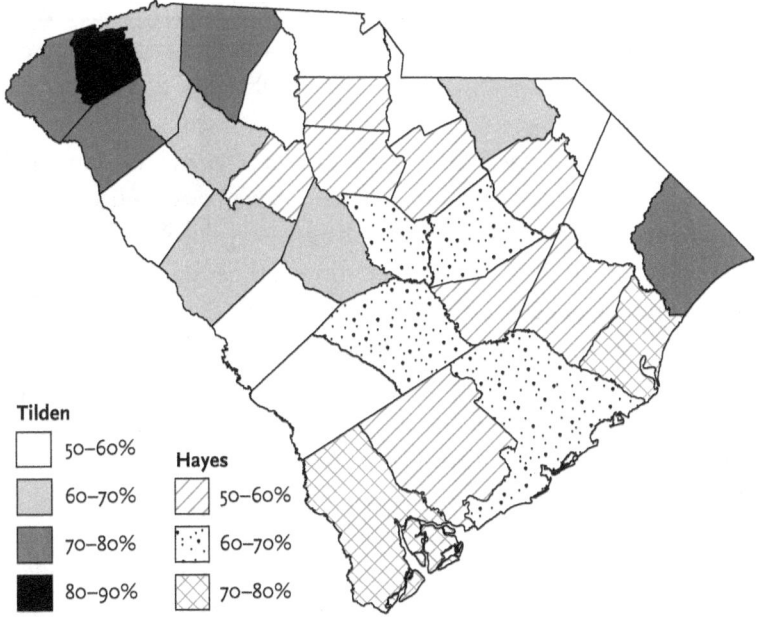

1876 presidential election results in South Carolina by county. The counties with patterns were won by Republican Party candidate Rutherford B. Hayes. The counties with solid colors were won by Democratic Party candidate Samuel Tilden.

Savannah and Charleston Railroad into a new "judicial and election county" called "Palmetto County." The territory of the proposed county had been an antebellum stronghold of both white yeomen and large planters and was less densely Black than the coastal section of Beaufort County. "The whole upper portion of this county is jubilant over the prospect of forever being separated from their sable brethren of the islands, by a division of the county," remarked one white resident of Beaufort County. Confident that the new county would weaken the Republican Party's strength in the Lowcountry and give the Democratic Party a footing in the region, Democrats across the state supported the measure.[32]

The plan for a new county, which had circulated since the early 1870s, picked up steam after the 1876 election of Wade Hampton, the Confederate hero whose gubernatorial victory represented the state's long-awaited "Redemption" from Republican rule. "What better name than Hampton!" exclaimed an editorial in a Beaufort County Democratic paper that wanted the new county to memorialize the governor. "A name dearer to Carolina than ever were the Colletons, the Berkeleys or the Ashleys of our provincial history." More than a symbolic victory for the Democrats, the creation of Hampton County significantly shrank the jurisdiction of Beaufort County's Republican Party, created a Lowcountry county with a significant white minority (34 percent), and set in motion a process that would ultimately allow its white residents political domination.[33]

Approved by both houses of the South Carolina General Assembly in February 1878, the newly created Hampton County gave Lowcountry Democrats a visible symbol to fight and defend in the upcoming fall election. The county's namesake visited the "baby county" several times during the 1878 campaign, and entire families clad in the infamous "Red Shirt" would reminisce as Hampton spoke glowingly about "redeeming" the state. Boasting at least ten Democratic rifle clubs of its own, Hampton County also attracted paramilitary organizations from across the state who sought to make the region as hostile as possible to Republican politicians. "There is scarcely a doubt but that Hampton County will go almost unanimously Democratic," argued one of the county's residents. "All breaches in Hampton County are healed. Every Democrat is falling into line, and there will be no straggling nor skulking," announced a "Red Shirt" writing to the state's paper of record.[34]

The new county would reshape the state's geography of violence. On October 26, 1878, Hampton County's Republican Party organized a political rally in the town of Gillisonville for the upcoming midterm election. Once the seat of Beaufort County during the antebellum era, Gillisonville was now part of the first county created since the state had been "redeemed." The town was the de facto border between the predominantly Black southern portion of the county, which included Beaufort and the Sea Islands, from the more white-dominated part that bordered Barnwell County. Moreover, Gillisonville was seen as the potential tipping point in the Fifth Congressional District race between Robert Smalls and his Democratic opponent George Tillman. Still reeling from the violent 1876 campaign, the leaders of the state Republican Party chose not to run a gubernatorial challenger to Hampton's reelection and focused their energy on the Lowcountry congressional race.[35]

Smalls likely knew that he was entering unsafe ground when he decided to canvass in the "baby county" of Hampton. Despite Wade Hampton's official support for racial reconciliation, his Red Shirt followers were determined to use violence to intimidate Republicans in Hampton County. In one instance, Smalls had to cancel an October 18 campaign rally with William Whipper in a nearby town in Hampton County. At an October 15 campaign event in Barnwell County, assailants opened fire on Smalls and his supporters. He considered suspending his campaign and exiting the race.[36]

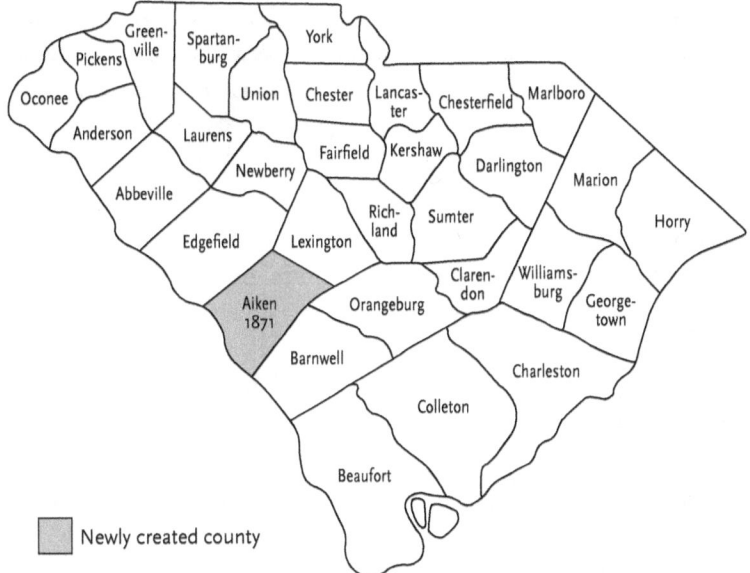

South Carolina counties, 1871–1877. South Carolina Department of Archives and History, www.archivesindex.sc.gov/guide/CountyRecords/1871.htm.

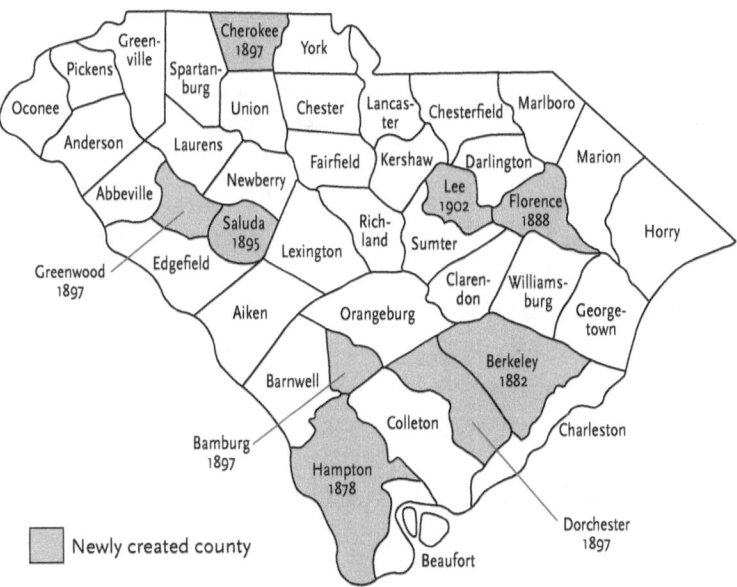

South Carolina counties, 1878–1907. South Carolina Department of Archives and History, www.archivesindex.sc.gov/guide/CountyRecords/1878.htm.

On Saturday, November 2, Robert Smalls arrived in Gillisonville for a Republican rally with forty men from Beaufort—many likely Union veterans or former members of the Lowcountry's Third Regiment of the state militia. The congressman had barely begun his campaign speech when the loud rumble of galloping horses forced him to cut his remarks short. Eight hundred Red Shirts under the command of former Confederate Lt. Col. Joseph Kirkland "came dashing into the town." The Red Shirts who patrolled Gillisonville included an assortment of newly reformed rifle clubs from around the state, some of whom had ridden for as many as three days from the state's Upcountry or neighboring counties in Georgia. They included some of state's "leading men," among them Smalls's opponent George Tillman. Having dragooned the county since September, the Democratic Clubs and Red Shirts in the state believed that any disarray in Democratic Party ranks would "throw Hampton into the hands into the radicals" and potentially give Republicans a majority in the US House of Representatives.[37]

The mob of 800 transformed the Republican rally into bedlam. Not satisfied with simply "whooping and hollering" or "scouring down the street on their horses," the Red Shirts began attacking the Black men and women in the audience by knocking off the hats of men and slapping women in the face as they rode by on their horses. These acts of disrespect incensed the men, who were ready "to pitch right into a fight with the eight hundred," but Smalls preached caution as he saw that his constituents were outmanned and outgunned. Rather than accede to mob's demand for a "division of [speaking] time," Smalls and his forty followers retreated to the store of Z. T. Morrison, a white Republican who had been a longtime ally of Smalls. With Colonel Kirkland announcing a ten-minute countdown before violence would ensue, Smalls and his armed associates barricaded the door, set up sentries behind the store's counters, and patiently aimed their weapons at the violent mob that waited outside. After ten minutes of waiting, the Red Shirts and rifle clubs threatened to set the store on fire, began trying to break down the door, and riddled the building with bullets. Fortunately, no one in the store was killed.[38]

Such anti-Black violence had become commonplace in the post-Reconstruction South Carolina. However, what occurred after the initial attack in Gillisonville may have had no parallel in the late nineteenth century. Following the late morning assault, several of Smalls's supporters in the crowd "ran to raise the alarm in every direction," and by the early afternoon the news had spread to "the most distant parts of the county" that Smalls's life was in jeopardy. By 6 p.m. that evening, hundreds of Smalls's supporters had arrived from Beaufort County. Armed with guns, axes, hoes, and other makeshift weapons, these men and women outnumbered and repelled the Red Shirts. Robert Smalls's second great escape would rival his wartime flight to freedom in its theatricality. When the Lowcountry politician discovered that a final column of the white mob was awaiting him at the Gillisonville train station to prevent his return to Beaufort, he managed to evade his would-be assailants by slipping past the entryway on the passenger platform and sneaking into the eastbound train's coal car. Once safe and seated, Smalls was heartened to see that at every station he "met troops of negroes, one and two hundred together, all on their way to Gillisonville to the rescue." Upon hearing Smalls tell this story at a rally in Beaufort, one sympathetic audience member noted, "I think if Robert S. does meet with any violence there will be hot times between the Blacks and rebs."[39]

Despite the clear effort to carve out a safe county for white Lowcountry Democrats, many of the region's Black residents remained undaunted by the shift in the Lowcountry's political geography. During the 1878 election season, Hampton County's Republican Party continued to organize political rallies, and Black voters continued to participate in the wide-ranging political culture that had defined the region since Reconstruction. Under constant surveillance and violent intimidation from Red Shirts and rifle clubs, Black voters organized "Blue Shirt" organizations to demonstrate their fearlessness toward their Democratic rivals. Donning a uniform designed to mirror, if not mock, the red canvas shirt worn by the supporters of Wade Hampton, the Blue Shirt organizations appeared in Hampton, Barnwell, and Richland counties during the 1878 campaign to defy the visual grammar of Redemption. When unable to purchase a solidly blue shirt, Black Republicans in the upper Lowcountry chose to accentuate the color blue somewhere else on their person. "The women wore, many of them, blue veils . . . blue shoulder knots, blue belts or blue scarfs," noted one observer. "The men were gorgeously attired in shirts, shoulder knots, or bat bands of the same ominous color."[40]

Part of freedpeople's longer tradition of postemancipation self-fashioning, the Blue Shirts' act of sartorial resistance was coupled with a willingness to meet white paramilitary forces with equal measures of violence. At an October 18 rally in the town of Lawtonville, a white observer remarked that the main street was "Black and blue," with men, women, and children all wearing the new uniform of resistance. At an October 22 rally, Red Shirts and Blue Shirts clashed and Black members of the crowd drew pleasure from the prospect of "tearing the Red-Shirts off" their enemies. Far from simply retreating and accepting the death of Reconstruction, Black residents of the Lowcountry were resolved to meet violence with violence and resist the Democratic Party's efforts to erase the region's legacy of Black political power.[41]

While the paramilitary efforts by Black South Carolinians were able to save lives and preserve the Lowcountry's rival political geography, these tactics alone were not enough to secure a Republican victory in the 1878 Fifth Congressional District election. Having defeated the Democratic challenger George Tillman by a 1,500 vote margin in 1876, Robert Smalls would lose his reelection bid by 15,000 votes in 1878—the largest margin of victory by any candidate for the Forty-Sixth Congress. While the Southern Democratic press attributed Smalls's loss to his spurious 1877 bribery conviction, outside observers recognized that widespread polling place irregularities, ballot box stuffing, and broad election fraud as the central reasons for Smalls's defeat. For example, not only had the number of polling places in Beaufort County been halved from eighteen to nine, requiring many voters to walk more than twenty miles to cast their ballot, but also several polling places had been deliberately left closed so that those who made the extraordinary effort to vote were forced to trek even further to find another precinct. Even more pressing were the questions of tissue ballots and Election Day voter intimidation. One observer highlighted that in Edgefield County, the September 5 Democratic primary vote total of 3,000—nearly every registered Democratic voter in the county—more than doubled to 7,500 in the November 5 general election.[42]

The rampant election fraud that occurred in South Carolina and other Southern states in 1878 triggered demands for greater federal oversight of the region's elections. A committee led by Colorado Democratic senator Henry Teller was convened and given the power to subpoena witnesses. Over the course of two months, the Teller Committee interviewed more than 100 South Carolinians, including several residents of Hampton and Barnwell Counties who testified to voter intimidation and polling place irregularities that occurred during the 1878 campaign. "It is probable that within a short time there will be important changes in the Federal officials in the South," one Northern newspaper wrote of the Teller Committee's findings. "The President and his intimate advisers are not well satisfied with the manner with which a number of the more prominent officials there have performed their duties in Georgia, South Carolina, and Louisiana." Popularizing the term "bulldozing," meant to highlight the more unrestrained nature of post-Reconstruction voter intimidation in the South, the Teller Committee captured a long and ongoing Redemption, reminding Northern Republicans that the full political and moral cost of abandoning Reconstruction in the South was still being calculated.[43]

Ultimately, this effort to provide a "fully-loaded cost accounting" of Redemption-era violence would remain an unfinished project. Well into century's last decade, former Red Shirts, white Northerners, and members of the Reconstruction generation continued to debate the meaning of the earlier era's violence. Benjamin Tillman, the Democratic US senator who led paramilitary mobs during Reconstruction, would defend the violence of 1876 in glowing terms. "We took the government away. We stuffed ballot boxes. We shot them. We are not ashamed." In his old age, Daniel Chamberlain would repeatedly lament Black political power as "a grave mistake" and would support the lynching of Black men accused of sexual assaulting white women. On the eve of disfranchisement, Robert Smalls would stand before the South Carolina statehouse and provide a radical countermemory of Redemption, declaring that "since Reconstruction times" more than 50,000 Black Southerners had been killed—a figure that surpassed any contemporary or current estimate of postbellum violence.[44]

In Columbia, South Carolina, a quieter memory persisted in Randolph Cemetery, which been established to commemorate the legacy of Benjamin Randolph and served as the final resting place for many of the era's Black political leaders. The violence of Redemption had been formative for those who lived—and not everyone lived—through the end of Republican government in South Carolina. In the century's final decades, many of these struggles would continue, albeit in quieter, more quotidian ways. Battles in the public sphere would transform into more intentional struggles over collective memory and countermemory, as the Reconstruction generation shifted their struggle to new terrain.[45]

CHAPTER THREE

The Rise of the Black Seventh
Racial Gerrymandering, Rival Geography, and the Struggle over the Republican Party's Destiny in South Carolina

On January 1, 1880, Ulysses S. Grant made a whistle stop in Beaufort as part of a then-unprecedented third-term presidential campaign. Canvassing the Southeast on his national railway tour, Grant returned to Republican Party politics after seeing the disarray brought about by the administration of Rutherford B. Hayes. Hayes's failures to appeal to any of the major factions within his party, from the defenders of the spoils system to the advocates of civil service reform and the proponents of hard money policy, left him without a pathway for a second term. Grant's popularity and strength were seen as an antidote to the weak and indecisive tenure of his successor, and many Republican Party operators began setting the stage for the former Union general's return to the White House.[1]

Coordinating his visit to coincide with Emancipation Day, Grant likely recognized that his pathway back to the presidency would depend on re-animating the world of Southern Republicanism—making Beaufort, the Reconstruction-era Republican stronghold, an ideal campaign stop. Upon arriving in the Lowcountry, Grant, his wife Julia, and his brother Fred were greeted by a spectacular parade replete with a brass band, two Black military companies in full parade regalia, and a cavalcade of carriages and horse-drawn buggies. The vehicles made their way from the center of the town of Beaufort to the Port Royal Railway train station at Yemassee Junction.[2] Before a crowd of more than 5,000, Grant delivered a speech that explicitly evoked the history of the Civil War, emancipation, and Reconstruction—likely with the understanding that the Black voters in attendance were the base of the Reconstruction-era Republican Party. "It has afforded me great pleasure to pay a visit to the town of Beaufort," he told his listeners. "It is a place that has occupied a conspicuous place in the history of our country for the past twenty years, and it is to be hoped that it is a place where the best of the newly enfranchised race are to be developed. I hope that they will become worthy and capable citizens." Undeterred by the broader attacks on the Republican Party in the state, Beaufort's Black citizens came out in great numbers to see Grant in person and show the former president that the Lowcountry still had a robust Republican political culture. "We got Him! We's got him!" shouted one attendee. "You's all right, General. We is going for ye. We's all Republicans, hurrah!" exclaimed another.[3]

The Lowcountry's leaders were equally aware that Grant's reelection would offer the Reconstruction generation a chance to rebuild the statewide party. Leading the procession to and from the train station, Robert Smalls, who had recently been returned to Washington after a congressional committee determined that his 1878 opponent had won fraudulently, "looked the monarch of all he surveyed," according to one reporter. More than planning a parade, Smalls also sought to broadcast a pointed message to the nation about Southern Republicanism broadly, and the Lowcountry's unique political world more specifically. In an interview with a national reporter, Smalls did not mince his words: The state's Democrats had "bulldozed our people last time [in 1878]," he said, "and got things in their own hands." He challenged white Northerners' commitment to racial justice, stating, "If we could only get some Northern Republican to come and stand there to watch things it would go all right for they're afraid of you folks." Most important, Smalls made sure that the reporters covering Grant's presidential campaign recognized the power that Black voters in the Lowcountry continued to hold. "They can't bulldoze us here," Smalls said of his home district, "for we're too strong." Skillfully connecting the recent past with the present, Smalls made Grant's presidential campaign a referendum on the legacy of Reconstruction and reminded national Republicans that while Black voters in the South had been betrayed by the Hayes administration, Republicans could mobilize that powerful regional bloc if they remained committed to civil and voting rights.[4]

This chapter examines both Republican leaders' desire to preserve their political power in the Lowcountry during the early 1880s and South Carolina Democrats' efforts to circumscribe that still active political world. Still possessing a Black majority, South Carolina, especially in its coastal regions, continued to see Republican officials elected to local and state office during Wade Hampton's governorship. While the statehouse and governor's mansion had been "redeemed" by the Democratic Party, postbellum white supremacy remained an incomplete political project. Divided by class and region, some portion of the state's white voters could be drawn into a coalition with the Republican Party, spelling a return to Reconstruction.

To prevent this, the Democratic Party embarked on a series of voting rights attacks that, while falling short of total disfranchisement, severely curtailed the strength of the state Republican Party and eliminated the possibility of a third-party challenge to Democratic Party dominance. By both making voter registration more difficult and adding additional barriers to casting a ballot on Election Day, South Carolina's Democratic Party pioneered a series of antidemocratic measures that would anticipate the more robust suite of voting restrictions implemented in the century's final decade. The most sinister innovation of these policies would be the redrawing of new congressional districts to pack as many of the state's Black-majority counties as possible into a single congressional district. With no respect for geographic or spatial consistency, the newly created Seventh Congressional District would serve as the late nineteenth century's capstone in racial gerrymandering. While not singular in its creation of a "Black district," South Carolina Democrats' redistricting exceeded earlier efforts and reflected the deep tactical innovation that the legacy of Reconstruction inspired among the state's white leaders.

While the 1882 gerrymander eliminated Black voters' ability to influence statewide and federal elections in the other six districts, it also increased the Lowcountry's importance as a Black geography in the national imagination. Now the home of one of the South's few remaining Republican pathways to Congress, the Lowcountry and its leaders stood as a bastion of the Reconstruction generation's legacy. Inextricably connected to discussions about the race's destiny in the national Black press, South Carolina's "Black Seventh" would serve as both a battleground for the first phase of disfranchisement and a still burning ember of the earlier movement's political dream.

Early Disfranchisement, Third-Party Politics, and the South Carolina Republicans in the Political Wilderness

Robert Smalls's observation that the Lowcountry's base of Black voters still retained considerable political strength reflected a broader belief among Black Southern leaders that they had suffered only a temporary loss in 1877. In 1880, Frederick Douglass publicly expressed disappointment with President Hayes before endorsing Ohio congressman James Garfield for president. Across the nation, Black leaders in the press began to follow closely the career of Senator James G. Blaine of Maine, believing that after Grant, he would be the most ardent voice for civil rights and stronger federal election laws. In Washington, DC, the "Blaine Invincibles" would remain a powerful social club that dominated the city's local Black political culture during the 1880s.[5]

A relatively minor political figure in the party before the 1880 Republican National Convention, Garfield defeated both Grant and Blaine for the party's nomination and Democratic candidate Winfield Hancock in the fall. Although Garfield lost South Carolina to his Democratic rival by an almost two-to-one

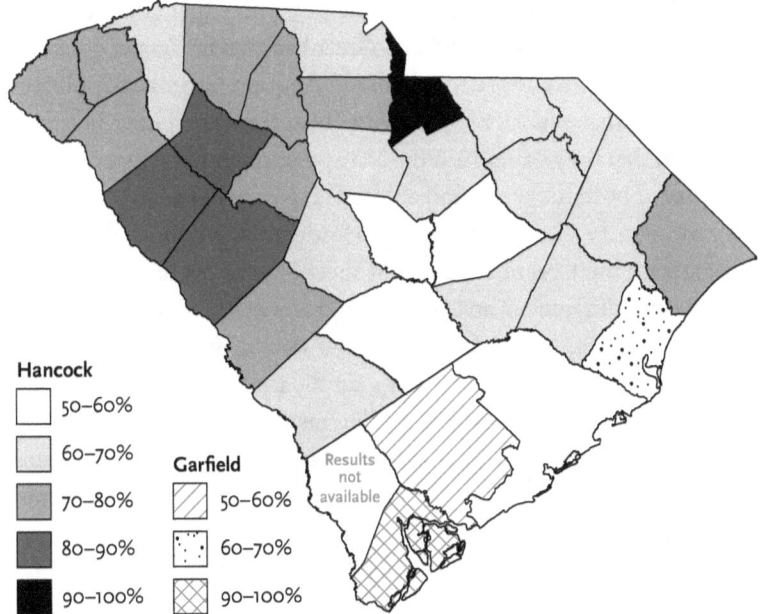

1880 presidential election results in South Carolina by county. The counties with patterns were won by Republican Party candidate James Garfield. The counties with solid colors were won by Democratic Party candidate Winfield Hancock. The Lowcountry counties of Beaufort, Colleton, and Georgetown would provide a majority of their votes for Garfield. No election data available for Hampton County.

margin, he had his strongest turnout in the Lowcountry, winning popular vote majorities in Beaufort, Colleton, and Georgetown Counties.[6]

While this election highlighted the weakness of the statewide Republican Party, it also offered a potential roadmap for a third-party challenger that ran through the Lowcountry. "Even united," remarked historian Stephen Kantrowitz of the state's white voters, "they remained a minority." Any split in the white Democratic coalition threatened the long-term future of the party. The Greenback-Labor Party saw small political window opening and tried to take advantage of this new, and still fluid, political order.[7]

Formed to oppose monopolies and the gold standard, the Greenback Party saw its success in South Carolina tied to its ability unite the state's poor white and Black people against the large landowners and Lowcountry elites who controlled the Democratic Party. Largely composed of white yeoman farmers in the state's Upcountry, the Greenback-Labor Party hoped that the economic and political issues that afflicted the state's poor white people would lead them away from the Democratic Party, which could offer the slogan of white supremacy and not much else. "The prejudices that could deprive the colored man of his vote," declared one Greenback leader, "cover contempt of the fortunate classes for those less favored." Another Greenback politician in the state argued that elite Democrats were "foster[ing] prejudice between the two races" so that they could "run the state government for their own benefit to the injury of both the white and colored taxpayers of the state."[8]

The Lowcountry's Reconstruction-era leaders also recognized the promise of aligning with the Greenback Party. Robert Smalls saw that despite the regional and racial differences, an alliance could serve the economic and political interests of his constituents. At a September 1882 rally, he invited J. Hendrix McClane, the Greenback-Labor Party's candidate for governor, to Beaufort, where both Smalls and Thomas E. Miller gave speeches in support of McClane and the Greenback Party's platform of soft money. Likely remembering the 1876 Combahee rice strikers singing in support of receiving greenbacks over paper scrip, Smalls broke from his party's hard money orthodoxy and briefly aligned with this new populist political party. "We cannot elect a [statewide] Republican ticket," Smalls argued in the campaign leading up to the election. "But by combining with the Greenbackers we may be able to effect something."[9]

While the Greenback-Labor Party was soundly defeated in both the 1880 and 1882 gubernatorial elections, it gained more than 13,000 votes and won Beaufort County with the assistance of Smalls's Lowcountry political machine. More important, the party's growth provided a glimpse of an alternative political path for the state. Like the Readjusters in Virginia, as well as the later Farmers' Alliance and Populist movements, the Greenback-Labor Party exemplified the vibrancy of the century's penultimate decade for third-party challenges in the South.[10]

In the face of these challenges, South Carolina's Democratic Party instituted a series of measures designed to disfranchise African American voters without violating the Fifteenth Amendment. A voter registration and election law enacted in 1882 became the cornerstone of this effort. It required all citizens of the state of South Carolina to register to vote by the end of 1882. Those who missed the initial registration deadline were given a single one-day window per month until the July preceding a November election; after that, new voters would be prohibited from voting in that year's election. While ostensibly color-blind, the law's stringent registration provisions were designed to have a disproportionate impact on the state's Black wage workers and sharecroppers because it required them to reregister every time they moved (even if the move was on the same farm). Another provision, which became known as

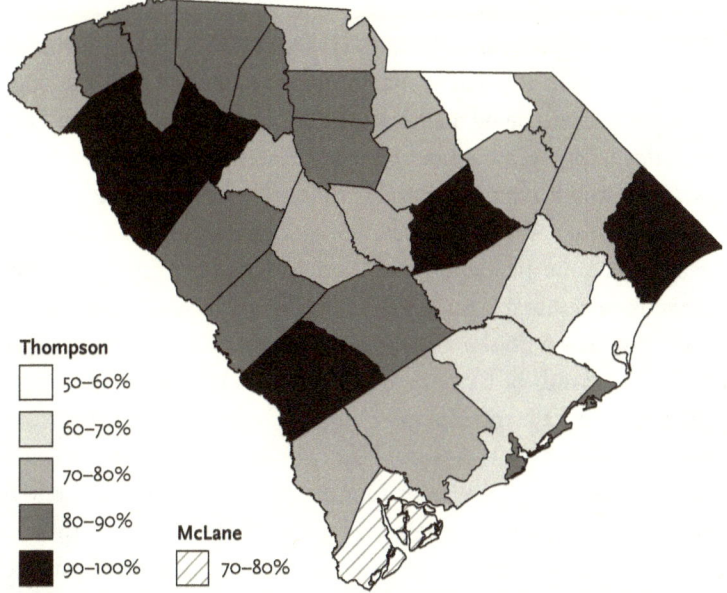

1882 South Carolina gubernatorial election results by county. The counties with solid colors were won by Democratic Party candidate Hugh Thompson. Beaufort would be the only county to provide most of its support for J. Hendrix McLane, the Greenback-Labor Party candidate.

the "eight-box law," required voters to deposit a properly marked ballot in a separate box for each of the eight electoral races at the local, state, and federal levels. By requiring voters to recognize each box's label, the law effectively established a literacy test; ballots placed in the wrong box were invalid. While the law managed to disfranchise large swaths of illiterate voters across racial lines, it had a disproportionate impact on Black voters.[11]

Alongside the registration and election laws, a new stock law, which required all livestock owners to fence their animals, also had a dramatic impact on the state's agricultural working class. Pushed forward by the state's white landowning elites in the fall 1881 session of the state legislature, the stock law caused a veritable uprising among the state's poor white farmers. A "stock law kuklux" took to destroying existing fences belonging to white landowners and heightened class tensions within the state. "This element in favor of the act don't raise any stock nor do they want to raise any but they want it fixed so as to make the poor people pay for their bacon in the rents of their lands. Their object and intention is to keep the poor white man poor and the negro poorer." As several scholars have noted, South Carolina's stock law, as well as similar fencing laws passed in other Southern states following Reconstruction, gave pause to the cross-class coalition among white Southerners in the Democratic Party. In eliminating free-range grazing, a practice that had long been essential for white yeoman farmers across the South, the stock law added strength to the populist argument being made by the nascent Greenback-Labor Party.[12]

Less noticed, however, has been the way the new stock law impacted Black farmers. In addition to causing a sizable exodus from the state, the new stock law spurred another wave of intrastate migration, leading the Lowcountry to once again became an anchor for a Black exodus from the South Carolina Upcountry. In response to a poor crop in the fall of 1881, a new stock law and a new registration law passed in the state legislature, and ongoing violence and voter fraud, thousands of Black South Carolinians left Edgefield County. At least 5,000 left the state entirely and migrated to either Atlanta or the trans-Mississippi West, where they would join the larger exodus that had been started by Benjamin "Pap" Singleton. One newspaper reported that 1,000 Black residents of the Upcountry had migrated to Beaufort County in a three-week period. The *New York Times* argued that the central reason that Beaufort had emerged as site of in-migration "is because the country is almost exclusively republican." Similar to the wave of emigration that occurred in the immediate aftermath of Redemption, the 1882 exodus reflected the Lowcountry's ongoing symbolic power as a site of Black freedom in the South—a site of counter-memory that continued to reflect the hopes and aspirations of freedpeople.[13]

In this moment of economic turmoil and regional reordering, Republican leaders in the South Carolina Lowcountry framed their region as a mecca where the promise of Reconstruction persisted. At an 1882 Emancipation Day celebration in Beaufort, Robert Smalls; J. W. Collins, intendent for the town of Beaufort; and Thomas E. Miller all encouraged Exodusters to settle in the county and promised affordable land and the ability to exercise their political rights without interference. Smalls went so far as to connect the 1882 exodus to the larger story of emancipation. Where the initial emancipation nearly twenty years earlier had been physical, Smalls argued that the 1882 migration reflected an ongoing "moral emancipation" that saw Black Southerners rejecting injustice and actively seeking "to go elsewhere where their labor would be better renumerated" and where they "would be better appreciated and more fairly dealt with." The *Charleston News and Courier*, the state's Democratic newspaper of record and a harsh critic of Smalls, saw a more sinister and political motive in the day's events. Calling the Gullah statesman's speech "perfect caravansary," the paper insinuated that Smalls and his allies were seeking to buy land and houses in the upper portions of Beaufort County for the migrants and thus grow the number of votes that his Lowcountry machine could wield in future elections.[14]

South Carolina's Seventh Congressional District and the Rise of Racial Gerrymandering

Deeply aware that ongoing white rule in the state was jeopardized by changing state demographics and the threat of new federal election laws, South Carolina's Democratic Party looked at the upcoming federally mandated redistricting as a way to address the new demographic reality. At a special session of the legislature convened on June 7, 1882, state senator J. F. Izlar of Orangeburg introduced a bill dividing the state into seven congressional districts. Samuel Dibble, a Democratic congressman from South Carolina, was the plan's architect. Hoping to ensure Democratic control in six of the seven new districts, Dibble drew the boundaries so as to concentrate a full 25 percent of the state's Black population into a single district, the new Seventh Congressional District, thereby diluting Black voting strength in the other six districts.[15]

Unconstrained by any calculus other than racial concentration, the proposed Seventh District presented a fantastic cartographic spectacle. The Seventh District not only encompassed all of the state's most heavily African American coastal counties of Beaufort, Georgetown, and Colleton but also snaked several hundred miles inland to incorporate portions of six other counties in the state that had significant Black populations. Not surprisingly, the new congressional district map placed the relatively new Hampton County outside the Seventh District, thereby ensuring that its white voters would have a Democratic congressman. Thus, in reserving the Seventh District for "ex-convicts and scalawags," white elites in South Carolina used the power of cartography to reduce Black political power without resorting to fraud and violence.[16]

Political gerrymandering has had a deeply fraught history in the United States. Introduced into the Constitution to prevent the formation of rotten boroughs, shrinking or already marginal districts that exercise outsized power in the legislature because there was no means for redistricting based on population change, gerrymandering almost immediately took on an explicitly partisan contour. Most famously in Elbridge Gerry's efforts to draw amphibian-shaped districts in Massachusetts, the early nineteenth century saw a wide variety of states create outrageously shaped political districts. At the height of the Second Party System, Whigs accused Democrats of dividing the congressional districts in North Carolina in a patently unfair way; Democrats pointed to the lines drawn by Whigs in Kentucky that gave Henry Clay's party control over nine of the Bluegrass State's ten house seats. During Reconstruction, Southern Democrats accused Gen. John Pope, then military governor of the Third Military District, of unfairly giving the Republican Party a partisan advantage through the redistricting of Florida and Georgia. With no legal precedent for challenging the constitutionality of partisan gerrymandering, state political parties used the decennial redrawing of districts as an opportunity to punish their enemies and further entrench their own power.[17]

While the gerrymandering of congressional districts was an immediate feature of government-mandated redistricting, the post-Reconstruction moment gave rise to what we would now call racial gerrymandering. The burning desire to redeem Southern state governments from Republican rule led Southern Democrats to realize that extralegal violence would not be enough to maintain political power. Still faced with large Black populations—and thus a large reserve of Republican voters—Democratic leaders sought to pack as many Black voters as they could in a single congressional district. In 1875, the Mississippi Democratic Party's "shotgun plan" of overthrowing the duly elected Republican state government was accompanied by the creation of the "shoestring" Sixth Congressional District, which encapsulated nearly all of the majority Black counties that ran the length of the Mississippi River. In 1876, Alabama's congressional districts were redrawn in a way to force Jeremiah Haralson and James T. Rapier, Black men who had represented different parts of the state's Black Belt for most of the decade, to compete against one another in the state's new "Black Fourth District." While apparently violating the spirit of the Fifteenth Amendment, these districts were not challenged in state or federal courts during the nineteenth century. As historian J. Morgan Kousser has demonstrated, what we now know as racial gerrymandering began occurring almost immediately after the Fifteenth Amendment was passed. A response to the specter of Reconstruction's return, these New South redistricting efforts highlight the long and uneven road to disfranchisement.[18]

As an interim step before full and total disfranchisement, the rise of racially gerrymandered districts in the post-Reconstruction era signaled a profound shift in how the nation understood the terrain of Black politics. The creation of hypervisible Black districts reminded observers of the recent past when Black voters had more robust political rights. "I am in a very 'Black region,'" wrote one white resident of Eutaw, Alabama. "I am unable, thus far, to find any distinct evidences [sic] of improvement among the colored people in any of the 'Black districts,' except that, of course, they are of late giving far less attention to politics than they formerly did." White Southerners saw this as reminder of the continued danger of the Black franchise. Many Northern Republicans understood the efforts to concentrate Black voters into single districts as part of a larger assault on the free and fair ballot. "In the colored districts, where the Republican majority is overwhelming, the votes of the colored men do not seem to have been counted," reported one Northern newspaper.[19]

Lowcountry Republicans criticized the proposed gerrymander and highlighted the detrimental effect it would have on Black political power. Reflecting on the impact of the impact of the gerrymander before a congressional committee in 1891, Thomas Miller of Beaufort claimed that the 1882 redistricting had to be understood alongside its "twin companion," the state's election and registration laws, and seen as an all-out assault on the Fifteenth Amendment. "It was the high-water mark of political ingenuity coupled with rascality, and the merits of its appellation, 'Fraud made easy and safe.'" Other critics castigated Dibble's plan for packing 25 percent of Black South Carolinians into a single district; with a total population of 187,535, the new Seventh District would be the most populous congressional district in the state, with between 20,000 and 69,000 more people than each of the other districts. Miller offered an alternative plan that would have allowed for four Democratic districts and three Republican ones, rather than the six-to-one division of the proposed gerrymander. That call went unheeded, and by July 5, 1882, the gerrymandered map of the state had been approved by both houses of the South Carolina Legislature.[20]

South Carolina's Democrats celebrated their victory. "If the full white and colored Democratic vote be cast for Congressman," boasted Francis Dawson, editor of the *Charleston News and Courier*, "only the Seventh district would go Republican." Other Democrats in the state saw the gerrymander as high political art and a welcome effort to preserve "good government" in the state of South Carolina. As one white Lowcountry leader explained, "It was . . . determined that the negroes should be massed in what is termed the 'Black district' and that this region of darkness should be given over to the republicans." Another observer remarked, "Any Congressional district in South Carolina which can be carried by the Republicans is sure to send to Congress some low Blackguard or self-confessed thief." Speaking in the revanchist language of Redemption, one "tax payer" declared his support for the gerrymander in explicit opposition to Reconstruction: "Will our Legislature hesitate for a moment to redistrict our State in such a manner as to prevent the possibility of its falling into the clutches of this vulture crew, for at least the next ten years?" Going further, the writer warned that Radical Republicans could once again gain control of the levers of state power. "They have never changed their skin nor their spots, and could they by any possibility, get another hold upon the State they would profit by the experience of the past, and with death grip would cling to power until deprived of it by a revolution more memorable than that of 1876."[21]

Northern Republicans focused on the district's outrageous cartography, using the monstrous shape of the Black Seventh to make their own arguments against voter suppression. "The district is shaped like a bat with outstretched

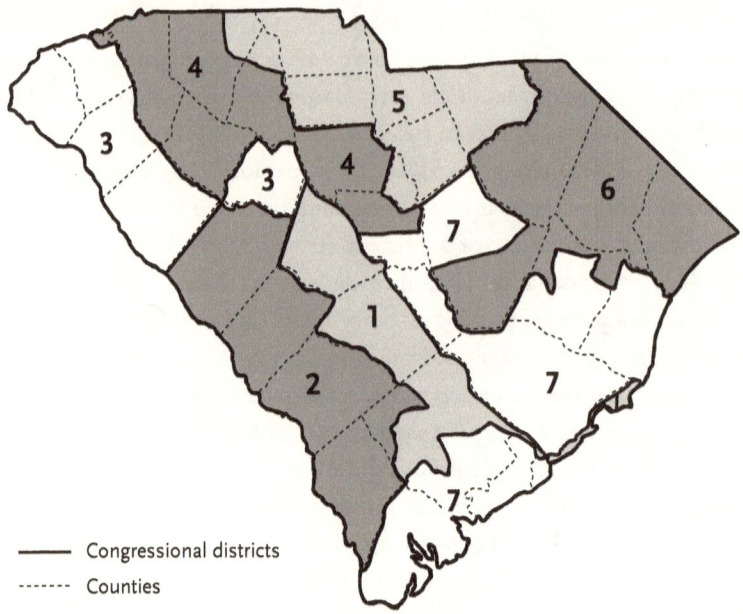

"The Congressional Districts of South Carolina as 'Gerrymandered' by the Democracy in 1882." Control no. 2015588077, Geography and Map Division, Library of Congress, Washington, DC.

wings," remarked the *Chicago Daily Tribune*. "It is backed like a camel, and from one point of view is very like a weasel." In the summer of 1882, during House debates over the contested 1880 election between Robert Smalls and George Tillman in the state's old Fifth Congressional District, Republicans used the most recent gerrymander as more evidence of the unabashed theft by South Carolina's Democrats. "It was not pretended that any prospective redistricting in 1882 had had any effect upon the vote for Smalls or Mr. Tillman two years before but served the Republicans as evidence of the total depravity of the white people of South Carolina in 1882," reflected the *Charleston News and Courier* on the debates in Congress.[22]

The map of South Carolina's newly gerrymandered districts was an invaluable tool in these congressional debates. "Maps illustrating the recent gerrymander in South Carolina played an important part in the day's proceedings as part of the Republican argument against the indorsement of such methods in preventing free elections," remarked one reporter who witnessed the debates on the floor of the Forty-Seventh Congress. Three different maps of South Carolina's newly gerrymandered districts were displayed on the Speaker's desk, with one congressman using his cane as pointer to draw attention to the outrageous features of the new districts. Map 3.3., most likely created by

Republicans specifically for the aforementioned congressional committee, highlights how access to the ballot box in the South continued to be a live issue for the post-Reconstruction Republican Party.[23]

While it is impossible to say with certainty when this map was created, it seems likely that the map above was designed with a pedagogical purpose. With each of the state's seven congressional districts brightly color-coded, and each county line framed with sharp bold outlines, this map offered a clear argument against abandoning the party's Black voters.

Sensing that they could make political hay out of the gerrymandering issue, the Republican Party's 1882 campaign textbook recapped and summarized the House debate over South Carolina's 1882 gerrymander. As a tool to help party operatives find explosive topics that would engage the party's base, the campaign handbook played an outsized role in shaping the order of platform issues that were debated on the campaign trail. Most important, the 1882 Republican Party textbook highlighted that this gerrymander was part of a multipronged "Bourbon plan" that began almost immediately after the passage of the 1867 Reconstruction Acts. In a reprinted speech from Massachusetts congressman George Frisbie Hoar, the Republican Party document closed its attack on the recent gerrymander by emphasizing a now-fading strand of Union memory that challenged Southern redeemers' extralegal efforts and defended the right of Black Southerners to pursue their political destiny. "You commenced by every conceivable means, by kukluxism, tissue ballots, intimidation, red-shirt brigades, and shot-gun companies to prevent the voice of her loyal people from being heard, and to prevent the colored men in your state from having any voice in choosing their rulers."[24]

The Black District's First Election

The gerrymander had an additional negative consequence: disorienting the Black political sphere in South Carolina and making former allies into enemies who had to compete over a shrinking electoral landscape. The ensuing battle royal over the Seventh Congressional District became even more crowded by the entrance of Edmund William McGregor Mackey. A white native of Charleston born into the Lowcountry plantocracy, Mackey betrayed his class background and joined the Republican Party after the war. Over the course of Reconstruction, he served as a chair of the state Republican Party, a congressman from the state's Second Congressional District, and an assistant US district attorney. Long despised by white South Carolinians for betraying white supremacy by marrying a biracial woman, Mackey found that his home in Charleston County had also been gerrymandered into the Seventh Congressional District. Outside observers clearly recognized that the three-way battle royal was intentionally designed so that "Mackey, Smalls, and [former speaker of the South Carolina House of Representatives Samuel Lee] will all run, and that they will cut one another's throats, giving the seat to the Democratic candidate." Another Northern reporter remarked, "The boa-constrictor Seventh District has born several stings. Besides massing the colored vote, it coils around the three Republicans who will hold seats."[25]

The road to the nomination in the Seventh Congressional District was a chaotic combination of anger, ambition, and intraparty conflict. At an August 1882 mass meeting, Smalls railed against both Mackey and Lee, as well as the Democratic press for their racist description of his Gullah dialect as "Congo talk" and argued that his ability to codeswitch for his Lowcountry constituents was a skill that allowed Beaufort County's Republican Party to weather the Red Shirt counterinsurgency of 1876. Going further, he attacked the "hellish election law" that had created a de facto literacy test. Most interestingly, Smalls exhibited a copy of the map of the new Seventh Congressional District at the rally so that his constituents could understand the consequences of the recent gerrymander. At various moments compelling, anxiety-ridden, and defensive, Smalls both represented a storied history associated with Reconstruction in the Lowcountry and a deep fear that he was out of step with where the party was heading.[26]

Some leaders in the district felt that the top candidates for the nominating convention left much to be desired. At the same rally where Smalls exhibited the map of the Seventh Congressional District, he got into a physical altercation with a rival politician who represented the "reform" faction of the Beaufort Republican Party and was forced to flee the speaker's platform when the crowd turned against him. At a September 1882 mass meeting, William Whipper argued that Mackey "had no moral right to come into this district and run for Congress," that Smalls "was totally unfit . . . to represent the colored race," and that Lee was no more than "a very good speaker." Himself a candidate for probate judge in Beaufort County, Whipper had long sought to craft the state party in his aristocratic image and likely loathed that men he saw as his intellectual inferiors were being rewarded with a chance to represent the state and the race at the nation's highest level.[27]

At another September meeting in the Lowcountry, the Republican Congressional Convention of the Seventh District brought forth a clash of local rivals. On the first day, Lee accused Smalls and Mackey of forming a secret alliance to defeat him; one of Lee's allies from Sumter County vowed to "turn the district to the Bourbons" if Lee were defeated. Despite the demand by several delegates for "a Black candidate for the Black district," Mackey led the first day's vote for the nomination by one vote over Lee and by five votes over Smalls. The delegates who had pledged support for Smalls, Lee, and Mackey reached a deadlock that could not be swayed or broken after multiple rounds of voting. On September 27, after more than 250 votes had been cast at the contentious convention, Robert Smalls bowed out and told his delegates to throw their support behind Mackey. "Mackey is nominated. I blame Lee," Smalls told a crowd outside of the church. Samuel Lee accused both Mackey and Smalls of foul play, claiming that delegates had been bribed by his white opponent and that Smalls had betrayed the Republican cause.[28]

The division within the Lowcountry's Republican Party was cheered by the state's Democratic press. The *Palmetto Post* considered it sign of Black incapacity that Mackey, "the excrescence of the Caucasian," was nominated over Lee. "To elect him, or any colored man," the paper said of Lee, would be "to express to the world the desire [of the Lowcountry's Black voter] to elevate his race in the political scale." Mocking the ironic outcome of the Seventh District's first election, the Southern newspaper not only argued that Mackey's victory was evidence that Black men were "not the intellectual peer of the white" but also claimed that the defeat of Lee and Smalls was a missed opportunity for a Black candidate to "occupy the topmost round of his race's destiny." The Black public sphere also expressed dissatisfaction that the Seventh District's racial destiny would remain unfulfilled. The *Washington Bee* had declared in the summer that it wanted "Lynch, Smalls, Haralson, Lee, O'Hara, Witherspoon, and a dozen other colored men in the next house of representatives." While no editorials were published in the paper in direct response to Mackey's election, the January 1883 meeting of the Bethel Literary and Historical Society, which ended in a heated exchange between William Whipper and Robert Smalls and was covered by the *Washington Bee*, likely involved a confrontation about Smalls's failure to secure the Seventh District's nomination and his loss of an important platform to represent the race in the upcoming Congress.[29]

While Mackey would go on to win an uncontested race in the November election and receive support from the Black press, he was unable to sponsor much legislation in the first session of the Forty-Eighth Congress. At the beginning of the second session, Mackey died at the age of thirty-eight from peritonitis. With a special election needed to fill his seat, the debates about the Black district and its role as an avatar for racial destiny resumed. "Mr. Mackey is dead but a few days only and already the white flag is raised," lamented Daniel Augustus Straker, a prominent member of South Carolina's Republican Party. For defenders of racial destiny in the Black press, there was considerable fear that the events of 1882 would be repeated, and the district's Republican Party would once again fail to elect a Black man.[30]

The heated battle within the Republican Party for the Seventh District was counterbalanced by the party's larger retreat in that year's election. While leaving the Seventh District race uncontested, the Democratic Party easily captured the state's other six congressional districts—producing the exact results that the architects of the 1882 gerrymander intended. Even more humbling, the Democratic Party's candidate for governor won every county in the state except for Beaufort, which overwhelmingly supported J. Hendrix McClane, the Greenback-Labor Party's star-crossed leader. Having failed to elect its desired candidate in a hypervisible congressional race and abandoned any statewide ambitions, South Carolina's Republican Party was badly wounded by both the ongoing and multipronged disfranchisement and partisan infighting that reanimated debates about the party's Reconstruction-era ideals and the long-term viability of those tenets in the new political moment.[31]

A product of a prolonged struggle over the meaning and the future of postbellum Black political power in the South, South Carolina's Seventh Congressional District emerged as an effort to disfranchise Black voters and permanently defeat the Republican Party. Part of a larger suite of political and economic measures that made the state hostile to democratic rule and economic mobility, the 1882 redistricting effort served as a capstone of a new flurry of events that sought to move the fight against Black political power away from paramilitary violence and Election Day fraud to more discreet and legally acceptable means of shrinking the electorate.

The rise of the Black Seventh provides a complicated portrait of the battle over Reconstruction's legacy. The racially gerrymandered congressional district was part of the Democratic Party's larger counterrevolution that maliciously deprived Black voters in South Carolina's other districts from electing their preferred candidates. At the same time, the Black Seventh would serve as the most hypervisible site of Black politics in the post-Reconstruction nation. Anchored by Beaufort County, which remained a hub for Black migration, grassroots politics, and electoral ambition, South Carolina's Seventh District would be one of Black politicians' few pathways to Congress during the Gilded Age. In the national press, it remained a model for larger discussions of demography, Republican Party politics, and racial uplift. Most important, it preserved a political counterbalance to a vision of the New South that sought to erase the story of Reconstruction. Inextricably linked to a raucous and often violent struggle against white supremacy, the "Black district" preserved a struggle that increasingly appeared out of step with the more whiggish political strategies preferred by a new generation of race leaders.

Part II

The Postbellum Public Sphere and the
Production of Black Countermemory

CHAPTER FOUR

Reconstruction's Last Congressman
The Gilded Age Black Public Sphere and the Battle over Robert Smalls's Legacy

On August 9, 1884, just two days before his forty-second birthday, Robert Brown Elliott was found dead in his New Orleans home. Once the most prominent and celebrated leader in South Carolina's Reconstruction-era Republican Party, he, like many Black elected officials from that era, experienced a harrowing and ignominious fall from public life in the years that followed the Grant presidency. Appointed customs inspector in Charleston in 1879, he was unexpectedly transferred to New Orleans and then dismissed altogether from the federal government in 1882. The following year, the Supreme Court overturned the 1875 Civil Rights Act, a law which outlawed discrimination within sites of public accommodation, including theaters, hotels, and railway stations. Elliott had famously championed the bill from the well of the House of Representatives, calling the measure a "cap-stone" for the nation's "temple of liberty." In his final months, he witnessed the judicial demolition of his generation's crowning legislative achievement alongside the collapse of his own personal fortunes.[1]

Elliott's sudden death from malaria marked a tragic end to a remarkable life. The funeral service in his home on the corner of Villere and Le Sharpe Streets was sparsely attended. While the Southern press could only remember Elliott as figure who had "darkened the atmosphere in the halls of Congress" and delighted that the estimable politician spent his last years "living miserably as a police court lawyer," there was larger celebration of his life and legacy among Black leaders. His longtime friend and law partner T. McCants Stewart lamented of Elliott, "In our Reconstruction history, there stands alone a man who was successful and as great as a jurist as he was eminent as a statesman." Frederick Douglass also mourned the loss of Elliott. "From under his dark brown eyes there blazed an intellect worthy of a place in the highest Legislative hall of the nation," he reminisced. "We can only hope that the same power that gave us one Elliott, will give us another in the near future."[2]

The largest memorial to Elliott's legacy occurred in Columbia, South Carolina. On October 1, dozens gathered at the Bethel AME Church, a building that stood only a few blocks from the state legislature that Elliott had once commanded as the Speaker of the House. Daniel Augustus Straker, a longtime friend and former law partner of Elliott, served as both the president of the memorial committee and the deliverer of the eulogy. Having first met Elliott in 1874, when Elliott represented South Carolina's Fifth Congressional District in Washington and Straker was a law student at Howard University, Straker movingly placed Elliott's death within the broader story of postemancipation Black life. "His loss seems irreparable reaching in its effects from the human classes to the uppermost ranks of society and government," Straker praised. He went further and claimed Elliott's impact would not only be felt on "the entire memory of these United States" but also "wherever the oppressed sons and daughters of Africa had a dwelling place." More than anything else, Elliott embodied the highest promise of Reconstruction, and Straker used his eulogy to place the memory of the South Carolina leader at the cornerstone of the postbellum racial destiny story.

> The life of Robert Browne [sic] Elliott is inseparably woven with the history of the conduct of the United States and of this State for the past twelve years, and with the history of the Negro race as a distinct race of people the world over. From the commencement of the new era of our peaceful life in this state, as it changed from slavery to freedom, from chattel to man, from bondage to citizenship, through the period of ten years of Republican rule to the downfall of the Republican party, he was in sum a brave defender of our rights.

However, while the Black press reported that "a large and appreciative audience" attended the memorial service, the state's most prominent Black politicians were absent. Just blocks away, South Carolina's Republican Party was holding its state convention, with its leaders engaged in a deep debate over the future of the party. With electoral politics largely focused in the Seventh District, the state's Republican Party now largely served as a vehicle for doling out patronage and sending delegates to the party's national convention. "Ever since 1876 when the Bourbon Democracy overcame us by fraud and violence, our party has been like a ship drifting without purpose or progress," argued one Lowcountry leader. Despite this lack of direction, the party had decided to nominate a full state ticket in 1884 and would challenge the Democratic Party's candidates for governor, lieutenant governor, and attorney general for the first time since Reconstruction. In the midst of the fierce and contentious battle between the rival factions, it was determined that an hour and a half recess to attend Robert Elliott's memorial would be too difficult, and the convention's delegates voted down the measure nearly unanimously.[3]

Elliott's funeral was accompanied by a larger sense of loss among the Reconstruction generation. Martin Delany, who had left the South for Ohio, died the following year from tuberculosis. In 1882, Aaron Alpeoria Bradley, who split time during Reconstruction between Savannah, Beaufort, and Charleston in both law and politics, would be found dead in St. Louis with twenty-five cents in his pocket and "a lot of papers of no value." Many of the movement's surviving leaders were struggling personally and professionally. "Frank Moses is an outcast drifting from one jail to another.... [Jonathan] Wright is eking out a scanty living in the Trial Justice courts in Charleston; [William] Whipper is doing about the same thing in Beaufort.... [Richard] Gleaves is somewhere forgot and unheard; [Henry] Purvis was a wretched vagabond about Charleston at last accounts," reported one Upcountry newspaper. "The remainder of the evil is scattered from one ocean to the other, honored and prosperous nowhere." Georgia Lowcountry leader Tunis Campbell was indicted on trumped-up charges by his political enemies and sentenced to hard labor on a Georgia prison chain gang. "During the whole time I was in dread of the ku-klux, or parties of men who broke open jails and prison camps to get the persons that they wanted out of the way," he later recalled.[4]

In this growing and palpable void entered Robert Smalls, who now became the undisputed inheritor of the Reconstruction generation's legacy. Unanimously renominated to Congress by the Seventh District's Republican Party just one week earlier, Smalls, who had previously succeeded Robert Elliott as the representative of South Carolina's old Fifth Congressional District, provided a contrasting vision of Black political destiny. Where Elliott had died penniless, Smalls had become one of the wealthiest men in the town of Beaufort. Where Elliott had been rebuffed by James Garfield in 1881 for a federal appointment, Smalls had the ear and audience of the national party and artfully navigated the patronage system. Finally, where Elliott had been a soaring rhetorician who would represent the political heights of the Reconstruction era, Smalls, who had no formal schooling and was most readily identified with the region's Gullah-speaking freedpeople, came to embody the more earthbound realities of grassroots democracy.[5]

For his constituents, this lack of pretense was a deep part of Smalls's continuing appeal. A political survivor who had already experienced an assassination attempt, the first wave of postbellum disfranchisement measures, and an almost endless stream of personal attacks in the Southern press, Smalls embodied the unvanquished spirit of the Lowcountry's rival Black world. As Joanne Freeman has argued, "Congressmen *were* their constituents, states, and regions personified; they practiced a kind of *performative representation*, acting as physical surrogates for all that they represented." As the Black Seventh's congressman, Smalls brought his Lowcountry constituents to the nation's capital at a moment when their political concerns had largely been abandoned by the Republican Party.[6]

In doing so, Robert Smalls not only preserved an earlier vision of his party's platform but also exercised tremendous cultural influence over the story of Reconstruction in the Black public sphere. As a vaunted war hero, Smalls's daring flight from slavery would be told and retold across the nation—often by Smalls himself. As a stand-alone Civil War story, Smalls's capture of the CSS *Planter* exemplified the highest promise of the Black military experience. For Northern Republicans who were increasingly disillusioned by the perceived failures of political Reconstruction in the South, Smalls's courageous war story provided a stark reminder of why emancipation could not be separated from the larger Union cause.[7]

More than a war hero, Robert Smalls now occupied a peculiar place in the nation's political landscape: the last Reconstruction-era Black congressman. Having been first elected to the House of Representatives in 1874, Smalls was the only Black member of the Forty-Eighth and Forty-Ninth Congress to have held a federal office before the 1880s. Conscious of this unique position, Smalls connected his story of political survival to larger narratives of racial destiny. Here, Smalls was inextricably bound to the changing gender politics of the Black public sphere. As elite men reshaped the institutions that anchored Black social and associational life toward a narrower politics of racial destiny and respectability, the histories that they produced placed a greater emphasis on figures who embodied masculine virtues such as wartime courage and political strength. From this perspective, Smalls and his story appeared ready-made for the new political moment.[8]

For many in the national Black press, however, Robert Smalls was the wrong figure to represent the race's post-Reconstruction political destiny. Unlike Elliott, who had received a classical educational in Boston and England, Smalls gained his education of the world in bondage, the wharves and waterways around Charleston, the Union navy, and the rough-and-tumble political world of the Reconstruction-era Lowcountry. While his background granted him a unique and valuable set of political skills, including the ability to code switch before his Sea Island constituents, empathize with the specific horror of slavery, and connect politics to the freedom dreams of Black South Carolinians, Smalls's opponents saw him as a crude demagogue who represented the worst excesses of Reconstruction. Part of a larger criticism of both stalwart Republicanism and "bossism," the generation of Black politicians, journalists, and intellectuals who came of age after Reconstruction sought to pursue a whiggish vision of racial destiny that would place a narrower band of elite men in positions of leadership.[9]

This hypervisibility brought greater scrutiny to Smalls and the Lowcountry as a coterie of influential Black leaders sought to turn the page on his generation. As a machine politician who drew influence from charismatic rhetoric, grassroots mass democracy, and doling and denying, Smalls came to appear as an illiberal demagogue in the eyes of his opponents. Increasingly, the Lowcountry's longtime congressman became a symbol for an old guard out of step with late nineteenth-century ideas of racial destiny. This battle over Smalls's legacy occurred in both the national press and at the local level in the Lowcountry. Part of a larger discussion about the failures of the Reconstruction-era Republican Party to secure the civil and political rights of its Black constituents, the battles over Robert Smalls the politician were always struggles over the meaning of Reconstruction's nascent countermemory in the Black world.

Robert Smalls: National Political Celebrity

Robert Smalls rise as a national political figure corresponded with a parallel expansion in the scale and scope of the Black press. The beginning of a high tide in Black journalism, the late nineteenth century not only saw the rise of powerful new periodicals like the *New York Age*, the *Indianapolis Freeman*, and the *Richmond Planet* but also saw the beginnings of the journalistic careers of Ida B. Wells, T. Thomas Fortune, and John Edward Bruce. These figures would be pioneers in muckraking journalism, correcting the red record on lynching and challenging the Republican Party's failure to protect civil and political rights in the South. Critical in shaping ideas of a collective racial destiny, the Black press saw Reconstruction and its afterlife as a critical part of the countermemory that organized its political coverage of the South.[10]

For old guard Reconstruction-generation figures like Smalls, this increased attention was a double-edged sword. He, as much as anyone in Black America, understood the importance of preserving and sustaining the Lowcountry's ongoing political world. However, a new generation of leaders began to reject the straightforward Unionism of the Civil War–era Republican Party and openly questioned the efficacy of aging lions like Smalls who seemed to be stuck in an earlier chapter of the race's history. Partially responsible for the rise of his national political celebrity, the Black press now played a major role in painting Smalls as unwilling to step aside for the new generation of Black political leaders. A conflict animated around lines of class, education, and regional identity, the battle between Robert Smalls and the Black press embodied a larger struggle for Reconstruction's memory and would reshape both Smalls and the Black public sphere in following decades.

No figure in the Black press more fully embodied the spirit of the new generation than the journalist T. Thomas Fortune. Under Fortune's leadership, the *Globe*, and its later iterations as the *Freeman* and the *Age*, would become the most widely circulated newspapers in Black America. The son of a prominent Reconstruction-era officeholder from the Florida Lowcountry, Fortune would use the pages of his newspaper to highlight the political events in the South and excoriate the Republican Party for abandoning Black voters in the South. As Shawn Leigh Alexander has noted, Fortune's newspaper served as a site of "counter-memory of the [Reconstruction] period" that provided its Black readership both an unflinching account of Southern violence and a fiercely independent perspective on the current state of the race's political destiny in the South. "It is in the South that the largest number of our people live; it is there that they encounter the greatest hardships," remarked Fortune. "Consequently, the colored statesman and the colored editor must turn their attention to the South and make that field the center of speculation, deduction and practical application."[11]

At the cornerstone of Fortune's national journalistic influence was the care and detail his newspapers placed in local reporting of the New South. "*The Freeman* was decidedly the most popular paper published among Afro-American journals," remarked the esteemed journalist and historian Irvine Garland Penn. "In typographical make-up it . . . contained all the most important news about the Afro-American, sent by trustworthy and brilliant correspondents." Perfecting the new mode of Black political journalism that first emerged during Reconstruction, Fortune's newspapers reflected a new vision of racial destiny that not only sought to cover Black political candidates in the South but also aspired to shape the larger debates over what these elections meant for the Black collective future.[12]

As the number of congressional districts that could still send Black politicians to national office dwindled, the remaining few Black officeholders in the South began to occupy an even more outsized place in the Black press's political coverage, which viewed these congressman as important barometers for the race's larger destiny. When North Carolina's Second Congressional District had an opportunity to send a Black congressman to Washington for the first time, the *Washington Bee* framed the election as a critical moment in the race's larger political destiny. "We don't wish to be understood as drawing the color line, but we do say that no white man should receive the nomination for Congress from that district," the newspaper argued.

When Edmund Mackey, the white Charlestonian who represented the Lowcountry's newly gerrymandered Seventh Congressional District, unexpectedly died before the end of his first term, many in the national Black press assumed that local and state Republicans would "leave the field for General Smalls" and that Smalls, who had already won a special election to finish Mackey's term, now had a "flattering opportunity" to return to Congress.[13]

Almost as soon as the seat became open, however, a coordinated whisper campaign in the Northern Black press emerged that sought to torpedo Robert Smalls's bid for reelection. "Gen. Robert Smalls, in spite of reports to the contrary, will by no means have a 'walk-over.' He will not carry his own county for the nomination without bitter struggle." It is likely that many of the attacks on Smalls in the Northern press were planted by his Republican Party challenger, Daniel Augustus Straker. A graduate from Howard University's law school, Straker had traveled to South Carolina during the last years of Reconstruction to become a professor and dean of the law department at the AME Church–founded Allen University. Viewing the Seventh Congressional District as a "Black Republican Mecca," Straker was drawn to the growing mythology around the Lowcountry's political promise. Fully imbibing the elixir of racial destiny, Straker believed that his election to the Seventh District's congressional seat would contest the "growing evil" that Black Americans were "incapable of becoming anything more than hewers of wood and drawers of water."[14]

In this mission, Straker had several allies in the Northern Black press. T. Mc-Cants Stewart, a free-born, Northern-educated Charlestonian who returned to the Lowcountry during Reconstruction before moving back north to New York, served as a corresponding editor for the *New York Globe*. A former law partner with Straker and Robert Elliott, Stewart was likely responsible for the shaping the positive coverage for his longtime friend. "Mr. Straker is a lawyer of ripe experience and would do not only his immediate constituents credit but the entire race if sent to the National Legislature," argued the *Globe*. "He is a man decided views, fearless and independent, our people owe it to themselves to select for their representatives the men best equipped in every sense to do them credit."[15]

For the younger generation of Black journalists, leaders from the Reconstruction era embodied an outdated and misguided fealty to the Republican Party. Without mentioning Smalls by name, the *Globe* placed the Gullah statesman on the wrong side of the growing generational divide in Gilded Age Black politics. "Let the citizens therefore of the 7th district send their best and most intelligent man as their exponent at our Nation's capital," declared one editorial in the paper. This pessimism not only reflected the elitism embedded in the philosophy of racial destiny but also captured a broader rejection of the ironclad faith Black voters placed in the Republican Party. Believing that the Republicans had taken their Black constituents for granted, T. Thomas Fortune and his generational cohort would regularly lambast the lions of the Reconstruction generation for their perceived obsequiousness to a party that had failed to protect the civil and political rights of Black Southerners. "A new generation is coming to the front," remarked one writer in the Black press. "We want the Republicans to understand that we no longer follow the dictates of [Frederick] Douglass, [John Roy] Lynch, [Robert] Smalls, and others."[16]

To the shock of the *Globe*'s Northern audience, Robert Smalls handily defeated Straker in the Seventh Congressional District's nominating convention. Receiving thirty-five votes to Straker's one, Smalls and his vision of stalwart Republicanism delivered a powerful rejection to a reform movement led by the race's younger intellectual class. After Straker's embarrassing loss, the *Globe* rationalized his defeat by leveling charges of corruption and bossism at Smalls. A letter from pseudonymous "observer," declared that "the people [of the Seventh Congressional District] left alone would have nominated Hon D. A. Straker, but the demagogues who corrupt the party with whiskey and the purchase of votes in convention thwarted the people's wish."[17]

Deeply offended by Straker's hubris, some of Smalls's supporters challenged the elitist premise at the core of his vision of racial destiny. In the pages of his Washington-based newspaper *Grit*, the journalist John Edward Bruce defended Smalls against the charge that he was part of a generation whose time had passed. A self-educated former slave and dyed-in-the-wool Republican, Bruce developed what would become a life-long friendship with Smalls based on their similar backgrounds and shared values. To this end, Bruce mocked the pretentious, would-be leaders such as Straker whom he viewed as possessing high ambition and low political ability: "We have a great deal of sympathy for men with swelled heads for those of our race, who, because they enjoyed the benefits and privileges which were denied the greater number of us in antebellum days of getting 'eddycashum' boastfully allude to ignoramuses who are intelligent enough to outgeneral them and make their heads ache very very badly." In a letter responding to Straker's earlier *Globe* editorial, Samuel Jones Bampfield, Robert Smalls's son-in-law and lieutenant in his Lowcountry political machine, challenged Daniel Straker's claim that his loss to Smalls in the Seventh District's recent congressional convention was a larger setback for a racial destiny helmed by rising educated elite: "Among the supporters of Gen Smalls in the 'Black District' are numbered some of South Carolina's brightest and best sons, men who have long since learned to earn their bread by the sweat of the brow, and who supported him upon principle, and principle alone, and are to-day as highly respected by all classes of our citizens as one need be." As willing as some Black elites had been in drawing the line on education, the leaders who depended on the votes of freedpeople were equally willing to craft a political narrative that valorized the history of those who had once been enslaved and now represented the South's rural working class.[18]

While the harsh words directed toward Smalls in the pages of the *Globe* highlighted unresolved tensions over Reconstruction's legacy, the Lowcountry politician's return to Washington as a congressman was largely greeted with celebration and fanfare. He was welcomed to the nation's capital by a sizable parade led by the city's famed Capital City Guards, who met him as he got off the train at Union Station and marched him to his residence at 1512 L Street NW. Over the course of his tenure in Washington, Smalls was feted with numerous honors and regularly rubbed shoulders with the city's Black elite. A recent widower, he brought his youngest daughter, Sarah, to Washington with him and enrolled her in the prestigious Miner Normal School. At various moments during his terms in the Forty-Eighth and Forty-Ninth Congress, Smalls marshaled the Washington's annual Emancipation Day parade; attended a banquet in Van Ness Park to celebrate the fourth anniversary of the Washington Cadet Corps, where he delivered a keynote address before more than 5,000 Black Washingtonians; and was invited to replace Frederick Douglass as the keynote speaker at the 1884 National Encampment of the Grand Army of the Republic. Smalls's closeness to the Douglass family would become even more evident when Frederick Douglass Jr. and his wife Virginia named their seventh child after the South Carolina congressman.[19]

As one of only two Black Americans serving in Congress, Smalls felt the burden of Black America's racial destiny squarely on his shoulders. In addition to sponsoring several pieces of legislation, including bills that would outlaw racial discrimination in Washington's public accommodations, establish a memorial for Black soldiers, and provide a pension for Gen. David Hunter's widow, Smalls used his platform to speak out against the injustices Black South Carolinians continued to face in the post-Reconstruction years. Before the 1884 Republican state convention, he lambasted the South Carolina's "hellish election laws" as well as the stock law instituted by the "Ku Klux Democrats." In an interview with a Northern reporter, Smalls offered a more nuanced analysis of how the 1882 "eight box" election law had disfranchised Black voters in his state. "Most of our people—I mean the negroes—can't read; haven't had any chance to read," Smalls explained to his interviewer. "The eight ballot boxes are properly labelled, but the negro can't read the labels," he continued.

In another interview with a Northern reporter, he drew "the color line" and defended the right of the Seventh District's voters to elect a Black politician to represent the majority Black district. "We—the colored men—feel that it is a reflection upon ourselves if we cannot find one man out of thirty-two thousand voters capable of representing us in Congress," Smalls argued.[20]

In speaking with anger, clarity, and precision about the antidemocratic features of the New South, as well as defending the Black majority's unencumbered access to the ballot, Robert Smalls preserved core ideals from the Reconstruction era—grassroots democracy and protection of the ballot. Where many national leaders sought to retreat from Reconstruction and distance themselves from the perceived rough edges of "Negro domination," Smalls continued to uphold the legacy of the nation's radical experiment with multiracial democracy and sought to educate an increasingly disengaged national audience on the shifting terrain of disfranchisement in the South.

A stalwart Republican, Robert Smalls had a deep faith in the machinery of party politics and saw both his political future and the memory of Reconstruction inextricably linked to his own patronage network in the Lowcountry. A strategy to keep the post-Reconstruction South within the protective orbit of the federal government, the patronage system was also a means to secure loyalty at the grassroots level in the Lowcountry. While his rivals mocked that Smalls's supporters only received "some minor appointments . . . which nobody else wants," the longtime Lowcountry leader understood the ability to appoint talented individuals to highly visible political positions as a central component of nineteenth-century racial destiny. For example, as a sitting congressman, Smalls could make the coveted and prestigious appointment to the US Military Academy—a position that immediately signaled upward mobility and racial progress to the nation. He could also fight against the removal of federal employees from appointed positions. After a series of Black federal employees—who likely received their positions in part due to Smalls's lobbying—were fired at the beginning of Grover Cleveland's administration, the Gullah statesman wrote a scathing letter to the *Washington Bee* that connected the Black employees' being fired with a larger uncertainty about post-Reconstruction political progress. "I can see nearly every colored person who has been appointed from the State of South Carolina removed from official positions for no other than partisan reasons," he fumed. The battles over patronage and power offered another lens on the struggle over the legacy of Reconstruction and the effort to preserve a specific idea of Black progress rooted in the power of men like Robert Smalls.[21]

Smalls's Gilded Age political power was coupled with a growing sense of his national celebrity and increasing importance in the pantheon of Black history.

Already well known for his heroic capture of the CSS *Planter* during the Civil War, Smalls during the Gilded Age chapter of his political career increasingly found himself placed near the top of the list of the nation's Black heroes. In 1883, he began writing a memoir—a work that he never completed. In the *Indianapolis Freeman*'s competition to determine the "Ten Greatest Negroes" in history, Robert Smalls was a popular favorite among the reader-generated lists but failed to register in the final top ten produced by the paper's panel of judges.[22]

Among Smalls's most powerful cultural legacies would be in the nascent visual iconography of Reconstruction. In the Black and Republican press, lithographs of Smalls appeared with greater regularity following his 1884 reelection to Congress. Like those of Frederick Douglass, who carefully produced and curated his image over the course of the nineteenth century to combat the powerful current of anti-Black images in the press and popular culture, Robert Smalls's lithographs challenged the outrageous images of the Black politician that had proliferated during the Reconstruction era.[23]

No image captured this visual countermemory more than the 1881 chromolithograph *Heroes of the Colored Race*. An era-defining illustration, *Heroes of the Colored Race* tells a panoramic story of postbellum Black progress. The lithograph centers the profile portrait of Frederick Douglass, who is flanked on each side by former US senators Blanche K. Bruce and Hiram R. Revels. Four fellow Reconstruction-era congressmen are placed in each corner of the image: John R. Lynch, Joseph H. Rainey, Charles E. Nash, and Robert Smalls.[24]

An ode to the generation that saw Reconstruction as the defining political event of their lives, *Heroes of the Colored Race* couples a hagiographic depiction of the era's great men with a broader visual story of the era's grand achievements. Each of the lithograph's corners contain a vignette that frames a different aspect of postbellum Black life: freedpeople farming for themselves, USCT soldiers leading a courageous charge during the war, families being reunited, a Black teacher delivering a lesson to a classroom of Black students. Additionally, a figure in each of the vignettes gestures back toward the pantheon of great men. The constellation of political figures in portrait—as well as the broader stories told in the lithographs vignettes—highlight a postbellum story that portrays the world made by Reconstruction as a high tide moment in the long march of the racial destiny.[25]

Produced by the Philadelphia-based print publisher Joseph Hoover, a German-Swiss American and one of the nation's most prolific chromolithographers, *Heroes of the Colored Race* would have been just one of the many mass-produced images churned out by the successful publishing house. Recognizing the growing market for affordable images among middle-class

Heroes of the Colored Race (Philadelphia: Joseph Hoover, 1881). The portrait of Robert Smalls is in the chromolithograph's lower left-hand corner. Library of Congress, Washington, DC.

Americans, Hoover likely saw this specific lithograph as meeting a growing consumer demand. Although we do not know who commissioned *Heroes of the Colored Race*, or how many copies of the lithograph were sold, the expansion of the Black public sphere during the nineteenth century's final decades suggests that the market demand for such an image was probably robust. As an affordable piece of ready-made countermemory, prints of *Heroes of the Colored Race* would have not only found their way into middle-class Black homes but also likely circulated across the late nineteenth-century Black public sphere, appearing in school classrooms, churches, and lyceum halls.[26]

As this generation of leaders left public life, Robert Smalls stood as one of the last remaining pillars of the previous political era. As a result, he not only became an important figure in the story of the race's political destiny but also served as a cultural symbol in the late nineteenth century's lithographic landscape. Following his 1884 reelection to Congress, Smalls posed with greater regularity for photographs and the circulation of his image expanded across the Black public sphere. Like Frederick Douglass, who carefully produced

Lithograph of Robert Smalls in Simmons, *Men of Mark*.

and curated his self-image over the course of the nineteenth century to combat the torrent of anti-Black images in the press and popular culture, Robert Smalls was likely aware of his historical importance and thus actively shaped his public image during the century's penultimate decade.[27]

One such lithograph appeared in Rev. William J. Simmons' 1887 *Men of Mark: Eminent, Progressive and Rising*. Smalls' story of embodying Reconstruction's political legacy becomes abundantly clear. The image, which was drawn from his congressional photograph, depicts a side profile of Smalls wearing a three-piece suit and gazing contemplatively past the camera. Showing the signs of age, he was now a heavier man with grey in his hair and beard. Smalls appeared distinguished and statesmanlike, conveying both his own sense of dignity, esteem, and self-possession, as well as the maturing of the postbellum Black political story that he embodied. Like *Heroes of the Colored Race*, the *Men of Mark* lithograph reflected a growing gender hierarchy in the Black public sphere. As the more radically democratic Reconstruction-era vision of progress gave way to a more conservative vision of racial destiny that emphasized ideas like civilization, educational attainment, and respectability, journalists and nascent historians turned to the production of a pantheon of "great men" to challenge the prevailing white supremacist accounts of the era.[28]

Smalls's growing celebrity reflected a unique moment in late nineteenth-century Black cultural life. The Black press had reached its nineteenth-century apex, and the profession of journalism was now infused with an almost existential duty to correct the national record on race. During the 1880s, a thriving Black history movement had emerged, and members of the Reconstruction generation like Joseph T. Wilson, George Washington Williams, and Benjamin Tucker Tanner would produce the first monographs to provide sweeping narrative accounts of African American history. Both Frederick Douglass and William Still responded to the growing market demand for Black history by writing updated accounts of their well-known lives in the antebellum abolitionist movement. In 1884, T. Thomas Fortune provided his own critical reinterpretation of postbellum Southern history in *Black and White: Land, Labor, and Politics in the South*. In his study of the Reconstruction era, Fortune argued that freedpeople's economic struggles were not simply the result of a broad racial animus on the part of white Southerners but instead the consequence of the Republican Party's shortsighted policy platform, which allowed the former slaveholding class to retain near-total control of the region's land. Read together, the writings of this generation of self-taught historians show that they experienced the century's penultimate decade as an intellectual turning point—precisely because their era's great political project was now in jeopardy.[29]

No event captured this shift in late nineteenth-century African American intellectual life more than the rise of the Bethel Literary and Historical Society. Founded in 1881 by AME bishop Daniel Payne, "the Bethel Literary," as it came to be known, quickly became the cultural North Star of the Reconstruction generation. Part of a larger rise of Black literary societies across the nation's major urban centers, the Bethel Literary's weekly evening meetings not only attracted a wide swath of Black Washingtonians who filled the Metropolitan AME Church's Bethel Hall to hear poetry, music, dramatic selections, and other performing arts but also drew a growing national audience. "Every Washington correspondent of the Colored press, and there were more then than now, gave conspicuous notice to this institution, and the editors of their home papers often continued the discussion," observed the Bethel Literary's historian.[30]

As we saw in William Whipper's January 1883 address, the most exciting portion of these meetings was usually the lecture. Designed to solicit audience participation and encourage debate, the lectures made the Bethel Literary a popular forum that gave structure to the larger cultural feeling of racial destiny. As one attendee observed, "Bethel Literary, while it consists of clerks,

Metropolitan AME Church at 1518 M Street NW, Washington, DC, 1899. From 1881 to 1913, the Bethel Literary and Historical Society met in the Metropolitan AME Church's Bethel Hall. Library of Congress, Washington, DC.

schoolteachers, professional men and others occupying higher grades of labor, offers inducements and entry to all persons who desire to avail themselves of the benefits it has to offer. As a consequence, the Bethel Literary is the most popular and at the same time the most influential and worthy institution which has ever been instituted among us."[31]

The intellectual and cultural center of Black Washington, the Bethel Literary became a crucial site for the production and preservation of Reconstruction's countermemory. During the Bethel Literary's 1884–85 season, separate lectures were delivered on Robert Elliott, the legacy of the Freedmen's Bank, the rapid disappearance of Black officeholders from the political landscape, and "The Wit and Humor of Reconstruction." Political leaders from the Reconstruction generation, many of whom now resided in Washington, regularly attended the meetings and gave lectures. In addition to the address by William Whipper, other Reconstruction-era luminaries like Blanche K. Bruce, P. B. S. Pinchback, Francis Cardozo, and John Mercer Langston also addressed the organization. Reaching its zenith during the same period that Robert Smalls served as one of the last remaining Black politicians in Congress, the Bethel Literary embodied the golden era of the Black public sphere and anchored the production of the Reconstruction generation's countermemory.[32]

Keenly aware of the precarity of remaining Black political centers in the South, as well the growing chorus of attacks on Reconstruction in the Northern press and the American historical profession, members of the Bethel Literary and Historical Society, along with leaders in the Black press and larger national Black public sphere, responded to the uneasy cultural landscape of sectional reconciliation by crafting their own accounts of what Reconstruction meant. These accounts not only rejected white supremacist attacks on Black self-government in the South but also introduced Reconstruction-era Black officeholders like Robert Smalls into their new accounts of the Black past.

Robert Smalls's Lowcountry Political Machine and the Legacy of His Last Congressional Race

In contrast to his growing stature in the Black public sphere, Robert Smalls remained a derided figure in the white South. Southern newspaper editors continued to demonize and degrade Smalls in racist language. For these white Southern writers, Smalls embodied the spirit of "Negro domination." Often referring to him as the "Convict Congressman" or the "Beaufort bribe-taker," the Southern press repeatedly slandered Smalls with old attacks of political corruption that had long been proved false. After Smalls won his March 1884 special election, the *Charleston News and Courier* claimed that the Seventh District's voters sent to Congress "possibly the worst man they could find" and a "positive disgrace to his race." Sumter's *Watchman and Southron* called Smalls "a disgrace to the civilization of the nineteenth century." These accusations of corruption, part of a long strategy in the Southern press to paint Reconstruction-era Black leaders as corrupt and incompetent, were a constant thorn in Smalls's day-to-day life. Encountering *News and Courier* editor Narciso Gonzales on the streets of Charleston one Christmas Eve, Smalls and his most unrelenting critic got into a shouting match that devolved into a fistfight.[33]

The most pointed charges by the Southern press framed Smalls as a demagogue who used Black solidarity to "draw the color line" and mobilize his working-class base of voters. According to one former slaveowner, Smalls "rules like a king among the colored people who know him." Describing Smalls as both "smart as a whip" and "crooked," this Southern observer feared that Smalls could "make a good speech, and any day could set South Carolina by the ears if he chose." The perception that the Black voters of the Lowcountry were incapable of exercising independent judgment was pervasive among the Lowcountry's white elite. "The ignorant voter who forms the bulk of the farming population on these islands and in the Savannah rice fields" was incapable of "voting anything else than what the local leaders of the party dictate," reported one newspaper in the state. The accusation that Smalls actively "drew the color line" and appealed to Black voters' sense of racial solidarity in his political campaigns not only conjured the bogeyman of "Negro domination" but also justified a white supremacist backlash. "Now, then, if Smalls' Black face entitles him to the support of the colored voters, what becomes of the distinction of race forbidden by the constitution and denounced by the colored people themselves?"[34]

In highlighting past accusations of corruption and drawing upon Gilded Age anxieties over democratic excess, South Carolina's Democratic leaders believed they had landed on a powerful new argument for redeeming the state's Black district. "The eyes of all South Carolina are upon the negroes in the Black District . . . as long as they show such utter unfitness for choosing Representatives," warned one of the Lowcountry's leading Democratic papers following Smalls's return to the Forty-Eighth Congress. When Smalls was renominated by his party that fall, the state's paper of record argued that "a strenuous effort is to be made to redeem the Seventh Congressional District." Choosing William Elliott Jr., a Harvard graduate, former Confederate lieutenant, and scion of one of South Carolina's most prominent slave-owning families, Lowcountry Democratic leaders hoped that their nominee could conjure the same antebellum myths that endeared Wade Hampton to the state's white voters during his 1876 political campaign. "Why should the district be Black?" asked the *Charleston News and Courier*. "Is it not plain to every man's good sense, be he colored or otherwise, that an intelligent, presentable citizen like William Elliott could achieve more in Congress for all the peculiar interests of the district than could Smalls?"[35]

Most outside observers accepted the idea of a Black district and likely viewed the Lowcountry congressional seat as an acceptable concession to the fading spirit of Reconstruction-era multiracial democracy. "The negroes in that district want a Black man to represent the Black district in all things," wrote one Northern reporter. Even Democrats in other parts of the South Carolina saw it as a mistake to challenge Smalls. "We have now six out of seven Congressmen—of course, we would prefer all seven if we could get them," argued a writer in Columbia, "but there were sound political reasons for the formation of the Black District, and those reasons are of as much force now as they were at the time the State was redistricted." When asked by a writer from the *Atlanta Constitution* about Elliott's prospective campaign, Robert Smalls rejected the plot as farcical. "It is in my opinion a false rumor designed to frighten me, but it don't scare me worth a cent," the Gullah statesman exclaimed. Going further, he made a robust argument about his political staying power in the Black district.

> I am going to be my own successor in this district, and don't you forget it. Suppose the democrats are such fools as to place a nominee of their party in the field against me what do you suppose it would amount to? My constituents would elect me or raise hell; that's all about it. You white folks may expect to see the devil stirred up if you attempt to deprive me of my place. There is another thing, too, you may as well make up your minds to divide some of the offices with us. We mean to make a fight this year. We count on carrying the state for Blaine and Logan. We are going to beat Cleveland out of his boots.

This "incendiary" speech by Smalls highlighted the statesman's sophisticated interpretation of the New South's political landscape. While overstating the political strength of presidential candidate James G. Blaine, Smalls recognized that white supremacy remained an unfinished project and that the Black voters in his district recognized that the Reconstruction-era hero could only be defeated by illegitimate and extralegal means. When the final votes for the 1884 race were tallied, Smalls received more than double those of his competitor Elliott—8,900 to 4,100—leaving no doubt as to his continued popularity among his constituents.[36]

Despite his commanding 1884 victory, many white elites in the Lowcountry continued to believe that Smalls's political power was illegitimate. The *Palmetto Post* claimed that Smalls not only controlled Black vote "by his patronage" but also "added to his influence by having men appointed to federal offices heretofore that he can use for party purposes." In 1885, it was reported that an opposition movement was developing against Smalls. "The colored people are forming clubs all over the county to get rid of Smalls and the smaller planets that revolve around him." On the eve of his 1886 reelection campaign, the *New York Times* reported that Smalls was "gradually losing his hold on the people." Smalls's stalwart Republican allies attempted to challenge these attacks on the general's character and emphasize the continued importance he had for larger ideas of racial destiny. "There has been a disposition on the part of several Southern Negroes to discount the value and worth of Hon. Robt. Smalls, but to-day he is the boss of his State so far as the Negroes are concerned," remarked the *Washington Bee*.[37]

Political bosses and ring politics were central to late nineteenth-century politics. Most commonly associated with the sophisticated networks of patronage that revolved around institutions like New York's Tammany Hall, political machines had an equally important role in Republican political centers in Black America. Washington's Perry Carson, a saloon keeper and deputy US marshal, physically imposing at six feet, six inches tall, operated a robust political network that mobilized the District of Columbia's large Black working-class constituency within his "Blaine Invincibles" organization, while also offering protection from police brutality and Irish mobs. In both Boston's West End and Philadelphia's Seventh Ward, Republican Party leaders tapped community and precinct leaders to mobilize Black voters. For reform-minded critics, these political operations reflected barriers to modern racial destiny and entrenched corrupt men who brought politics into the populist mud instead of elevating the race. Even William Calvin Chase, a stalwart Republican in all other facets of his political life, saw a figure like Perry Carson as a poisonous influence on Black political culture and the rowdy Emancipation Day celebrations Carson organized as a "disgrace." "He may not suit the dandies of the colony," one observer remarked about Carson, "but he suits the bone and sinew."[38]

South Carolina's post-Reconstruction Republican Party reflected the uneasiness of the nexus between patronage and power, as the machine led by Robert Smalls had to negotiate with rival power centers in Charleston and Columbia, where William N. Taft and Ellery Brayton sat atop "rings" that provided patronage for Black supporters through the Internal Revenue Service and the US Postal Service. In Beaufort County, networks of patronage spooled out from the federal customhouse, the post office, and positions in local government—especially the public school system.[39]

For many members of the Reconstruction generation, Robert Smalls had ceased to be an effective avatar of the race's destiny. Some claimed that he had been ineffectual in Washington and had lost touch with the issues that mattered to the Lowcountry's Republican voters. F. D. J. Lawrence, a former slave who served in the Thirty-Fourth USCT, and later became an agent in the Freedmen's Bureau and an attorney, challenged Smalls for his failure to advocate for a more robust bill in Congress that would have compensated Beaufort residents financially devastated by the collapse of the Freedmen's Bank. W. H. Thompson, a Berkeley County Republican who challenged Smalls for the Seventh District's congressional seat, claimed to have asked Smalls about reimbursing the Freedman's Bank's depositors and was angered when Smalls told him that the federal government had no responsibility for the losses experienced by those who had banked with the failed institution. John C. Mardenborough, a New York–born Black attorney who initially moved from the North to Edgefield County before fleeing to Beaufort in 1877 in the aftermath of the Red Shirt campaign, claimed that the people of Beaufort "do not hear a single speech [Smalls] has made or a single thing he has done for the people of the State or this district."⁴⁰

These accusations misrepresented Smalls's long-standing policy commitments and continued efforts to use his power and connections in Washington to bring real benefits to his Lowcountry constituents. Having served four previous terms in Congress, including one term before the Compromise of 1877, Smalls had a deep knowledge of Congress, hierarchies of power within the Republican Party, and the broader world of political horse-trading in Washington. As a congressman, he objected to a bill that would have allowed segregation on interstate trains; he also pushed for stronger enforcement of federal civil rights law against businesses in the District of Columbia that discriminated against Black patrons. Most interestingly, Smalls was able to secure a fifty-dollar monthly pension for Maria Hunter—Gen. David Hunter's widow. When this request was denied by President Grover Cleveland, Smalls evoked a strand of Lowcountry countermemory that saw Hunter's legacy of declaring emancipation before President Lincoln was ready to embrace such a shift in the meaning of the war as a moment of Civil War history that the nation should remember. "It exposes the hypocrisy of the assurances for the colored man," excoriated Smalls, "by striking a blow at the nation's brave defenders and the colored man's best friend."[41]

In Robert Smalls's historical vision, defending the legacy of Reconstruction not only meant continuing the protect the Fourteenth Amendment but also looking beyond the narrow parameters of acceptable Union memory amid sectional reconciliation. In lifting up figures like David Hunter, who grasped the emancipationist meaning of the war before Lincoln, Smalls spoke to a more radical world of wartime countermemory in the Lowcountry that had become increasingly invisible to most Americans. Understanding the duty—and burden—of being the last Republican political figure to have held a Southern office during the 1870s, Smalls lent considerable moral and political gravity to the ongoing struggles to protect free and fair access to the ballot box, full equality under the law, and the larger promise of the nation's second founding.

A five-term congressman who had spent considerable time in Black Washington as it became the mecca of postbellum Black intellectual and cultural life, Smalls could speak to the racial destiny's soaring heights. He was comfortable in rooms like Bethel Hall and had friendly relationships with W. Calvin Chase of the *Washington Bee* and John Edward Bruce of the *Indianapolis Freeman*, who covered Smalls and his political career in largely favorable terms. His political career, military fame, and status as a Union veteran gave him access to upper echelons of the Republican Party, the Grand Army of the Republic, and the

Northeast's old line abolitionist world. In 1882, Charles Cowley, a white Massachusetts-born attorney who had served in the Union navy with Smalls, published *The Romance of History in "the Black County," and the Romance of War in the Career of Gen. Robert Smalls, "The Hero of the Planter,"* which offered a glowing account of Smalls, his political district, and his place in history. Historian Frederic Bancroft would interview Smalls while writing his 1885 dissertation on Reconstruction-era Black politics in Mississippi and South Carolina—a project that he completed at Columbia University under the direction of John Burgess, the intellectual grandfather of the Dunning School of Civil War–era scholars. Understanding that he was in the midst of a contentious cultural moment over the meaning of sectional reconciliation, Smalls used all the tools at his disposal to shape Reconstruction's legacy in the public record.[42]

Having survived assassination attempts, seen friends assassinated, and witnessed how unchecked white paramilitary violence had undone the Republican Party across his state, Smalls also understood that the lower political frequencies—particularly the language of political violence—and knew when to get down to the brass-tacks concerns of his constituents in his political rhetoric. Smalls's opponents observed that he not only waved the "bloody shirt" but also invoked the horrors of slavery to mobilize his voters. In one 1886 interaction Smalls warned one constituent, "If Mr. Elliott goes to Congress you will all be slaves, and the land will be taken away from you." At another 1886 political rally, Smalls described in graphic detail "the barbarities of slavery," giving lurid accounts of slaves being whipped, sent to the stocks, and separated from their families on the auction block. Smalls's Lowcountry addresses did not reach for the same soaring high notes as his speeches in Congress or Bethel Hall; instead he spoke to the immediate fears of freedpeople who had experienced bondage and thus could imagine a much deeper catastrophe if the Democratic Party were to capture the levers of political power in their Black district.[43]

In doing so, Smalls and his acolytes deployed a specific version of the "bloody shirt" that not only became a dominant theme in the region's postbellum political culture but also seeped into the more intimate aspects of Lowcountry life. Preachers who supported Smalls reportedly ostracized parishioners known to support the Democratic Party. Parents who had supported the Democratic Party reported that their children were bullied in school. One opponent proclaimed that Smalls told the women in the crowd at one of his mass meetings that "if the man courting you votes for a Democrat, do not marry him; get rid of him right off; he is not fit to be a husband." Even more scandalizing were accounts of Smalls telling married women in his audience to punish husbands who voted Democrat by not letting them "enjoy any of the privilege of the bed with you." A common feature of Reconstruction-era grassroots politics, direct appeals to women as wives and romantic partners drew the indignation of Democrats and were seen as a perversion of the public sphere. One of Smalls's opponents claimed that the congressman's speeches were "calculated to stir up women" and thus violated traditional ideas of not only gender and decorum but also of who could participate in the public sphere.[44]

Smalls's opponents were most offended by reports of violence against those who dared to challenge his political power. Thomas Reynolds, a member of the state senate and one of Smalls's top lieutenants, reportedly told a crowd of followers to go to the polls armed and prepared to wade "knee deep in blood if necessary" to carry the election. In another speech, state representative Joseph Robinson, also a Smalls supporter, was reported to have told a mass meeting, "Any man who votes a Democratic ticket on this island, I advise you to drive him off the island; if you can't get him off, get a gun and run him off." An October 22 Democratic mass meeting was broken up by a mob that filled the air with brickbats, leaving one person injured with a head wound. In another instance, Smalls encountered John Freeman on Bay Street, the town of Beaufort's central thoroughfare. Freeman had opposed Smalls at the Seventh Congressional District's Republican nominating convention. Freeman claimed that Smalls asked others on the street, "Do you know any Democrat n——by the name of Jack Freeman?" When Freeman announced his presence, Smalls supposedly commanded his associates "to tie him and lick him." While many of these accounts reflected the jaundiced opinions of Black Democrats and were obtained as witness testimony on behalf of William Elliott's campaign during a congressional hearing over the contested 1886 election results, they do suggest that some minority of residents opposed Robert Smalls and his methods for maintaining power.[45]

While it is likely that Smalls's supporters, like those of other nineteenth-century political machines, deployed some level of violence to intimidate opponents, patronage played the largest role in keeping constituents in Smalls's political fold. While it is impossible to reconstruct the full texture of Smalls's political machine from existing records, it seems clear that he maintained power by supporting longtime allies with money, patronage, and political support. His closest associates had all been born into slavery; these men spoke from the same register of historical memory as Smalls and understood the deeper fears and anxieties of Beaufort's working class. Hastings Gantt, a successful farmer on St. Helena Island who had served several terms in the general assembly, was often smeared in the Democratic press for being unable to read or write. Joseph Robinson, another member of the general assembly, and George Reed, who would later be the county's first Black sheriff, had all been aligned with Smalls since the 1870s and had held local offices or been elected to the general assembly.[46]

A handful of highly educated men also surrounded Smalls. Samuel Bampfield, a free-born Charlestonian who was educated at Philadelphia's Lincoln University, served as postmaster and clerk of the county court. Thomas Miller, another free-born Charlestonian who also attended Lincoln, had been associated with Smalls's machine since the 1870s and received a federally appointed position in Beaufort's Customs House when Smalls's returned to Washington. Riding the congressman's coattails, the individuals associated with his machine not only filled local offices in Beaufort but also were among the handful of Black politicians elected to the state's general assembly during the 1880s.[47]

Patronage played a critical role in keeping Smalls's political machine in power. Positions in the post office and the customhouse were likely the most prized places where Smalls could place loyalists. "I am just as much service to you all, while the Democratic [P]arty is in power, as that building is," Smalls told one group as he stood on Bay Street, the town's main thoroughfare. Having accumulated significant wealth during his lifetime, Smalls was accused by his opponents of unfairly weaponizing his financial strength. He paid speakers and confidential agents to canvas the district for his election, paying some as much as forty dollars a month. Facing a challenge for the Seventh District's congressional seat from W. H. Thompson, the chairman of the Berkeley County Republican Party, Smalls tapped the billfold in his pocket during a public confrontation with his opponent and remarked, "A fat dog can always beat a lean one."[48]

When Smalls lost his 1886 congressional election by a margin of fewer than 600 votes, his long-standing critics in the Black press immediately began to write his political obituary. Like its attacks on Smalls in 1884, T. Thomas Fortune's *Freeman* discounted Smalls's political virtues, suggesting his "sway of the masses" was simply an extension of his "rude plantation eloquence." Going further, the paper reported to have "dozens of protests" from intelligent young men of South Carolina who found Smalls's leadership "ignorant and dictatorial." The *Star of Zion*, the official newspaper of the African Methodist Episcopal Zion Church, also editorialized that Smalls was out of step with Gilded Age notions of racial destiny. "We fear that the defeat of Mr. Smalls was due in part to the belief that he entertained that no colored man was entitled to represent that District but himself, when there are many men there abler and equally as competent to fill the position." Generally hostile to the older generation of Black politicians, the *Freeman* and the *Star of Zion* put forward a vision of a Black political future led by a younger generation of highly educated politicians opposed to the perceived corrupting influence of stalwart Republicanism.[49]

Smalls's allies challenged the claims made by Fortune and other Black independents. "Mr. Fortune should remember that the educated and enlightened young men are vastly in the minority in Smalls' district," suggested one of Smalls's allies. "His rude eloquence and his blunt manners are more powerful and efficacious to his illiterate constituency than that of abler and better educated men," Smalls's friend continued. Joseph Robinson wrote to the *Springfield (MA) Republican* to challenge a story the paper reprinted from the *Charleston News and Courier* that claimed Smalls's loss was a result of an intraracial struggle between light-skinned and biracial elites from the North and the Gullah-Geechee freedpeople in the Lowcountry. While colorism tinged Black politics and may have influenced the political terrain in the South Carolina Lowcountry, it did so more as a proxy for class, education, and previous condition of servitude. Robinson, like Smalls, consistently argued that the base of the Republican Party was made up of freedpeople:

> I am proud to say that this town and county, Black as they are, and governed by republican officials, will not for progress, peace and good order, suffer in comparison with any others in the state. And now after my race has suffered more than 200 years in slavery and has had only 20 years of freedom, the threat is made by the democrats that they will at the next election capture this county in the same way they have stolen the election in this district. Our freedom, our rights as citizens, cost this country four years of a bloody war, and the struggle is not yet ended.

Mobilizing the memory of emancipation, Robinson rejected the idea that Smalls's defeat was somehow a larger victory for racial destiny and instead pointed to the political project in South Carolina's Lowcountry as the last hope for Black freedom in the New South.[50]

The national press also viewed Smalls's defeat as a turning point in Southern politics after Reconstruction. The *Boston Herald* explicitly challenged the *Atlanta Constitution* for its silence on the Black district election while being the loudest booster of the myth of the New South. "We want to know whether the seventh congressional district of South Carolina is part of the New South, or whether it still remains in outer darkness?" charged one of the *Herald*'s journalists. "What does the New South think of the men who stifled the Black vote in the Black district and threw out Robert Smalls?" the writer continued. "For an organ of the new revelation, the *Atlanta Constitution* has been strangely mute on the chief political outrage of the day in the South." The *Daily Inter Ocean* examined the cynical effectiveness of the voter suppression effort in the majority-Black Seventh Congressional District. "A neat but not gaudy democratic majority was manufactured; not large enough to be showy; just big enough to be useful; just the size to float the falsehood that in this naturally Republican district, the policy of Mr. Cleveland was indorsed by the negroes." While the Democratic Party lost seats in the House and only narrowly retained its majority, it gained seats in the South and left as the Republican Party's only remaining footholds the Mountain South and the former Readjuster stronghold of Virginia.[51]

For Black observers, Smalls's defeat was made more pronounced by the concurrent defeat of James O'Hara, the representative for North Carolina's "Black Second." With the incoming Fiftieth Congress the first without a Black representative since the Grant administration, Black leaders in the press rightfully feared that racial destiny was at a perilous juncture. "In the 50th Congress there will [be] a conspicuous absence of colored men," lamented the *Washington Bee*. "Since 1872 the number of colored congressmen has been gradually diminishing until now there is not one left." While the *New York Freeman* once again complained that neither Smalls nor O'Hara could be called "brilliant men," the paper understood their defeats as a setback for the race's political future. "It is an evil wind that blows us no good—this envy and lack of race pride." As far as a silver lining could be gleaned from the defeat of Smalls and O'Hara, it would be a revival of the Republican Party as a defender of civil rights. "The counting out of Congressman Smalls will not be an unmixed calamity, great as was the outrage upon the ballot-box, if it only serves to stimulate the Republicans of the State to concentrated action in behalf of their inalienable rights, and to place at their back all Americans, North and South, who love fair play and believe in the doctrine of equal rights," argued the *Cleveland Gazette*.[52]

The inheritor of the Lowcountry's robust postbellum political legacy, Robert Smalls came to embody the promise and the peril of the Reconstruction era. For his supporters, he represented the possibility of sustaining Republican political power in the Gilded Age South, bringing national attention to issues of voter fraud and anti-Black violence, and creating a heroic symbol of political courage in the emerging canon of African American history. For his detractors, he was a demagogic machine politician who stood as an obstacle to both a new generation of leadership and a broader, more modern vision of racial destiny.

For Smalls's allies in the Lowcountry, as well as for observers in the Black press, the stakes of his political success—and failure—reflected a larger anxiety over the meaning of the Reconstruction era. Despite his 1886 defeat, Smalls and the Lowcountry district that he represented continued to represent the long reach of Reconstruction and would continue to be a pivotal battleground for the South's last bastion of Republican Party politics in the century's final decade.

CHAPTER FIVE

More Good from Nazareth
The Lowcountry's Long Reconstruction, Disfranchisement, and Archiving Countermemory at the Century's End

On May 30, 1890, the town of Beaufort prepared to host a spectacular Decoration Day celebration. Twenty-five years had passed since a group of freedpeople in Charleston created the holiday at a makeshift cemetery to honor the Union dead. By the century's last decade, a spectacular social event had emerged around Beaufort's County's local honoring of the Union dead. Organized by the David Hunter Post, Number 9, a recently established local chapter of the Grand Army of the Republic, the celebration was attended by "tens of thousands" of visitors who descended upon the coastal county. The *Savannah Tribune*, the most widely circulated Black newspaper in the Southeast, advertised ferry excursions to Beaufort for seventy-five cents. "The trains were filled with colored people," remarked one reporter, "and as the three last trains were being moved down to Beaufort thousands were passed on the way, all bent on the pilgrimage to the capital of the Black Belt." The region's now robust system of railways brought revelers from Charleston, Columbia, Augusta, and many other parts of the Southeast. "No one perhaps ever saw before so many Black people together in the Southern States," reported the *Charleston News and Courier*.[1]

By the century's last decade, Decoration Day had evolved from a solemn moment of quiet reflection to a massively popular celebration of the promise of Black freedom. "Bands were marching in the streets, hucksters were screaming good things from their carts, the banjo was going." The normal routines of agricultural and domestic labor were interrupted as the "rice fields were abandoned" and the "cotton field, the corn field, hut and home of all kinds were absolutely emptied of their denizens." The region's numerous veterans and GAR members wore their Union blues and paraded from Bay Street to the national cemetery. Women were decked in holiday attire, wearing "bright dresses" that to outside observers that possessed "all the colors that could be seen." The GAR provided free barbeque to the revelers, and vendors sold lemonade and ice cream to those who wanted a cool refreshment on the warm day; it was likely that some of the region's many "blind tigers" were also selling stronger drinks. A series of boat races took place over the course of the day in the Port Royal Sound, providing entertainment for both the casual attendees and the gamblers in the crowd. To white observers, the "riotous reverence" of the day's events highlighted the region's broader racial regression. "It was quite easy to fancy that one was in the middle of a big town in Ashantee on a grand pagan festival," sneered one Southern journalist.[2]

What both Black and white observers were witnessing at 1890 Decoration Day celebration was the apex of the region's Black countermemory of Reconstruction. The day's keynote speaker, state Republican Party executive chairman Ellery Brayton, sought to harmonize this countermemory within what had once been a traditionally Unionist event. "Let us never fail to be proud that we belong to the adherents of the Union, and to maintain that the cause of the Union was everlasting right," the Southern-born white leader proclaimed. Far from simply delivering the standard anodyne platitudes to sectional reconciliation, Brayton's speech quickly began detailing the many crimes of the Democratic Party in the state. He described how the political leaders of the Reconstruction era had been "hounded," "abused," "vilified," and "misrepresented." "White supremacy has been secured at a fearful cost," Brayton cautioned.[3]

Echoing the political themes that Black political leaders in the Lowcountry had been making for nearly two decades, Brayton connected Decoration Day to the long and bloody struggle for Black freedom. "What say you, my Black friends, standing as you do about the graves of your race who fought to preserve this government," Brayton exclaimed. "Are you ready at the demand of those who would have destroyed it to submit to this treatment? Will you bow your neck to take this yoke?" Brayton's speech continued in this bombastic tone, invoking "two hundred years of bondage and the blood," "fathers [who] were brought in chains," and families "forced to raise children for the auction block." Brayton's bloody shirt proclamations were interspersed with cheerier descriptions of Beaufort County's exceptionalism. Highlighting the "constancy, devotion, and sublime faith" of the Northern missionaries who arrived on the Sea Islands during the Civil War, Brayton lauded the white Northerners for bringing "light out of the darkness" and the "pathway of life" that placed Black children in the region "years in advance" of other freedpeople in the South. Most optimistically, he told his audience that the federal government would once again take seriously its duty of upholding the Fifteenth Amendment. "We are cheered with the promise that the administration and Congress are at last aroused to the need of Federal legislation to protect us in the rights of suffrage, so far as pertains to national elections," Brayton promised.[4]

The white Republican leader's speech crystallized a generation of Black countermemory that now exposed the unfinished nature of sectional reconciliation. The Southern press denounced the speech for desecrating a supposed high holiday with party politics—and reminded the region's white elites that their recent political victories were not permanent. "It is true political demagogues seek to inject politics on every occasion, and when they do, the worst passions of the race are aroused." In sharp contrast, the *Washington Bee*, one of the era's most important Black newspapers, saluted the "good news from Nazareth." The *Bee*'s readers, composed of Black Washingtonians who attended lyceums like the Bethel Literary and Historical Society, regularly encountered former Reconstruction-era politicians in the city's society circles and now had spent a generation following the paper's coverage of the postbellum South. They would likely have had a deep knowledge of the Lowcountry's recent political history. The article's allusion to John 1:46—"Can anything good come out of Nazareth?"—would also have made sense to the *Bee*'s readers, who understood that the larger march of postbellum racial destiny linked the political fates of elites in the nation's capital with rural freedpeople in the New South. "The speech from Ellery M. Brayton, delivered on Decoration Day, at Beaufort, S.C., offers another instance of the fact that there are at least a few men at the South who are honest enough to think fairly of the colored people and who have the courage of their convictions," claimed the *Bee*'s editor, Calvin Chase. Part of a longer history of journalists who understood the importance of enshrining Reconstruction's countermemory in the Black public sphere, Chase captured the deep sense of political possibility that persisted in the Lowcountry.[5]

This chapter explores the changing shape of the Black countermemory of Reconstruction in the century's final decade. As both Brayton's speech and the actions of the attendees at the 1890 Decoration Day celebration make abundantly clear, the promise of Reconstruction could still be seen and felt in South Carolina's rival geography of race and memory. Despite recent setbacks, the Republican Party in the state's Seventh Congressional District remained active at the local level—and well connected to the national party apparatus. With Benjamin Harrison's 1888 presidential victory, and a Republican-controlled Congress, many felt the real possibility that the GOP would deliver an election bill providing federal monitoring of Southern voting. Additionally, a statewide farmers' movement threatened to splinter South Carolina's Democratic Party, thus giving the state's Black voters a continued role in shaping state politics.

Despite ongoing attacks from a more aggressive and explicitly racist state Democratic Party, the Lowcountry continued to embody both the promise of a Black political past and the lodestar of a possible political future. The South Carolina Lowcountry's Seventh Congressional District continued to elect a

Black congressman; Beaufort County continued to elect and appoint Black officeholders to state and a local positions; a robust grassroots political culture persisted in the region, as did the organizations and holidays that preserved emancipationist and Union memory, serving as anchors in the region's larger network of African American associational life; and the Black press continued to closely cover Lowcountry political events. As the 1890 Decoration Day celebration made abundantly clear, the vibrant world established by the Reconstruction generation remained alive in the region.

While the Reconstruction generation's cultural power in many ways reached its zenith in the century's final decade, the Lowcountry's political foundation was beginning to erode. A factional divide within Beaufort County's Republican Party would bring negative attention to the party leadership and raise new concerns among leaders in the Northern Black press. At that same moment, Benjamin Tillman, a new demagogic Democratic leader, sought to reanimate Reconstruction-era grievances against the Lowcountry's Republican political world. A participant in the 1876 campaigns of terrorist violence, Tillman would ride the broader currents of Southern populism to the governor's mansion. Able to leverage the disorder following the devastating 1893 Sea Island storm to a narrow 1894 political win, Tillman's Democratic Party accomplished one of its own generational goals—rewriting the state's Reconstruction-era constitution and eliminating universal manhood suffrage.

Those who lived in the Lowcountry and paid close attention to the region's political events could not have anticipated the fall of the Damoclean sword of disfranchisement. As Ellery Brayton's 1890 speech and the broader Decoration Day celebration highlight, Republican Party leaders and Black Southerners still celebrated the ideals of Reconstruction and deployed its memory as a useable past. Despite the rise of antidemocratic forces seeking to eliminate the state's Black electorate, the Lowcountry's Republican leaders, as well as members of the Reconstruction generation in the national Black press, remained committed to a politics powered by a countermemory of the region's earlier era. Faced with a final, unwinnable battle, a motley crew from the Lowcountry's Reconstruction generation turned the state's 1895 constitutional convention into a larger battle over the meaning of the postbellum past. While unable to turn the tide of disfranchisement in South Carolina, these Reconstruction generation leaders would win the applause and approval of their allies in the Black public sphere and ensure that their historical vision would play an outsized role in the production of turn-of-the-century African American history.

Robert Smalls, the 1890 Federal Elections Bill, and the Legacy of Radical Reconstruction

In the 1886 Seventh Congressional District election, Democrat William Elliott defeated Robert Smalls by just over 500 votes. Smalls deployed his connections in the national Republican Party to raise awareness of voter fraud and election irregularities. In 1887, he brought a federal suit against Elliott. The resulting hearings, which included over 900 interviews and produced an 800-page report, presented a story of rampant and unrestrained voter fraud. "The contestee, Elliott," Smalls's side argued, "is confronted at the outset by the undisputed fact of the 39,000 voters of the Seventh South Carolina District, 32,000 are of the colored race and at least 30,000 are Republicans in politics." At one of the district's busiest precincts, Democratic managers closed the polls for two hours; some precincts failed to open at all. One Lowcountry voter had to travel thirty-four miles to reach the county's registration office. Read in total, the evidence submitted by Smalls and his attorneys demonstrates that despite the Democratic Party's 1882 gerrymander of the state, which packed the Black majority state's Republican voters into a single congressional district, Democratic Party leaders were already abandoning the political détente and betraying the spirit of the earlier redistricting effort. Despite the overwhelming evidence that South Carolina's Democratic Party had won a fraudulently decided election in the Lowcountry, the contested election committee ruled against Smalls and left Elliott in possession of the Seventh District's House seat.[6]

Smalls pushed the GOP to enact federal protections for Black voters in the South. Despite the Republican Party's control of the White House and both chambers of Congress on the eve of the 1890 midterm elections, "in South Carolina there is neither a free ballot nor an honest count," explained Smalls in the pages of the *North American Review*. Framing the state's post-Reconstruction political history as "a continued series of murders, outrages, perjury, and fraud," Smalls used the pages of the national magazine to paint a lurid portrait of the New South. In counties with either white majorities or relative racial parity, the "shotgun and rifle" ensured Democratic victory. In counties like Beaufort where Black majorities continued to anchor Republican political power, Democratic Party–controlled election boards had stuffed ballot boxes and created flimsy pretexts to throw out Republican ballots to arrive at a "false count" that would ensure the victories of hopelessly unpopular Democratic candidates. In addition, Smalls outlined the broader structural transformations in the voter registration process that harmed Black voters. "Thousands of voters," Smalls warned, "after travelling fifty and one hundred miles to the county-seat, the only place for registration, have to return home after a fruitless search for the register on the days that the law requires him to be present." He noted that this system disfranchised not only the state's Black majority but also "the poor whites who form the bulk of the Democratic voters."[7]

More than simply diagnosing a corrupt and deeply antidemocratic system, Smalls demanded that Republicans in Congress act upon the federal elections bill introduced by Henry Cabot Lodge. Submitted to the House on June 14, 1890, Lodge's bill allowed constituents at the precinct level to petition a federal judge if they believed significant fraud or irregularities were occurring in a local election. "The first step . . . toward the settlement of the negro problem and toward the elevation and protection of the race is to take it [the issue of race] out of national party politics," Lodge proclaimed. Giving the federal government power to appoint supervisors who would oversee all phases of federal elections, from voter registration to the certification of results, the proposed bill was demonized by Southern Democratic leaders as a return to Reconstruction. "With both the Senate and the House Republican there might be some danger to us, but I don't think our friends, the enemy, will attempt any further reconstruction measures and even if they did, the South has advanced too far to be relegated back to negro domination," warned the *Charleston News and Courier*. Perhaps the *News and Courier* had reason to fear. The prospect of renewed protection for Black voting rights energized the Lowcountry's Republican voters. At a June 27 meeting of the South Carolina Republican Association, Robert Smalls "warmly indorsed" the federal election bill and was given an ovation when he told his constituents that with the bill in place, the Republicans could carry five of the state's seven congressional districts.[8]

National controversy over the contested 1886 election dredged up long-standing debates about the racial legacy of Reconstruction and the specter of "Negro supremacy." In a special 1888 issue of *Forum* magazine, Wade Hampton penned an article detailing the horror of Black-led Reconstruction-era governance. Where he had previously presented himself as a moderate Democrat who rejected direct appeals to white supremacy, his article "What Negro Supremacy Means" emphasized the most racist tropes from the past decade and leaned heavily on James Pike's *The Prostrate State* to support his argument. Hampton took particular aim at Robert Smalls, relitigating the spurious bribery allegation and calling into question his fitness for office. "I am happy to say that his constituents, apprised as they have been of his disreputable conduct, and recognizing the shame that attached to them in having such a representative on the floor of Congress, relegated him, at the last election, to the walks of private life, much to their honor." Supporting the claim by William Elliott and other Democrats that Black voters had turned against Smalls's corruption in 1886—despite their having had the same evidence available in 1884, when they gave him a landslide victory against Elliott—Hampton argued that the recent election results from South Carolina's Black district reflected a final rejection of Negro supremacy by both white Southerners and a growing number of responsible Black voters.[9]

Hampton's attack on Robert Smalls and the legacy of Reconstruction reunited the Northern defenders of Black political power. In July 1888, the *American Missionary* published a rebuttal to Hampton's effort to relitigate the Reconstruction era. "We make no defence of that carpet-bag Legislature, but does not Senator Wade recognize the change that has taken place in the condition of the Negro—a change that is going on at an increased ratio?" Danish-born Niels Christensen produced his own response to Hampton, challenging the existence of Negro supremacy and the implicit idea of racial regression at the core of the trope. He did so by offering data from the 1880 census and local government reports to show how freedpeople had made material progress in categories like population growth, property ownership, school attendance, and church membership.[10]

Leaders in the Black press also took direct aim at Wade Hampton's 1888 article. The preeminent journalist John Edward Bruce challenged the idea of Negro supremacy and defended his friend Robert Smalls in the pages of Thomas Fortune's new periodical, the *New York Age*. "Senator Hampton has resorted to methods which place him in the front ranks among the white Democrats of the South who do not hesitate to misrepresent and malign the Negroes of that section, whom they rob of representation in Congress—that rule of the white man may be undisturbed." Turning the argument for "Negro supremacy" on its head, Bruce saw the reanimation of the Reconstruction-era slogan as a new project to defend Southern disfranchisement efforts. "The Senator does not in his learned dissertation against Negro supremacy incorporate the whole truth of history," argued Bruce, "and the records of those times will show that his deductions and conclusions, aside from being fearfully and wonderfully made, are terribly inaccurate." In a self-published pamphlet, Bruce expanded on his *New York Age* editorial, offering competing evidence from court records, newspaper articles, and personal letters to highlight the shallowness of Hampton's claims. Recognizing that Black political destiny was tied to the future of the Seventh Congressional District, Bruce's response to Wade Hampton not only served as a specific intellectual defense of Robert Smalls and the fading political world he embodied but also offered a broader argument for a countermemory of Reconstruction that challenged both Hampton's narrow vision of sectional reconciliation and the Northern intellectual institutions that propagated his misguided portrait of the New South.[11]

Republican Party Factions, Fusion Politics, and the Reconstruction Generation's Competing Memories

Beyond its outsized place in national debates over the meaning of Reconstruction and its legacy, South Carolina's Seventh Congressional District continued to be the home of a vibrant Black political world. William Whipper served as an incumbent probate judge; Samuel Bampfield received considerable praise for how he ran the county clerk of court's office; and George A. Reed would become the first Black man to be elected sheriff of Beaufort County as well as one of the few to hold such a post in the entire South. Black men held the local offices on the school board, county commission, and the coroner's office; and the county's Black majority continued to send Black representatives to both houses of the state legislature. The region's robust grassroots political culture served as the bulwark of the local Republican Party. Perhaps the most visible symbol of this continued political vitality was the formation of a local chapter of the Grand Army of the Republic. Founded in 1888, the David Hunter Post, Number 9, would not only serve as a fixture in local mass meetings and political rallies but also act as a vehicle for political education for local veterans and widows about the Union pension application process. One white observer reported that "hundreds" of Black Lowcountry residents received ten to forty dollars a month from the federal government in pensions. "If the yankees of the north draw as much money to pensions in proportion to their population as the negroes of Beaufort the scarcity of money in the South can be easily explained."[12]

A new set of tensions, however, emerged around how the Republicans in Beaufort should strategically align with white South Carolinians to preserve the party's political future. On one side of the spectrum stood fusionists, who believed that the party should unite with the Lowcountry's white elites to form a whiggish coalition of the region's "best men." In Georgetown County, a longtime Republican stronghold just north of Charleston, local Black leaders created a power-sharing arrangement that fostered comity between white elites and moderate Republican Party officials.[13]

Robert Smalls was the first to move the Beaufort County Republican Party toward fusionism. Still contesting the results of the 1886 election, Smalls initially cleared the way for his protégé Thomas Miller to receive the Seventh

District's Republican nomination. Seemingly out of nowhere, Smalls sought the party's nomination for sheriff when it became clear that the party convention was going to shock friends and foes alike by bolting from the regular Beaufort County Republican Party and creating a fusion ticket with local Democratic Party. Identifying itself as the "People's ticket," the fusion faction offered the positions of probate judge and state senator to white Democrats; promised sheriff, coroner, clerk of court, and school commissioner to Black Republicans; and divided seats on the county commission and in the state general assembly between the two parties.[14]

While Smalls's decision helped deliver a victory in the 1888 election to his fusion coalition, it also severely tarnished his reputation both locally and nationally. Thomas Miller blamed his one-time political mentor for his defeat in the Seventh District's congressional race. "The so-called fusion ticket has no more right to the name than a gang of burglars out to rob a bank would have to be called the directors of the same," Miller excoriated. Several party loyalists grumbled to the Black press that Smalls was a Republican in name only and could not meaningfully represent the party at that year's national convention in Indianapolis. The most strident criticism came from William Whipper, Smalls's longtime rival. Defeated in his bid for reelection for county probate judge, Whipper rejected the legitimacy of his defeat and refused to vacate his office and turn over official records to the incoming candidate. Whipper was held in contempt and imprisoned in the Beaufort County jail. As the national Black press turned its attention to the bizarre political drama brewing in the Lowcountry, Whipper self-published a broadside that lambasted Smalls for abandoning the Republican Party. Once "the idol of the Republicans of this county," Smalls, Whipper argued, was now "going into the very arms of the blood stained Democracy that he has so long, so often and so roundly denounced ... a party [that] but a few years ago penned him and a number of his friends in a house in Gillisonville and riddled it with bullets." Returning to the memory of the 1878 Red Shirt attack on Smalls that required a heroic mass intervention by Beaufort's Black citizens, Whipper weaponized the past against his rival, casting him as a man who had lost his way and forgotten his own history.[15]

This battle over Smalls's legacy erupted into a full-fledged political scandal that rose to the attention of President Benjamin Harrison. "Robert Smalls does not represent the Republicans of the State, District, or County in any of the essential principles that go to make up Republicanism," argued a group of regular Republicans who had collected the signatures of nearly 600 Beaufort County residents on a petition condemning Smalls and arguing he should not receive a federal appointment. Julius I. Washington, who had been part of an earlier campaign to challenge Smalls, argued that "during the whole campaign, he did not make a speech in the County in favor of Genl. Harrison for President, nor [Thomas] Miller for Congress," and that Smalls's abandonment of the party was "a bigger steal in comparison than the fraud of 1876." For the Lowcountry leaders who remained loyal to the traditional party, Smalls had become an avatar for ego and selfish ambition. "There is no falsehood that he would not tell in his own interest and swear it was true. There is no person so pure or so high that escapes his slanderous tongue when he stands between him and a coveted prize and there is no friend so dear that he would not sacrifice for profit," denounced one Republican in Beaufort. Some of the most powerful testimony came from longtime allies who been beside Smalls since the 1870s. "I ask for no office," pleaded one freedman who had been one of Smalls's most loyal political associates, "but do earnestly ask and pray that you deliver us from the influence of such men as ex-Congressman Smalls and a few others who have so cruelly deserted us and joined the Democracy for the purpose of defeating the overwhelming majority of the voters of this county."[16]

Powerful national Republican leaders rallied to Smalls's defense. Ohio senator John Sherman remarked, "Though cheated, counted out and prosecuted, he is the best type of the native negro in South Carolina and has more claims upon the consideration of the Administration than anyone else I know." Rufus Saxton also vouched for Smalls's character. "He may be regarded as one of the representative men of his race," Saxton observed. "Should he receive the appointment he desires, I am confident that he will perform his duties with fidelity, and advantage to the government." The president of Beaufort's David Hunter chapter of the Grand Army of the Republic also issued a letter in support of "Comrade Smalls," arguing that the charges of Smalls's being disloyal to the Republican cause were untrue.[17]

Smalls and his allies attempted to rebut the charges against him by claiming that he had never abandoned the Republican Party but simply sought to preserve the South's last Republican Party stronghold from the scourge of Northern corruption. "The allegation that Gen. Smalls does not represent the Republicans of this county and State is simply ludicrous and grossly false," argued Smalls's son-in-law and political lieutenant Samuel Bampfield. "The truth is that those men who originated that paper are Republicans 'for revenue only' and are aggrieved because the general, as an honest citizen, preferred to vote the fusion ticket in preference to the regular, because it was composed of decent men." Smalls would tell the president that the accusation that he had abandoned the Republican ticket had no merit. Stunned by the betrayal by his former protégé, Thomas Miller, who not only "used me to help secure his nomination and election" but also joined a coalition with William Whipper,

Smalls's "political enem[y] for the last fourteen years whom I have fought and defeated in every State and Congressional Convention," Smalls stood his ground and defended his record. "[Miller] cannot injure me with the people of the State, who have known me through the long years of trials as well as triumphs ... [to] whose cause I have never proved recreant in the past and whom I will never desert in their struggle for their rights, their ballot, and for the victory of the party."[18]

As the national Black press published accounts of his critics, and a petition signed by hundreds of Beaufort County residents called on incoming president Benjamin Harrison to revoke Smalls's appointment to the local customhouse, the Gullah statesman struck back at his challengers in unsparing terms. He tarred the delegates who attended the 1888 Beaufort County Republican convention as "men of the lowest degree of character" and argued that the rival cohort of aspiring party leaders were a "stench in the nostrils of all honest and decent people." William Whipper, his longtime rival, was "a disgrace to Beaufort and an injury to Republicanism"; the "carpetbag and rum element" within the party who supported Whipper were nothing more than "Northern negroes who lead profligate and adulterous lives."[19]

In private, Smalls's allies went even further, claiming that if the Lowcountry was going to remain a North Star for the race's political destiny, men like Whipper could not be in party leadership. In a letter to the president defending Smalls's appointment to federal office, Samuel Bampfield disclosed that while Whipper was required to conduct official business as a probate judge at the county courthouse, he and other regular Republicans kept an illicit gathering spot above a local grocery store where drinking and gambling may have mixed with local politics. Bampfield further alleged that a male teacher sexually assaulted a female student in this secret headquarters and only escaped arrest by fleeing the county. At a moment when temperance not only provided an organizing moral principle within national Republican politics but also included an implicit critique of a suite of criminal and morally repugnant behaviors against women that were not discussed in the public sphere, the private challenges that Smalls and his allies leveled against their opponents made clear that they were waging a battle for the soul of the Lowcountry's Republican Party.[20]

For Smalls and his allies, the Lowcountry remained a site of social and political renewal within the larger Black South, and they actively sought to broadcast this narrative to the national Black press. In 1889, Bampfield, Robert Smalls's son-in-law, founded the *New South*, a weekly newspaper that sought to reflect a distinctly Black Southern perspective on the issues pertaining to the Republican Party and racial uplift. Anticipating Booker T. Washington's agrarian conservatism, the *New South* nursed the generational sense of betrayal Black Southerners felt toward the national Republican Party. Responding to Henry Blair's proposed House bill that offered federal funding for public education in the South, and thus partially alleviating the growing racial disparities in the region's schools, the *New South* argued that the Lowcountry's progress would be rooted in localism, not federal largesse: "There are more than 10,000 tax payers in Beaufort County, S.C., and fully two-thirds of them are colored persons. We are coming, Father Abraham, Blair bill or no Blair bill. We are coming anyhow."[21]

In defending the Lowcountry's late nineteenth-century political world, the editors of the *New South* took aim at the chauvinism of Black Northern leaders, who saw the rollback of Republican political power in the region as a sign that Black Southerners had failed the larger project of racial destiny. Acknowledging that Black Southerners alone could not "bell the cat" of lynching and white mob violence, Bampfield argued for a long-term approach to Southern politics that required working within the existing system. When an 1890 *New York Age* article criticized Black South Carolinians for not putting forth a statewide ticket, the *New South* reminded the paper that "such a State ticket would engender race friction, in which the Afro-American would get smashed." Arguing that "safety and success for the Negroes of South Carolina lie in conciliation and not antagonism in their dealing with the whites," the *New South* produced a fatalistic vision of Black Southern life that found honor in the ability to "grin and bear" the region's white supremacy. T. Thomas Fortune's *New York Age* reprinted the New South's editorial about abandoning statewide politics with concern and confusion. "Is the policy of the *New South* the safest and manliest one? We hesitate to decide," remarked Fortune.[22]

Fortune's comments reflected an ongoing struggle to reconcile the Northern and Southern nodes of the now national Black public sphere. By the 1890s, leaders in the Black press framed themselves, their journalistic institutions, and the history of their industry in the language of rising racial destiny. In 1880, the National Colored Press Convention held its first meeting in Louisville, Kentucky. By the end of the decade, the National Colored Press Association had been formed with the mission of more purposefully stitching together the national Black public sphere. In his 1891 history, *The Afro-American Press, and Its Editors*, journalist Irvine Garland Penn honored the long nineteenth-century tradition of Black journalism. An exhaustive compendium that gathered interviews and essays from every major and minor figure in the late nineteenth-century Black public sphere, Penn's history framed the journalistic industry's long march since the publication of *Freedom's Journal* as reaching its golden age in the decades that followed the Civil War. "To our mind, the greatest stride made in Afro-American journalism, was the decade which ends with the present year, 1890."[23]

In measuring this new zenith, Penn made clear that much of the expansion in the Black press was occurring in the South. Expanding from 31 newspapers in 1880 to 154 periodicals by the end of the decade, the Black press saw 91 of these new newspapers emerge in states that had once been a target of the Thirteenth Amendment. The inclusion of freedpeople among potential readers of the Black press not only increased the scale and scope of the Black public sphere but also reshaped the meaning of racial destiny. "The Afro-American press has guided a race of freemen who have been watching its course with unabated interest," Penn declared. In the same volume, T. Thomas Fortune contributed an essay that went further and argued that the expansion of the Black press had the potential to surpass Reconstruction as a moment of political progress: "A colored newspaper, with one hundred thousand subscribers, would be a greater power for good than any other agency colored men could create—than even fifty black members of Congress would be; and until we have newspapers equal in circulation to those controlled by our enemies, the contest for our just rights under the Constitution will remain pitiably unequal."[24]

The Lowcountry's journalists struggled to reconcile their region's place in this shifting public sphere. While some Southern writers like Ida B. Wells and John Mitchell Jr. were lauded by their Northern peers for their courageous and unsparing attacks on the white Southern press's defense of lynching, the Lowcountry's Black journalists still held grievances from the previous decade's battles with Northern elites like T. Thomas Fortune. When Ida B. Wells fled her native Memphis after her courageous investigative journalism put her life in danger, the Lowcountry's *New South* offered a dissenting perspective in the national Black press regarding the famed writer's flight from the South. "Miss Ida B. Wells says she is not going back to Memphis," bemoaned Bampfield. "We are compelled to remain in Memphis: indeed, we have never fled." Sensing that the perceived vanguard of the national Black public sphere was still based outside the Deep South—and likely resenting Wells for joining the staff of Thomas Fortune's *New York Age*—Samuel Bampfield repositioned the Lowcountry's political press as one of the few remaining beacons of Black journalism in the greater South. Emphasizing the material reality of the Lowcountry's remaining political world, Bampfield continued to confront a starry-eyed Northern vision of racial destiny that he believed was divorced from the conditions freedpeople continued to face in the New South.[25]

The Lowcountry's Southern Populist Moment and the 1893 Sea Island Storm

While Robert Smalls and his allies presented themselves as the last defenders of the race's political destiny in the South, a new vision of the South's Black political future emerged in the form of the Colored Farmers' Alliance. Founded on December 11, 1886, by a group of Black farmers in Houston County, Texas, the Colored Farmers' Alliance emerged in response to the failed promises of free labor ideology and the broken agricultural ladder that left the majority of the region's Black agriculturalists unable to climb out of sharecropping and debt peonage. Initially semiclandestine and organized largely through the preexisting infrastructure of the state's Black churches, the alliance grew to become a powerful regionwide mass movement, boasting 1.2 million members at its peak. Offering mutual aid, political and agricultural education, and, perhaps most important, solidarity in a moment of deep economic turmoil, the Colored Farmers' Alliance transformed Black Southern politics and shone a spotlight on the Republican Party's inability to offer concrete policy solutions to the harrowing shift in the postbellum cotton economy.[26]

Where fusionists sought to create a biracial alliance between old-guard Republican Party leaders and the Lowcountry's long-standing white elites, the Colored Farmers' Alliance hoped to build a form of interracial populism with white and Black agriculturalists struggling in the postbellum rural South. In June 1889, local Republican leader George Washington Murray hosted the first statewide meeting of the Colored Farmers' Alliance in the town of Sumter. Over 900 Black and white delegates from over twenty counties attended the meeting, where attendees were offered barbecue, a Black brass band playing "Dixie," and the promise of a biracial coalition that would defend a radically different vision of the New South from that presented by the Democratic or Republican Party. "A new era [has] dawned in which white and colored farmer [can] pull together for the good of South Carolina," announced Murray. White leaders of the South Carolina Farmers' Alliance rejected these overtures for biracial solidary. "We are not considering the negro [in South Carolina]," declared white populist leader J. W. Bowden. While most white leaders in the alliance had no interest in building a statewide biracial party, Murray's movement threatened the existing political consensus and caused considerable anxiety among the state's Democratic leadership.[27]

Murray broke the Reconstruction generation's hold on the Lowcountry's Republican Party and secured an unlikely victory at the Seventh Congressional District's 1892 Republican convention. Once thought to be an unserious

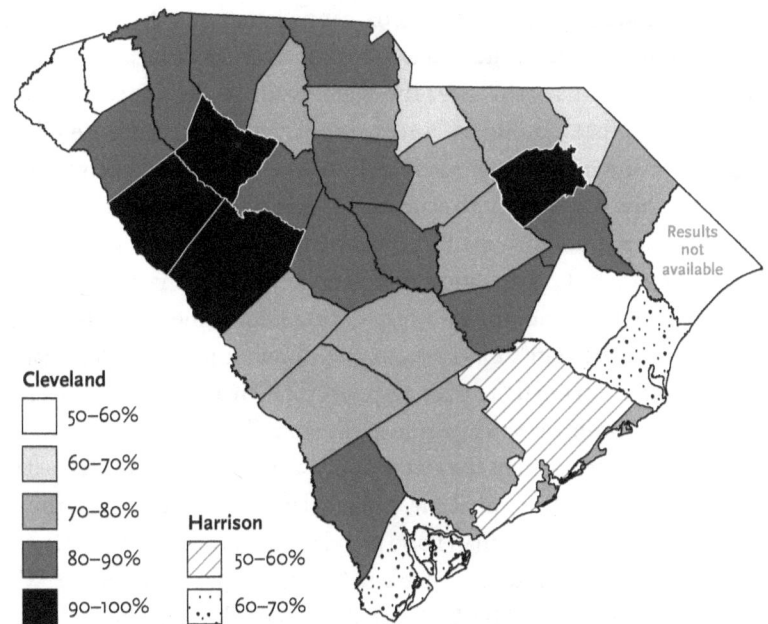

1892 presidential election results in South Carolina by county. The counties with patterns were won by Republican Party candidate Benjamin Harrison. The counties with solid colors were won by Democratic Party candidate Grover Cleveland. No election data available for Horry county.

candidate who would easily be defeated by the district's more seasoned politicians, the "Black Eagle of Sumter" would triumph over both Robert Smalls and Ellery Brayton, thereby transforming Sumter into a rival political center that challenged the Beaufort machine's dominance in the district. When Murray again defied the political odds by handily defeating his Democratic opponent, many wondered if Tillman had tipped the scales in favor of the Republican Party's candidate. Where the Seventh District's elections had been marred by Democratic Party-orchestrated voter fraud for almost a decade, Tillman's party chose not to challenge the results of the 1892 election. This was seen as a betrayal by many white South Carolinians who believed Tillman told the state party to stand down because the Seventh District's Democratic candidate was a member of the Lowcountry's long-standing planter elite—a group that the Upcountry Alliance man despised.[28]

While some accused Benjamin Tillman of being a political cynic willing to support a Republican candidate if it would hurt his intraparty enemies, the one-eyed demagogue understood Lowcountry Republicanism as an existential threat to his long-term project of building a white supremacist movement in South Carolina. During a June 10, 1892, campaign stop in the town of Beaufort, Governor Tillman addressed a crowd of over 800 Black citizens who "went wild with enthusiasm" over the Democratic leader's speech. Tillman denounced Beaufort County as "a niggerdom" and viewed the Republican stronghold as one of the chief roadblocks to the complete "redemption" of the state for white supremacy. The success of fusionism in the Lowcountry not only kept Black Republicans in office, but also bolstered local white elites who opposed Tillman and his coalition of Upcountry yeoman farmers and poor white people. In his mind, the 1882 registration law had not gone far enough in disfranchising the state's Black electorate; Republican voters, especially in the Lowcountry, remained "a frozen serpent" that if reanimated could strike a fatal blow to the promise of white rule in the state.[29]

Tillman's effort to reorient the state's political geography were assisted by a devastating category three hurricane. Making landfall in late August, the 1893 Sea Island storm killed more than 1,000 people in the Lowcountry and left tens of thousands more destitute and unable to harvest crops for the winter. While the relief effort coordinated by the Clara Barton and the Red Cross sought to offer scientific and impartial distribution of aid, many white Southerners saw echoes of "Black Reconstruction" in the relief effort. Writing a two-part series on the storm and the subsequent relief effort for the national magazine *Scribner's*, famed Southern color writer Joel Chandler Harris claimed that Black residents of the Lowcountry "remembered the days when the government poured its bounty through the Freedman's [sic] Bureau" and now viewed the Red Cross in a similar light.[30]

Seeking to exploit old anxieties about Reconstruction and federal intervention, Tillman's allies in the Lowcountry framed the Red Cross relief effort as a "Second Reconstruction," with white Northerners and freedpeople once again uniting at the expense of white Southerners. Thomas Martin, a Tillman supporter who lived in the town of Bluffton, wrote a letter to the *Charleston News and Courier* describing what he saw as systemic bias against white people and favoritism toward Beaufort County's Black residents. According to Martin, the Red Cross was giving aid to Black Bluffton residents who collected veterans' pensions from the US government, "drove double buggies," and owned property worth more than $1,000. Martin claimed that the Bluffton Relief Committee hurt not only poor white residents but also Black residents of Bluffton who were not part of the local Republican machine. Eugene Gregorie, a white planter from the Pocotaligo section of Beaufort County, asked the former Seventh District Democratic congressman William Elliott to seek an audience with Clara Barton to discuss the "common evil" the Red Cross was inflicting upon the county's white planters. Gregorie and his fellow planters believed that "indiscriminate issue of rations to the lazy negroes of this section" was hurting their ability to recruit Black workers during the pivotal spring planting season. Condemning the Red Cross as "an inflammatory failure," Martin concluded that "if wealthy politicians, republican pension drawers, carpenters, &c. are rationed and helped, and our poor white farmers have to suffer, I say God help such charity, we don't want any such here."[31]

These Democratic attacks were powerful and not only forced the Red Cross to spend time responding to charges of antiwhite racism but also helped strengthen Benjamin Tillman's grip on the Democratic Party. John MacDonald of the Red Cross responded to Martin's criticisms. After emphasizing that "the Red Cross cares not one iota whether a man is republican or democrat ... Methodist or atheist, Black or white," MacDonald described the nonstop hostility that white residents of Bluffton had directed toward the organization. During the spring of 1894, new reports of discrimination against poor white people began to emerge in the state's Democratic papers. The Columbia *Daily Register* published an article titled "Cursing the Red Cross! Bitter Feeling against It in Beaufort County." The article, written by an unnamed "special correspondent" and citing only one named source (Thomas Martin), savaged the work of the Red Cross and claimed that the organization was in league with Beaufort's Black Republican machine. "Bob Smalls," identified as a key agent of the conspiracy, had "risen largely in the estimation of the negroes of Beaufort in the last few months." Pointing to his recent failed congressional bid, the unnamed correspondent argued that the aid issued by the Red Cross would give the politically moribund Smalls enough support to return to Congress.[32]

With the 1894 election on the horizon, Tillman and the Democratic Party sought to strike a mortal blow to their political enemies in the Lowcountry by redrawing the lines of the "Black district." Having wrested control of the Democratic Party from the Lowcountry's Bourbon elites, "straight-out" Democrats in the legislature put forth a bill that shattered the old Seventh Congressional District and placed Beaufort County into a newly drawn First Congressional District—a district that included the long-standing Democratic Party stronghold of Charleston. Sponsored during the December 1893 legislative session, a moment when the Lowcountry's citizens were still reeling from the devastating August hurricane, Tillman's allies and enemies immediately grasped the partisan nature of the new gerrymandering effort. One state senator from Charleston opposed the bill "to put Charleston in the Black District" and pleaded with the bill's Upcountry sponsors to not take revenge on the white citizens of Charleston because they did not vote for Tillman. J. R. Rivers, a

Black representative from Beaufort, opposed the bill because it reflected both another act of overt hostility toward "the people of his section" and a betrayal of the détente that conceded the state's Black majority a single district where they could elect a Republican congressman. "The negroes had been quietly submissive to everything imposed upon them," warned Rivers, "but time was coming when forbearance would be no virtue." Passing easily in both houses of the state legislature, the 1893 gerrymandering bill exposed the paper-thin nature of the fusion alliance between Republican Party leaders and white elites in the Lowcountry. In the following years, Bourbon leaders returned to the Democratic Party fold rather than see historic Charleston "disgraced" by the possibility of being represented by a Black congressman.[33]

The 1893 gerrymander also intensified the preexisting rivalries within the Lowcountry's Republican Party. The following spring, Robert Smalls and George Washington Murray clashed over who should be seated to represent the new district. While the incumbent Murray initially secured more delegates in the new First District's May 2 nominating convention, Smalls refused to concede. He claimed that the recent redistricting effort "destroyed the Republican organization in the district" and that the convention that gave Murray the nomination was "irregular." With Republicans hoping to regain control of the House of Representatives in the upcoming midterm election, figures in the national party pressured Ellery Brayton to quickly resolve the dispute between Smalls and Murray. "It seems to me that it would be a political mistake, yes a political crime, not to sustain Mr. Murray," argued one national party leader. Corresponding with Whitefield McKinlay, a Black Charlestonian now residing in Washington, where he had become a real estate mogul and Republican Party donor, Murray explained that despite having "a powerful combination" set to defeat him, he expected and intended to win "because I have the people with me."[34]

The national Black press took notice of the First District's controversy and understood that the political drama taking place in the Lowcountry also reflected a deeper story about racial and political destiny. "Reports are current that ex-Congressman Robert Smalls, hero of the 'Planter,' is fighting the regular republican nominee of his congressional district—Hon. George W. Murray, the only Afro-American at present in congress," reported the *Cleveland Gazette*. The Lowcountry's current political battle, which turned on competing generational understandings of racial destiny, once again put Smalls on the wrong side of the Northern press's self-appointed intellectual vanguard. "We are loath to believe this, for we have always given the old 'General' credit for having a greater amount of common sense, race and party love than such action would indicate," lamented Henry Smith, editor of the *Cleveland Gazette*. Once again, the *New South* defended Smalls, calling into question the veracity of Northern reporting on the Lowcountry's Black voters. Writing for the *New South*, Samuel Bampfield remarked, "Will Brother Smith kindly inform us whence comes his information, that the Hon. George Washington Murray is the 'regular republican nominee' of his congressional district? As a qualified voter of the First district of South Carolina, our information is to the opposite effect and we feel pretty confident that he might well share a like condition of mind after the Ides of November shall have come."[35]

Smith used his bully pulpit to highlight the inadequacy of Bampfield's defense of his father-in-law. "It seems that there is a fight in that South Carolina congressional district, for even the *New South* does not say too loudly and strongly who, in its judgement, is the regular nominee," countered Smith. Like the earlier political controversies that followed Smalls in the 1880s, Smith saw the Lowcountry's political seat, then the only district that sent a Black man to Congress, as a battleground over more than simple party politics. The district's congressional race had become a referendum on "who was nearest in touch with our people" and what characterized "an ideal Afro-American representative."[36]

Ultimately, the Republican National Committee intervened and declared that Murray was the First District's Republican Party candidate. Facing longtime Democratic candidate William Elliott in the general election, Murray would be the victim of widespread voter fraud and election tampering. Once again, the Republican Party would take these contested election results to the House of Representatives in the hope of receiving justice. With the South Carolina Democratic Party sweeping the federal and statewide elections, the stage was now set to accomplish Ben Tillman's long-standing dream: rewriting the 1868 state constitution and delivering a final blow to the spirit of Reconstruction in the state.[37]

The 1895 Constitutional Convention and the Creation of Reconstruction's Rival Archive

With the Democratic Party in control of the governor's mansion, the state legislature, all seven congressional districts, and the state's two US Senate seats, Benjamin Tillman used his control over the state Democratic Party to call a new constitutional convention for October 1895. Tillman hoped to follow the model of Mississippi's 1890 constitutional convention, which had placed new draconian measures on voting rights that included literacy tests, poll taxes, and residency requirements. While ostensibly race-neutral, and thus not in violation of the Fifteenth Amendment, the new constitution effectively disfranchised the state's remaining Black voters. While the document's grandfather clause loophole for poor white voters was eventually deemed unconstitutional, the Mississippi Constitution served as a model for Tillman, who sought to make South Carolina the second Southern state to permanently enshrine political white supremacy.[38]

The Black delegates who attended the 1895 constitutional convention understood the insurmountable odds they faced in the Columbia statehouse and used the event to create a spectacle that would draw the attention of the national press. With 158 white Democratic delegates in attendance and just 6 Black leaders representing the vestige of the Republican Party in the state, disfranchisement was a fait accompli. Still, the Black delegates highlighted the logical inconsistencies and blatantly antidemocratic spirit of the new state constitution.[39]

At a moment when questions of memory and statecraft converged, the Black delegates who spoke against the disfranchisement measures used political philosophy, history, and humor to challenge the logic of their antidemocratic opponents. Highlighting the danger the proposed provisions would pose to poor and illiterate white people, Thomas Miller, a Black delegate from Beaufort County who had recently served in the US Congress, pointedly asked, "Do you wonder now, gentlemen, that the white vote in Mississippi fell from over 100,000 to less than 38,000 at the last election?" Robert Smalls suggested that he would endorse a race-blind literacy test or a property requirement if the convention was serious about building a foundation for good government in the state. "You charge that the Negro is too ignorant to be entrusted with suffrage," he proclaimed. "I answer that you have not, nor dare you make a purely educational test of the right to vote.... You dare not make a purely property test of the right to vote." William Whipper drew on the specter of Reconstruction and claimed that federal law and racial destiny could not be defied forever. "You cannot fool the country and the supreme court," he warned. "You know the year of Negro progress is approaching. You hear the rumble of its ponderous wheels, the screech of the whistle, and the sound of the steam, and you know that it is freighted with educated men who have been coming forth to grapple with the new idea of the world."[40]

Ultimately, the South Carolina Constitutional Convention served as the swan song of the Reconstruction generation's political mecca. All six of the Black delegates in attendance were from the Lowcountry—five of them came from Beaufort County. The Black press valorized the efforts of leaders who made the last stand for Black voting rights. Daniel Augustus Straker, Smalls's one-time political opponent who now resided in Detroit, wrote an essay in the *Indianapolis Freeman* arguing that the Black delegates at the constitutional convention had "shown themselves real heroes. They are among those who in 1876, did not fly from the State and look for fields of pleasure and stations of emolument but rather met oppression and all the sorrows following that eventful period," Straker wrote. Often at political odds with each other in two decades that followed the removal of federal troops from the South, the Black delegates at the 1895 constitutional convention had now become a heroic and cohesive front in the eyes of the larger public.[41]

As in the production of white Southern memory, women took the leading role in preserving and proliferating the stories of Reconstruction. Both the daughters of Robert Smalls and Thomas Miller self-published broadsides that collected the constitutional convention speeches of their fathers; they also catalogued the praise that these speeches received in a variety of corners across the nation. "That the country may read these speeches and learn to know these brave and true men, I have edited a few of their arguments and prepared this pamphlet," remarked Mary J. Miller. "I regard them as gems of negro eloquence." Sarah Smalls also placed her father's effort to defend Black suffrage in the larger movement toward racial progress and Black uplift. "Indeed, it may have been an object lesson, planned by the All-wise God, to teach the haughty, boastful sons of Carolina that there are Negroes capable and amply qualified in every respect to protect themselves whenever it becomes necessary to do so; that those few representatives of the race were but a very small part of the rising host that time and education are bringing forward day by day in spite of lynching, caste prejudice or any methods used against them." Offering more than simple accounts of racial uplift, Miller and Smalls placed the work of their fathers at the vanguard of Black America's political destiny, as central to a Black historical project that was being stitched together by Black elites in the larger Black press.[42]

The correspondence that Sarah Smalls included in her pamphlet shone a hagiographic light on her father and played a critical role in repairing his national reputation. A letter from a Black church congregation in Philadelphia praised Robert Smalls for the "dignity, courage, and singular ability" with which he had honored "the negro race and American patriotism" at the convention. Another newspaper commended Smalls for his heroic last stand. "Mr. Smalls was a potent factor in this convention and the ringing speeches made by him were masterpieces of impregnable logic, consecutive reasoning, biting sarcasm and fiery invective . . . his arguments were unanswerable, and the keenness of his wit, the cleverness of his arraignment, and the persistence with which he routed his opponents from one subterfuge to another astounded the convention, and showed its members that the negro's capacity for intelligence, courage and manhood was not inferior to the bluest blood in the old Palmetto State." A figure who had been on the wrong end of many of the previous decade's central political battles, the fifty-six-year-old Robert Smalls, who experienced the tragic loss of his second wife, Annie, in the month that followed the convention, finally gained the high honor from Northern elite leaders that had previously eluded him.[43]

This final fight for Reconstruction's legacy in South Carolina corresponded with a sharp turning point in the Black public sphere. Earlier that same year, Frederick Douglass passed away at the age of seventy-seven. Just a month prior to the South Carolina Constitutional Convention, a thirty-nine-year-old Booker T. Washington stepped into national fame after delivering a powerful address at the Cotton States and International Exposition in Atlanta that yielded the remaining political ground that the Reconstruction generation had fought to hold. The *Washington Bee*, perhaps the clearest defender of the Reconstruction generation's political project, looked on with dismay at what the Wizard of Tuskegee had wrought. "Prof. Washington would have us to devote all our energies, talents, and time to industrial education," the paper remarked. "He is like the South Carolina Constitutional Convention. He would have all the negroes disfranchised and allow the white people [to] hold offices, while 8,000,000 or more of negroes pay taxes and confine themselves to industrial education. While Prof. Washington was apologizing for the Southern white people[,] the South Carolina Constitutional Convention was disfranchising the negro."[44]

In many ways, 1895 marked the end of the long Reconstruction era. The following year, the Supreme Court upheld Louisiana's 1890 Separate Car Act, establishing a legal precedent that allowed the South's early twentieth-century social order to be built on de jure segregation. The dominoes of disfranchisement would continue to fall until all the states in the region had rewritten their Reconstruction-era constitutions to create more burdensome voter registration requirements—burying democracy in the region for the next half century. In 1898, Wilmington, North Carolina, a coastal community that had preserved local Black political leadership through a fusionist office-sharing arrangement similar to the pattern that developed in Beaufort, experienced a violent endpoint in the form of a coup d'état that began with an attack on a Black journalist's press office.[45]

While the remaining outposts of the Reconstruction generation's political world frayed and collapsed, the memory work persisted. Here, Black women often took the lead. In 1892, Frances Ellen Watkins Harper published her first novel, *Iola Leroy, or Shadows Uplifted*, which set its sentimental account of romance and racial passing in Reconstruction-era North Carolina within a larger reckoning with the anxieties over generational duty to postbellum racial destiny. Three years later, Ida B. Wells's *The Red Record* would place the violent overthrow of Reconstruction within a long history of disfranchisement that had reached a crescendo. "The blood chills and the heart almost loses faith in Christianity when one thinks of Yazoo, Hamburg, Edgefield, Copiah, and the countless massacres of defenseless Negroes, whose only crime was the attempt to exercise their right to vote." New England–born Pauline Hopkins worked within a similar band of countermemory in her 1900 novel *Contending Forces: A Romance Illustrative of Negro Life North and South*. Set in Boston, New Bern, North Carolina, and New Orleans, Hopkins's novel was an ambitious attempt to capture the scale and scope of the Reconstruction generation's lost world. "The colored race has historians, lecturers, ministers, poets, judges, and lawyers,—men of brilliant intellects who have arrested the favorable attention of this busy, energetic nation," Hopkins observed. "But after all, it is the simple, homely tale, unassumingly told, which cements the bond of brotherhood among all classes and all complexions." Hopkins would continue this role of preserving the Reconstruction generation's legacy as a leading contributor to the Boston-based *Colored American Magazine*. In this role, she not only provided biographical sketches of postbellum political leaders like Robert Smalls but also helped give the magazine a form and style that captured the literary spirit of the Reconstruction generation.[46]

In the face of the falling Jim Crow curtain, leaders in the Black public sphere recognized the deep importance of capturing the full cultural architecture of their generation's countermemory. When former Virginia congressman John Mercer Langston and former Mississippi senator Blanche K. Bruce both passed away in March 1898, the Reconstruction generation not only collectively mourned the loss of these two monumental figures but also tried to situate their lives in the broader arc of the race's political destiny. "The death of Mr. Bruce marks a further disintegration, and perhaps the disappearance as such of the illustrious 'Old Guard,' whose unfaltering courage and matchless statesmanship blazed a wide pathway through an almost impenetrable maze of prejudice and distrust, and gave our generation a standing in the economies of the nation," remarked one writer for the Washington-based *Colored American* newspaper. On March 29, 1898, the Bethel Literary and Historical Society held a memorial meeting for John Mercer Langston that included several remaining members of the "old guard," including P. B. S. Pinchback, John R. Lynch, and Henry P. Cheatham. The *Washington Bee* would put the deaths of Bruce and Langston in a triumvirate with that of Frederick Douglass and ask a larger question about the era that they marshaled. "Their wisdom, patriotism, statesmanship, their race love may not be fully appreciated by the present generation," remarked the *Bee*, "but the men of the future will look in amazement and wonder that these men could have been so brave, so true, so constant amid such adverse conditions."[47]

The most ambitious project to emerge from this turn-of-the-century outpouring of historical production was Daniel Payne Murray's unfinished *Encyclopedia of the Colored Race*. A leading member of Washington's postbellum Black elite, Murray joined the staff of the Library of Congress in 1871, and over the course of his fifty-year career with the library, he would dramatically increase its collection of books and pamphlets by Black writers. One of the late nineteenth-century's nation's leading expert on African American history, Murray spent the last twenty years of his life unsuccessfully striving to produce a comprehensive six-volume encyclopedia of the race's history. Emphasizing the progress and achievements of the larger Black diaspora from "the earliest period down to the present time," Murray and his team of thirty assistant editors created a bibliography that listed every known Black author—more than 6,000 in total. Even more impressive, Murray promised to include more than 25,000 biographic profiles, which would serve as the cornerstone of the encyclopedic series.[48]

Reconstruction's countermemory seeped into almost every corner of this monumental historical project. Murray's team of assistant editors included both the famed journalist John Edward Bruce and Bethel Literary and Historical Society's president John W. Cromwell. While repeating much of the gendered hierarchy that had become a defining feature of the late nineteenth-century Black public sphere, Murray's compendium also captured some of the expansiveness of the Reconstruction generation's earlier world. "I thank you sincerely that you deem me worthy to be inscribed among those who have contributed to the progress and uplifting of the race," Frances Rollin Whipper wrote to Daniel Murray. "I have always classed myself among those who never reached the mark they had in sight."[49]

Whipper had become a fixture of Washington's Black elite social world and had spent the last decade working for the federal government. When Daniel Murray contacted her in 1901, she had recently returned to Beaufort to reunite with her husband William, who was helping her recover from a slowly worsening case of tuberculosis. Reflecting on her generation's political high tide, Whipper was both sober and sentimental: "I can honestly say at this distance from those stirring times, that with all the errors growing out of the lack of experience in Legislative matters, the colored leaders are worthy of the highest praise." She connected the lost promise of the Reconstruction era with something more subtle—a personal sense of success and contentment. "From 1868 to 1876 I was prosperous and happy," she reminisced.[50]

Over the course of the Ulysses Grant's presidency, Frances Whipper published her first book, served as an editor of a prominent Lowcountry newspaper, married a rising political star, and hosted the state's most prestigious salon. In many ways, she had experienced and shaped the highest cultural frequency of South Carolina's postbellum political world. As much as anyone of her generation, Whipper understood both Reconstruction's grand poetry and the harrowing descent of its collapse. In the years that followed, she would experience the unravelling of an unhappy marriage, the stalling of her once-promising writing career, periodic unemployment from the federal government, and, eventually, serious illness. She succumbed to tuberculosis in October 1901, just weeks before her fifty-fourth birthday.[51]

Frances Whipper's meditation on her generation's political dream captures a strand of countermemory that would disappear in the national memory of the Reconstruction era. As white supremacy gained new traction as a political movement in South Carolina and disfranchisement became a fait accompli, the Lowcountry's remaining Republican Party leaders transformed their political defeat into a new story of what the era meant. These figures, along with their family members and their allies in the Northern press, produced a rival history of Reconstruction that offered a radically different account of the postbellum past. And, in creating new archival practices to mark the end of their political era, the Reconstruction generation would lay the seeds for the modern discipline of African American history in the new century.

Part III

The Afterlife of the Reconstruction Generation

Antoinette Norvell teaching a history class, 1906. Penn School Papers, Southern Historical Collection, Wilson Special Collections Library, University of North Carolina at Chapel Hill.

CHAPTER SIX

The Jim Crow Generation
Black Teachers, the Industrial School Movement, and the Educational Battle over Reconstruction's Legacy in the Segregated South

During the Penn Normal, Industrial and Agricultural School's 1904–5 school year, Antoinette Norvell was photographed while teaching a history lesson to her elementary school classroom. Born in 1883 in Amherst County, Virginia, she graduated with Hampton Institute's 1902 class. Shortly thereafter, Norvell would join a larger cohort of teachers seeking to replace the Penn School's Reconstruction-era curriculum with the more conservative educational vision of the industrial school movement—an evolution reflected in the school's recent name change. The photograph captures the relatively new teacher as she guides three grade school students building a model of Abraham Lincoln's boyhood cabin. The chalkboard to Norvell's left has her lesson plan; to her right, three other children intently observe the lesson in progress; just above them is a portrait of Lincoln, who watches stoically over Norvell and her students.[1]

Almost perfectly staged to embody the spirit of the Hampton mission, the photograph of Antoinette Norvell's history lesson also highlights an additional story about her generation of Black teachers. Taken for the Penn School's 1906–7 annual report, the picture depicts postbellum racial progress in a way that would have appealed to the Northern donors who funded the expansion of industrial schools across the South. By framing the march of Southern Black education within a children's story of Lincoln, the photograph silences the more complicated road of Reconstruction, Redemption-era violence, and Jim Crow. The white photographer, Leigh Richmond Miner, a teacher and director in Hampton Institute's Applied Art Department, had mastered the visual aesthetic of the industrial school movement, which emphasized the quiet, unpretentious dignity of Black rural life. Rounding off the rough edges of the postbellum past, Miner's photograph provides an easy, elementary-school vision of emancipation and its afterlife for an audience eager to forget the late nineteenth-century political struggle to make Black freedom meaningful.[2]

A deeper examination of Miner's photograph, however, highlights the various ways that Reconstruction's countermemory lurked just beyond the camera's frame. The Penn School, until recently, had been led by Laura Towne, one of the most radical white abolitionists of her era, and her longtime educational partner Ellen Murray. These two women had been deeply involved in the previous era's politics, and it is unlikely that their legacy could be erased all at once. In addition, the school remained in a community where Reconstruction's social and cultural architecture persisted. A not-insignificant number of Black men in Beaufort would continue to cast ballots in local elections; Decoration Day remained a powerful regional holiday that brought thousands of Black Southerners to Beaufort's mecca of Black countermemory; and living members of the Reconstruction generation were still leaders in the community and would have certainly provided their own history lessons to the rising generation.

Finally, Antoinette Norvell would have brought her own countermemory of the long Reconstruction era to the South Carolina Lowcountry. Her birthplace in Virginia's Piedmont had been part of the larger hub of the Readjuster movement of the 1880s. In addition, she would have experienced the election that sent John Mercer Langston to the US Congress in 1890. One of the last Black men elected to the House before Jim Crow, the Oberlin-educated Langston built a robust political network in the state's Southside region while serving as the president of Virginia Normal and Collegiate Institute. Although just seven years old at the time of Langston took office—roughly the same age as her students in the Miner photograph—Norvell would have likely remembered the buzz of election season and the communal excitement when the news spread that Langston would be the first Black Virginian to represent the commonwealth in the US House of Representatives. Long before she received an industrial school education at Hampton and became an apostle for this new educational movement, Norvell would have almost certainly received her own history lesson on the meaning of Reconstruction.[3]

Entering a world on St. Helena Island that had been built by the Reconstruction generation, Antoinette Norvell was part of a new cohort of teachers who crisscrossed the Jim Crow South establishing and staffing industrial schools for Black children. In the case of the Penn School, their educational project required confronting a site of preexisting countermemory. One of the enduring symbols of the earlier generation's radical wartime vision, the Penn School was increasingly seen as an outdated relic of a misguided political movement. Following Towne's death in 1901, the Penn School was placed under the stewardship of a new board of trustees led by Hollis B. Frissell, then president of Hampton Institute. Under this new executive board, the Penn School deemphasized its previous focus on academic subjects and instead turned its attention to agricultural training, introductory training in trade skills, and guidance in home and domestic economics. Veteran teachers affiliated with the abolitionist movement and Reconstruction were replaced. New teachers who had graduated from Hampton were hired and soon dominated the teaching staff. These changes to the Penn School's curriculum and leadership not only brought economic success and higher levels of donor giving but also made the Penn School a hypervisible symbol of the industrial school movement as the new face of Southern education. It also put it at odds with the remaining members of the Reconstruction generation.[4]

While a great deal has been written about the rise of industrial education and its relationship to the Jim Crow order, less has been said about the teachers who were the foot soldiers for the industrial school movement. Often viewed as a top-down structure that emphasized the political and cultural power of Booker T. Washington, the industrial school movement was given its shape and meaning by the generation of teachers who saw it as their duty to spread the message of industrial school education across the South. Coming of age in a world where segregation and disfranchisement were now enshrined in the New South's social and political landscape, these teachers embraced the gospel of Booker T. Washington and saw industrial education's dissembling pragmatism as the new North Star for the race's destiny. Armed with the educational pedigree, social capital, and powerful philanthropic networks aligned with the nation's leading industrial schools, these teachers were charged with uprooting the old modes of Black education in the South and providing a new generation of schoolchildren with the agricultural and mechanical skills that would lead to economic independence—at the expense of the academic and civic training that marked the highest-frequency version of the previous generation's schooling.[5]

The hard-won educational world of the Reconstruction generation, however, did not fade gently into the Jim Crow night. Over the course of the early twentieth century, the Hampton-trained teachers and their Northern allies had to confront the rival educational vision that anchored the region's specific countermemory of the Black past. They entered a Lowcountry that increasingly bore the marks of disfranchisement and segregation, but crucial aspects of the earlier era remained unbowed. Black voters continued to vote in local elections, and Black officeholders held key federal patronage positions when the Republican Party was in the White House; a robust grassroots political culture continued to organize around holidays like Decoration Day; and Black Union veterans—many of whom were also former members of the Reconstruction-era state militia—continued to march in local parades and meet in one of the South's few remaining chapters of the Grand Army of the Republic. Finally, major Reconstruction leaders like Robert Smalls held onto the light of the Reconstruction era, connecting the current struggle against Southern racism to their generation's earlier fight for multiracial democracy.

This struggle took unexpected twists and turns. Beholden to an educational worldview that held a deep antipathy toward the perceived excesses of Reconstruction, the teachers and school leaders who arrived in the Jim Crow Lowcountry might have been expected to embark on a straightforward and didactic educational mission that demanded the erasure of Reconstruction's legacy at all costs. But, while the industrial school movement established several schools in the Lowcountry, its educators had to confront, and in many cases accommodate, the ideas of parents and community leaders who held on to the previous generation's faith in educational Reconstruction. While some of these teachers struggled with this tension, many could trace the Lowcountry's countermemory of Reconstruction to hidden transcripts of postbellum Black politics that appeared in earlier chapters of their own lives. Far from silencing the past, they found ways to incorporate the Reconstruction generation's vision into the conservative-presenting mission of industrial education.

In so doing, the Reconstruction generation continued to produce a countermemory of their political world during a low-tide moment of Black history. Still in the shadow of what Rayford Logan has called the nadir of Black life—a metaphorical low point drawn from an astronomical alignment when celestial bodies are below one's sight horizon and thus invisible. Despite the fall of the Jim Crow curtain, local leaders in the Lowcountry and national figures in the Black public sphere continued to fight for the ideals of the Reconstruction generation. As this struggle took place in the region's schools, a new generation of teachers and students encountered the story of Reconstruction. Contrary to what we might expect, the industrial school–trained teachers would help bolster the countermemory of Reconstruction by more closely tying the region's schools to the Lowcountry's broader countermemorial landscape. In doing so, the Black teachers who began their careers in the Lowcountry did more than spread the gospel of industrial education; they extended a powerful thread of the Black past into the future, preserving a vision of racial destiny that had organized a previous generation's historical practices and offered a new North Star for a postnadir world.

The Hampton Idea and the Industrial Education Movement's Attack on Reconstruction

The industrial school movement emerged as a hostile response to the world made by the Reconstruction generation. Samuel Chapman Armstrong,

Hampton Institute's founder, held a deep disdain for Black officeholders and believed that freedpeople had been given the ballot before they had reached the proper civilizational level to exercise the privilege of the franchise. In the pages of the *Southern Workman*, Hampton's monthly magazine, Armstrong argued that Black Southerners could "afford to let politics severely alone" and made the claim that Black participation in politics in South Carolina resulted in a "shameless legislature" that had "ruined the credit of a great state." A Williams College graduate, Union veteran and former employee of the Freedmen's Bureau, Armstrong's views on Reconstruction reflected a broader rightward turn among Northern white elites. Armstrong's politics reflected a conservative, but far from atypical, antislavery political world that would moderate the Radical Republicans' approach to Reconstruction. He would be among the first to abandon the Southern-facing aspects of Reconstruction in the face of accusations of corruption and redeemer violence. A son of white missionaries stationed in Hawaii, Armstrong also viewed the various Indigenous nations of the greater United States as groups that required the civilizing influence of industrial education and enrolled hundreds of Indian American students at Hampton during his tenure as president.[6]

A central node in the story of the New South, the Hampton-led industrial school movement established a network of Black schools in the region. This wide-scale shift in Southern education reflected a deeper moment of cultural capture within the Jim Crow–era public sphere. Historians have long debated the extent to which the movement should be considered accommodationist, pragmatic, or even covertly radical. Eric Anderson has highlighted how since Hampton's 1868 founding, Armstrong intentionally aligned himself and his school with the conservative elite in the state's Democratic Party with the hopes that this alliance would provide the school the necessary political protection in a commonwealth where the state Republican Party was much weaker than in its Southern neighbors. Whether inspired by the widespread racial animus of his Northern social class, a dour pragmatism over Virginia's postbellum political order, or a combination of the two, Armstrong's anti-Reconstruction worldview seeped into the very fabric of Hampton Institute.[7]

Nowhere was this anti-Reconstruction vision more evident than in the ideas of Armstrong's most famous protégé, Booker T. Washington. His account of the era in his best-selling memoir *Up from Slavery* mixed broad and abstract recollections of his childhood with secondhand stories and handed-down myths that circulated through Hampton's intellectual network. Largely a defense of industrial education, Washington's autobiography lamented the misguided attention paid to academic subjects like Greek and Latin among the first generation of freedpeople and the rise of poorly trained teachers unqualified to instruct elementary school students. In one anecdote, Washington told the story of a Black mason in an unnamed Southern city haranguing his assistant, "the governor," to hurry up with a wheelbarrow of bricks. The story's punch line revealed that the mason's assistant had once been lieutenant governor of the state. Not every former Reconstruction-era leader, however, was reduced to a simple comic figure. "Some of them," Washington acknowledged, "like the late senator B. K. Bruce, Governor Pinchback, and many others, were strong, upright, useful men." Recognizing the continued importance of figures like Bruce and Pinchback in national Black memory, and likely having met both men in his travels in the nation's Black elite circles, Washington offered much more deference to Black countermemory of the Reconstruction era than his mentor.[8]

Here, Washington was likely trying to communicate his interpretation of Reconstruction's legacy to two different audiences. The first, Northern donors and New South elites, would have also viewed Reconstruction as a cartoonishly misguided political project and would have already been familiar with the hostile tropes of Black officeholders that appeared in both highbrow and lowbrow culture of the Gilded Age. The second audience would have included his Black critics and potential recruits for the industrial school movement. Engaging positively with the legacy of Blanche K. Bruce and P. B. S. Pinchback was a clear signal to his Black readers that he was a part of their same Black worldbuilding project—albeit with a different set of political commitments. Describing his 1878 teaching experience at the Malden School in Washington, DC, his tone and analysis became more sober. As he recalled his students, children of the capital's emerging class of Black strivers, the social world that orbited around institutions like the Bethel Literary and Historical Society, Washington offered a Southern-facing vision of Black America's future that contrasted with the loftier and less grounded vision of postbellum Black life that flourished in Washington. While the Malden students had "more money," the "latest style of all manner of clothing," and were in some cases "more brilliant" than his Hampton classmates, they lacked a grounding in the earthbound duty of racial uplift in the South. "They did not appear to me to be beginning at the bottom, on a real, solid foundation, to the extent that they were at Hampton," Washington argued. More than anywhere else in his public writing, *Up from Slavery*'s chapter on "Reconstruction" wrestled with the more complicated moral lessons of both the industrial school movement and the race's larger postbellum collective destiny.[9]

A hidden transcript of Black countermemory was also embedded in Hampton's institutional landscape, challenging the more conservative accounts of the institute's history. During the Civil War, nearby Fortress Monroe became an early beacon for wartime refugees from slavery, leading to the rise of the military's first set of contraband policies and refugee camp policies. This pushed Congress to pass the Confiscation Acts and gradually led President Lincoln to see that emancipation, not simple preservation of the Union, had to be the true aim of the war. Like the Lowcountry, coastal Virginia attracted a cohort of free-born Black teachers who saw the next stage of the abolitionist struggle as providing missionary and educational uplift to Black Southerners. Mary Peake, a daughter of Hampton Roads' free-born elite community, joined the American Missionary Association and began teaching the children of former slaves who had congregated in the sprawling contraband camp just outside of Fort Monroe. The oak tree where she held her first outdoor class would later become a major site of emancipationist countermemory on Hampton's campus, both identifying the school's entrance for new students and visitors and subtly highlighting that the roots of their education went deeper than Armstrong's industrial vision.[10]

The next generation of industrial-school teachers would find themselves balancing the rival histories of Hampton Institute, first as they moved through their undergraduate education, and later as they fanned across the South to spread the school's educational philosophy. Pinckney W. Dawkins, an 1886 graduate of Hampton, captured the most recognizable version of the "Hampton Idea" at the school's 1900 commencement: "I have been trying to show my people that there is an honest and better living in the sod they tread, pure air and better sunshine in real life, greater happiness and independence in owning the soil and driving their own plows than in chasing the flitty, changeable, sham life we so often see." And yet, beneath the surface, competing versions of the Hampton Idea persisted. Across the nineteenth century, students at Hampton received a history education that included lessons about Black Reconstruction-era leaders like Blanche K. Bruce and P. B. S. Pinchback. The students who entered Hampton often came from communities where they would have encountered members of the Reconstruction generation; upon beginning their teaching careers in the South, they would have almost certainly met former politicians, teachers, and voters who experienced Reconstruction as a history-defining moment. In his biography of Booker T. Washington, Robert J. Norrell highlights that despite largely denigrating Reconstruction in his biography, the Hampton-trained educator would have found it impossible to navigate the late nineteenth-century Alabama Black Belt without confronting Reconstruction-era churches and schools and individuals who had either once held political office or remembered the terrorism that left the scars of generational trauma on families and communities in the postbellum South.[11]

The first generations of Hamptonites likely had little space to archive their countermemories of Reconstruction within the school's gates. But they certainly understood that both their home communities and the places they served after graduating held hidden histories of the postbellum Black past. While these rival accounts of Reconstruction might have been initially undetectable to outside observers, the teachers who traveled to the Lowcountry encountered a world where political history was everywhere. To be effective teachers, they had no choice but to incorporate the region's specific countermemory into their classrooms, schools, and broader reflections of the industrial education movement's place in the race's larger destiny.

Disfranchisement, School Segregation, and the Survival of the Reconstruction Generation in the Lowcountry's Jim Crow Era

The Hampton-trained teachers who traveled to the Lowcountry had to confront a sharp-edged but still inchoate world of Jim Crow. In the Lowcountry, a region with an outsized Black majority, a long history of armed community defense, and a robust Republican political world that persisted longer than in most parts of the former Confederacy, the defining marks of the Jim Crow order—disfranchisement, segregation, and state-sanctioned anti-Black violence—did not take the same shape as in other parts of the South. Due in large part to the persistent strength of the Reconstruction generation, disfranchisement remained an unfinished project in the Lowcountry, the color line—in the law, local school system, and social custom—was drawn with dashes and never unequivocal. And, able to confront mob violence with their own retribution, residents of the Lowcountry made it one of the safest places in the South, with regards to the threat of lynching.[12]

South Carolina's 1895 state constitution delivered a severe, but not quite mortal, blow to the Lowcountry's Black political culture. While the state's Republican Party ceased to have influence on statewide politics, and the 1894 gerrymandering effort had already splintered the Lowcountry's Black Seventh District, Black voters in Beaufort County continued to impact local elections and Black officeholders in the Lowcountry affected the direction of the national Republican Party. The town of Beaufort saw Black men elected to the city council until the century's second decade, and the town's mayoral races required white politicians to campaign for Black votes. As late as 1908, Republican voters in Beaufort County elected a Black man to be the town's marshal. Across the greater Lowcountry, federally appointed officeholders continued to serve; Black Republican leaders held valuable and visible customhouse

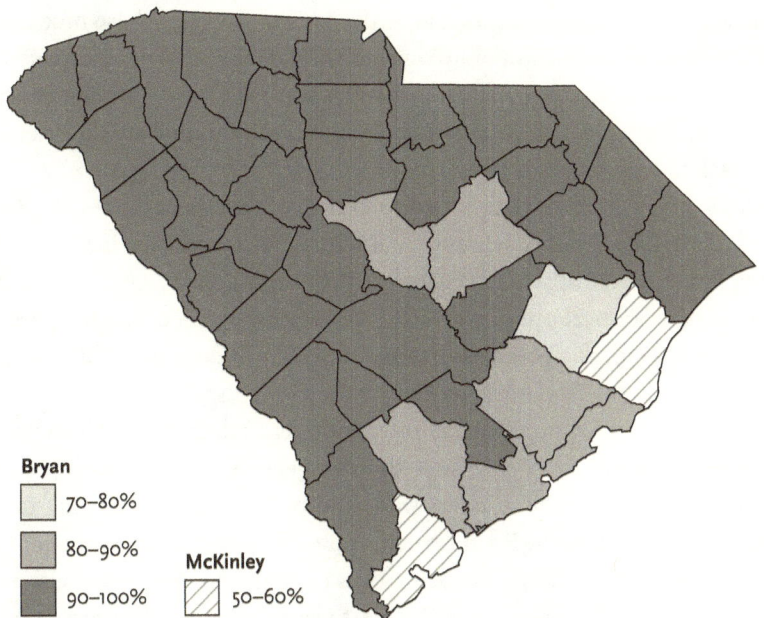

1900 presidential election results in South Carolina by county. The counties with patterns were won by Republican presidential candidate William McKinley. The counties with solid colors were won by Democratic presidential candidate William Jennings Bryan.

positions at the ports of Charleston, Beaufort, and Savannah. Elizabeth Smalls Bampfield, Robert Smalls's eldest daughter, served as Beaufort's postmaster for six years during the century's first decade. White Democrats, realizing that disfranchisement was only a partially won battle, began to clamor for an all-white primary, a clear sign that the 1895 state constitution left white political supremacy a half-finished goal in the Lowcountry.[13]

Segregation was also an incomplete project in the early twentieth-century Lowcountry. In South Carolina, a separate car act for the state's railway system would not be enacted until 1904—nearly fifteen years after Louisiana had established the new legal standard for "separate but equal." Educational inequality, however, preceded and anticipated Jim Crow–era segregation of the Lowcountry's public schools. As in many parts of the South, redeemers had cut funding for Beaufort County's post-Reconstruction public school system, exacerbating the racial divide in educational access. At the turn of the century, only one of the county's nine school districts served Black students. This school effectively stopped at the sixth grade; students who desired a high school education would need to attend the Penn School, Charleston's Avery Institute, or travel to Orangeburg, South Carolina, to attend the state's Colored

Normal, Industrial, Agricultural, and Mechanical College. These preexisting disparities had begun compounding with the passage of the 1895 state constitution and its codification of disfranchisement. By 1900, only 18 percent of the state's nearly 120,000 elementary school–aged Black children attended school; the Black illiteracy rate hovered near 50 percent.[14]

In the face of this inequality, and sometimes precisely because of it, Beaufort County's Black public schools became an important theater in the broader struggle over Reconstruction's memory. William Elliott Jr., whose father had been a chief political opponent of Robert Smalls, claimed that the accreditation process for the county's Black schools was "a disgrace" and fought to institute a more stringent teacher certification process when he served on the Beaufort County School Board in the early twentieth century. When half of Black teachers retired in protest of the stringent new examination process, Elliott argued that these teachers were "old political hacks" clinging to the misguided excesses of the Reconstruction era. "Many of the old negro political war horses protested . . . but the better class of negro cheered me on, although secretly." Both Black men and white Northerners continued to serve on the school board until the century's second decade, exacerbating fear among white South Carolinians that the specter of Reconstruction still hovered over the Lowcountry.[15]

This countermemory of Reconstruction was also embodied in the region's Black schools. In Charleston, the Avery Normal Institute, an institution founded in 1865 by the American Missionary Association and initially led by Reconstruction-era leaders Thomas and Francis Cardozo, continued to provide a broad academic education for Black students. The newly formed Colored Normal, Industrial, Agricultural, and Mechanical College of South Carolina (now South Carolina State University) was led by Thomas Ezekiel Miller, the former congressman from the Lowcountry's Black Seventh District. In Beaufort, Public School Number 1, a building that Robert Smalls had purchased in 1867 to educate freed children, continued to educate Black children in the twentieth century. Local Black leaders retained the deed to the school building, despite efforts by white school board members to reclaim it. Once completely under the leadership of a predominantly Black school board and able to draw postbellum funding from the Board of Missions for Freedmen of the Presbyterian Church, the school was transferred to the Beaufort County School Board at the end of the nineteenth century—forcing the Reconstruction-era institution to confront new limitations from New South white elites. "[It] takes all we can do to keep it going," Robert Smalls lamented in 1906.[16]

These new headwinds did not prevent Reconstruction's countermemory from entering the historical curriculum of the Lowcountry's Black schools.

Working with his longtime friend and prominent journalist John Edward Bruce, Robert Smalls fought to have Bruce's book *Short Biographical Sketches of Eminent Negro Men and Women in Europe and the United States*, assigned in Beaufort County's Black public schools. "The moral portraits which are here offered will present such features as will call for the thoughtful attention of the younger generation of the Negro race here and abroad," Bruce declared in the opening of his 1910 book. An edited collection of largely previously written historical profiles, the book not only summarized the lives and accomplishments of well-known figures like Crispus Attucks, Toussaint Louverture, Frederick Douglass, and Ida B. Wells but also preserved accounts of the fading figures from the Reconstruction generation. It reproduced parts of Frances Rollin's 1868 biography of Martin Delaney, as well as portions of the William J. Simmons's 1884 history, *Men of Mark*—the work that helped Robert Smalls rise to new cultural heights during the Gilded Age.[17]

In addition to offering hagiographic portraits of major Black leaders, *Short Biographical Sketches* led its school-aged readers through a series of questions to demonstrate mastery of the historical content. After a section in the book on the life of Reconstruction-era political icon Robert Elliott, Bruce crafted a series of questions designed to help students see the postbellum past through the lens of Black countermemory that Bruce had helped shape as a journalist in the 1880s and 1890s. Some questions were "Why was [Robert Elliott] in demand in South Carolina during the reconstruction period in that State? To what office was he elected by the Constitutional Convention? When was he elected to the Forty-second Congress, and by what political party? How did he distinguish himself as a member of the Lower House of the Congress, and what is said of his speech in April 1871? Of what prominent secret organization was he a member? When and where did he die? When was he buried?"[18]

It is unclear how widespread *Short Biographical Sketches* became during the Jim Crow era—or whether it was in fact adopted in the Lowcountry's Black public schools. Despite challenging the core tenets of the Lost Cause, it should not be impossible to imagine such a book making it into a Black classroom during the Jim Crow era. For those committed to racial destiny through education, such a book would have likely been part of the cultural arsenal of what educational historian Jarvis Givens has called a "fugitive pedagogy." Seeing themselves as a part of a longer struggle that ran counter to antebellum law and Jim Crow school policy, Black teachers were often willing to risk their careers to challenge the misrepresentations of the race embedded in the nation's standard social studies curricula.[19]

These efforts to keep Reconstruction's history in Black classrooms were coupled with the last political struggles over Reconstruction-era public policy.

In 1901, when Congress agreed to transfer the remaining funds left in the long-defunct Freedmen's Bank to Howard University, Robert Smalls used his understanding of the legislative process, and the Lowcountry's countermemory of Reconstruction, to argue that some of those funds should be placed in the hands of the trustees of Beaufort's Black public school. "We respectfully call your attention to the fact that a branch of said bank was established in the town of Beaufort," Smalls explained, "and that a large number of the freedmen in this section were depositors of the same, and, at the same time of its failure lost between $75,000 and $100,000." Despite the deep sense of betrayal that many Black residents of Beaufort, Charleston, and Savannah still felt toward the federal government and the Republican Party for the collapse of their local branches of the Freedmen's Bank, Smalls believed that formal political channels and networks of patronage could still benefit Black Southerners during the Jim Crow era.[20]

Perhaps most important, the cultural architecture of the Lowcountry allowed the memory of Reconstruction to persist in day-to-day life. The region's Decoration Day celebrations continued to attract thousands of Black visitors from across the region. The David Hunter Post of the GAR continued to organize Beaufort County's Decoration Day celebration, and Macon Allen Jr., the son of the Northern-born Black attorney who played a key role in shaping the Lowcountry's postbellum legal culture, continued to lead the town's brass marching band for the day's festivities. The county's public schools were closed for the holiday and revelers increasingly viewed the day as a "regular jubilee occasion," and not a solemn moment of quiet observance. Reconstruction-era leaders continued to deliver speeches and occupy a visible position in the day's festivities, suggesting that the fabric of the region's nineteenth-century political culture remained intact.[21]

Recognizing that the vestiges of the region's late nineteenth-century political culture threatened the nascent Jim Crow order, the county's white elites began seeking to use a broad range of legal and political attacks to diminish Decoration Day's cultural gravity. Using the new state dispensary law, which prohibited the sale of alcohol except by state-licensed vendors, local law enforcement increasingly arrested Black visitors for possessing alcohol and public intoxication. Local police also sought to make an example out of the "blind tigers" that illegally sold alcohol—in large part because the county closed the legal liquor dispensaries on Decoration Day. Black visitors also felt the hostility of the more sharply drawn color line in the region. At the 1906 Decoration Day Celebration, a Black man attempted to book a room at the Sea Island Hotel. When denied access because of his race, the man reportedly demanded access

USCT veterans marching in Beaufort, South Carolina, March 28, 1904. Julian Dimock Image Collection, American Museum of Natural History Library, New York.

to the hotel's telegraph office so he could send a message to President Theodore Roosevelt about this civil rights violation.[22]

The Lowcountry's surviving Reconstruction generation leaders remained connected to the national Republican Party and often used the pages of the national Black press to hold the GOP accountable to Southern Black citizens. Robert Smalls regularly corresponded with the *Colored American*'s editorial page to remind Northern readers of the ongoing effects of the "iniquitous constitution of 1895." Branding itself a "National Negro Newspaper," the *Colored American*, not to be confused with the *Colored American Magazine*, had financial backing from Booker T. Washington and the Tuskegee machine and imagined itself serving a national Black public interested in political reporting, historical accounts of Black progress, and coverage of social and cultural events among the Black elite. The paper's editors allowed Smalls to use its editorial section to address national Republican leaders. Deploying his stature as a Civil War hero and most prominent living member of the Reconstruction generation, Smalls brought attention to a USCT veteran who was disenfranchised for supposedly mispronouncing the word "agriculture" during a literacy test. He also offered statistical data on how much the statewide Black vote had been reduced since Reconstruction and pushed for Congress to reduce the proportional representation of the South in the House if the Fifteenth Amendment remained a dead letter. In reporting on the region's ongoing party activism and organization, the *Colored American* reminded its readers that the spirit of Reconstruction remained alive in the South.[23]

The previous era's political architecture also persisted in both the Lowcountry's formal political institutions and within the region's grassroots political culture, which remained a powerful bulwark against anti-Black violence. When Beaufort County experienced its first lynching in 1900, white observers in the region reported that the threat of retributory violence was in the air. One account claimed that Black leaders were "counselling, advising and urging their husbands, sons, and brothers to wholesale slaughter." Another one claimed to have overheard a group of Black women at the Yemassee train station promising vengeance for a Black man who was abducted from a Beaufort County jail cell by a lynch mob. One Southern paper reported that one of the Black women demanded that every white woman and child in this town "be hacked in pieces." This potential race war was supposedly being orchestrated by Robert Smalls, William Whipper, and Julius I. Washington. In 1907, another moment of white racial paranoia erupted when a Black fireman was shot and killed by a white security guard in the aftermath of a devastating fire that decimated much of downtown Beaufort. A series of mass meetings calling for justice stoked white anxieties for a potential "uprising" and the town's mayor called National Guard troops to restore order. These two instances suggest that, for many white Southerners, Beaufort's political leadership and Black majority remained the embodiment of Black Reconstruction's undead specter.[24]

White elites in the region and the state thus increased their attacks on the cultural afterlife of Reconstruction. *The State*, the leading newspaper in South Carolina, founded by the scion of one of the Lowcountry's most prominent white families, ran a twenty-nine-part series of articles on "Reconstruction in South Carolina." The author, John S. Reynolds, had been a student of William Archibald Dunning, and his portrait of postbellum South Carolina cohered to the broader framework of the Dunning School's revision of Reconstruction's history. In the final essay, he concluded that "smart negroes" from the North had played a crucial role in Reconstruction's corruption and downfall.[25]

The Southern press was not the only site of white supremacist historical revision. Daniel Chamberlain, the former Republican governor of South Carolina, denounced Reconstruction in increasingly vitriolic terms. In a 1904 interview with the *Springfield (MA) Republican*, Chamberlain argued that "no ray of hope for peace" could exist in the South as long as the "nameless crime" of Black men sexually assaulting white women "continued to be of frequent occurrence." He supported the expansion of industrial education and claimed that "the three r's are all the average negro needs." Most damningly, he attacked his former political allies in the Lowcountry and viewed the region as a place where "the negro educated rogue is tolerated and honored to the end by the negroes who surrounded him." Reviving his old attack on William Whipper's character, Chamberlain not only described Beaufort as a place where republican political virtue was corrupted but also cast the region as an ongoing moral threat to the still unfinished project of white "redemption" of the South.[26]

The Lowcountry's Industrial School Movement and Reconstruction's Regional Legacy

At first glance, it appears as though the Hampton-trained teachers descended upon the Lowcountry to implement the most conservative vision of the Hampton idea. Helen Lou James, a 1901 Hampton graduate, viewed St. Helena Island's Black farmers as existing in a state of "ignorance, destitution and depravity." P. W. Dawkins and his wife Emma Jennie Fentress Dawkins, also a Hampton graduate, both joined the Penn School in 1901, but they refused to allow their children to attend the school because they believed the current teachers were of poor quality. Seeing themselves as a civilizing force, the Hampton teachers viewed the Penn School as a completely outdated institution that no longer served its students or the broader St. Helena community. When Helen Carnan Jenks, the niece of the Penn School's aging founder, asked Hampton president Hollis Frissell to take control of the institution, he privately complained that the school was "far behind the times" in its approach to educating Black students.[27]

When the white abolitionist educator Laura Towne died in 1901, control of the Penn School was transferred to Hampton's board of trustees, who proceeded to lead a radical overhaul of the school's curriculum and leadership. One of the few white Northern educators who remained in South Carolina long after the Port Royal Experiment, Towne remained committed to an expansive and antiracist vision of Black education—a position that drew considerable ire from the region's redeemer elite, who viewed Reconstruction-era schools as a Trojan horse for Black Reconstruction's return. After closely inspecting the school's day-to-day operations, the new board concluded that Ellen Murray, who had joined the Penn School during the Port Royal Experiment and succeeded Towne as principal, had to be replaced. "She has no conception of what the modern industrial school should mean," Hollis Frissell maintained. Over the next decade, the school's academic curriculum was deemphasized and replaced with a new focus on agricultural, mechanical, and domestic training. The new board highlighted this momentous shift by incorporating the school under a new name: the Penn Normal, Industrial, and Agricultural School. In 1904, Rossa Cooley and Grace House, two Northern-born white Hampton instructors, joined the Penn School's staff as assistant principals with the expectation that they would take over the school's leadership whenever Murray vacated the role.[28]

The lion's share of the work of transforming the Penn School fell to the Hampton-trained teachers who joined the school in the first two decades of the century. Antoinette Norvell, who joined the Penn School at the beginning of the 1904–5 academic year, was a part of a larger cohort of Hampton-trained teachers who were charged with reorganizing the school's curriculum around industrial education. By the beginning of the 1905–6 year, there were seven Hampton graduates on the school's staff. The following year, a "Hampton House" was constructed for the growing number of teachers who were joining the school's faculty. By 1917, twenty-five of the school's twenty-seven teachers were Hampton graduates, and the Penn School would be framed as the pinnacle of the industrial school movement in the South.[29]

"This ought to be an inspiration to students and workers at Penn School, Hampton, and wherever the call of service is sounded," remarked one Hampton-trained teacher. Two of the educators, Joshua Blanton and Linnie Lumpkins, would get married on St. Helena Island, a union that would embody a whiggish turn-of-the-century vision of romantic partnership. Part of a larger politics of respectability, the Black educated class increasingly embraced and defended a Victorian politics of family formation as part of the larger struggle for racial destiny.[30]

While the Penn School was the most notable force in the campaign for Black uplift in Beaufort County, the twentieth-century Lowcountry was dotted with institutions designed to provide industrial and agricultural training for Black children and the rural communities around their schools. In 1867, during Reconstruction, Rachel Crane Mather, a white woman from Massachusetts, had established a school for freedpeople in the town of Beaufort; fifteen years later, it was brought under the auspices of the Woman's American Baptist Home Mission Society and became a boarding school that offered normal and industrial education for Black girls. In 1894, Elizabeth Wright, then a student at Tuskegee, began her education career at a school in Hampton County, a jurisdiction created during Redemption and named to honor the Democratic governor who oversaw the overthrow of statewide Republican Party. Wright's tenure at the small Reconstruction-era school was cut short when

Penn School teachers' group, 1908. The pictured teachers were all graduates of Hampton. Antoinette Norvell is seated second from left in the first row. Penn School Papers, Southern Historical Collection, Wilson Special Collections Library, University of North Carolina at Chapel Hill.

the institution was burned down by hostile members of the local community. In 1898, she returned to the Lowcountry, where she founded the Voorhees Institute, her own "miniature Tuskegee," in Bamberg County. In 1901, three Tuskegee graduates established the Port Royal Agricultural School, an industrial institution that had the explicit blessing of Booker T. Washington and the backing of Abbie Holmes Christensen, a Northern-born abolitionist who was now the matriarch of the county's most powerful political family. "This school is not endeavoring to furnish a higher education that would carry individuals away from their homes," a 1905 pamphlet explained, "but to provide enough practical education, and cultivate habits of cleanliness, thrift, and industry, to enable the average child to go back to his home fitted to make a good living off the land." Indeed, by the first decade of the twentieth century, both Tuskegee and Hampton were establishing satellite campuses across the South, transforming the abolitionist schoolhouses founded during the Reconstruction era into models for their vision of industrial education.[31]

When teachers from the industrial school movement tried to enforce the most conservative aspects of their educational vision on residents of the

Lowcountry, they often faced stiff resistance. Despite being cloaked in both the prestige of the Penn School and federal authority as an agent of the US Department of Agriculture, Joshua Blanton found it difficult to change the farming practices of the island's older generation. Still a young man, Blanton was considered "a mere boy" by men who had come of age in the late nineteenth century and who treated him with "distrust and skepticism." On Hilton Head Island, a nascent industrial school named after Northern shipping magnate William P. Clyde, who had purchased much of the island's land so it could become a private hunting preserve, foundered when residents of the island repeatedly rejected the overtures of the Tuskegee graduate who oversaw the project. In a 1920s interview, a former resident of St. Helena Island who had left the Lowcountry during the Great Migration lambasted the Penn School for upholding the Jim Crow social order. "All southern people are against the colored," the young migrant lamented. "Been tryin' to hold them down. Want to keep 'em diggin' all their life. That's what [President Robert Russa] Moton does at Tuskegee. That's what the new teachers at Penn School do."[32]

In many ways, the Lowcountry's Reconstruction generation changed the industrial school movement more than the movement changed the Lowcountry. Robert Smalls maintained a decade-long correspondence with Booker T. Washington, and while Smalls flattered Washington with high praise for his national leadership, Washington was equally inspired by the elder statesman. Preparing a speech for Tuskegee's twenty-fifth anniversary, Washington asked Smalls for details about the 1876 Hamburg Massacre. Understanding the moral force of Smalls's countermemory of Reconstruction, Washington recognized that despite his public denunciation of the earlier generation's political leaders in his 1903 autobiography, any serious reflection on the recent Black past before a Black audience would require a firm grasp of the sustained historical argument Smalls and his generation had been making in the Black public sphere for nearly half a century.[33]

Perhaps the most poignant example of this concession to the region's preexisting fabric of countermemory occurred at Beaufort's 1908 Decoration Day Celebration. David Hunter Post, the local chapter of the Grand Army of the Republic, invited Booker T. Washington to be the day's keynote speaker. Likely making good on a promise to Robert Smalls to visit the area, Washington left for the Lowcountry immediately after Tuskegee's recent commencement exercises. Washington was joined by the sociologist Monroe Nathan Work, "Tuskegee Machine" power broker Emmett J. Scott, and *Savannah Tribune* editor Solomon C. Johnson. The most dominant figure in the early twentieth-century Black public sphere, Washington secretly bankrolled several leading newspapers. In a tragic alchemy, Washington's rising influence over the Black press coincided with the fall of the previous era's leading publishers. In 1907, following a long battle with alcoholism, marital issues, and financial struggles, Thomas Fortune suffered a nervous breakdown and sold the *New York Age* to a Washington ally.³⁴

While Tuskegee and the industrial school movement had a sizable presence at the 1908 festivities, Decoration Day continued to embody the previous era's rival vision of what Reconstruction meant. Several other high-profile educators, including John Hope, the president of Morehouse College, and W. T. B. Williams, a professor at Hampton Institute, also joined the Tuskegee cohort. The *New York Age* reported that more than 10,000 attendees had descended on Beaufort County. Washington was hosted by Robert Smalls and Julius Washington, two of the region's most prominent surviving members of the Reconstruction generation. While the text of his address has not survived, a reporter from the *Savannah Tribune* described Washington's address as a "practical one" and write that his speech "was generally applauded and met the hearty approval of all who heard it." Washington would have almost certainly understood the particular context of the Lowcountry's world of countermemory; he and his entourage would have likely traveled to Beaufort precisely because the pomp and pageantry around the region's long-standing holiday continued to highlight Reconstruction's enduring hold in an increasingly national Black countermemory.³⁵

In 1912, a similar celebration occurred at the Penn School's fiftieth anniversary. A weekend-long commemoration of both the school's Reconstruction-era founding and its perceived progress under Hampton's leadership over the previous decade, the Penn School festivities could not avoid the countermemory of the Reconstruction era that persisted throughout the Lowcountry. Robert Smalls served as the master of ceremonies for the formal Sunday event; veterans of the First South Carolina Volunteers marched and carried the US flag; and Penn School students offered a heartfelt rendition of "My Country 'Tis of Thee," a tribute to the spontaneous version of the song that local freedpeople sang on January 1, 1863, upon hearing Rufus Saxton announce the Emancipation Proclamation—a moment that came to embody the vernacular poetry of the day of jubilee. While paeans were made to industrial education and the Hampton Idea, the Penn School's semicentennial was inextricably linked to the broader memory of emancipation and Reconstruction.³⁶

The Penn School's curricular transformation had the ironic and unintended effect of preserving one the Reconstruction era's lost political figures. Born into slavery on St. Helena Island, Hastings Gantt had been a member of the South Carolina state legislature during the 1870s and 1880s as well as a key figure in Beaufort County Republican politics. Often sharing political stages with

Hastings Gantt, 1905. Penn School Papers, Southern Historical Collection, Wilson Special Collections Library, University of North Carolina at Chapel Hill.

Robert Smalls and William Whipper during the 1870s, he had been among the Republican leaders who led the petition against Smalls's 1889 appointment to Beaufort's customhouse and had been excommunicated from Smalls's political machine during the fusionist struggle over the future of the party. By the early twentieth century, however, he had largely been forgotten in local and state political memory. When Anthony Dimock, a Northern photographer, traveled to the Lowcountry to photograph its Black residents, he was surprised to discover that his taxi driver was the former member of the state legislature.[37]

Women viewing the Gantt Cottage, 1923. Penn School Papers, Southern Historical Collection, Wilson Special Collections Library, University of North Carolina at Chapel Hill.

While Gantt disappeared from local and state political consciousness, his legacy would become forever enshrined in the Penn School's landscape. In 1864, he sold land that he had acquired during the Port Royal Experiment to Laura Towne and the Penn School—land that would help serve as the foundation for the school's modern campus. That same year, he joined the school's board of trustees—a radical appointment by Towne that fully aligned the school's mission and leadership with the politics of radical Reconstruction. In 1902, amid the school's leadership change, Gantt sold another sixty-eight acres to the Penn School and in his will arranged for his remaining landholdings to be transferred to it. In 1923, when Penn School students took part in the Better Homes Competition, in which nearly 1,000 communities nationwide sought to build and decorate the most modern home, the Penn School's teachers and students chose to name their prize-winning entry the "Gantt Cottage."[38]

This choice to name their school's entry in a national competition after a forgotten representative of an era now demonized in the country's collective memory suggests that some sizable portion of the Penn School's current faculty understood the importance of embracing the region's Black countermemory of the Reconstruction era. Here, the Jim Crow generation of educators not only held aloft the legacy of the Reconstruction generation but also made sure to enshrine their predecessors' rival memory for future generations. An anchor of the modern Penn Center campus, the Gantt Cottage also served as a site of respite for later generations of civil rights activists. In the summer of 1963 Martin Luther King Jr. would write a draft of his "I Have a Dream" speech while staying in the building named after the Reconstruction-era leader. Planned to coincide with the hundredth anniversary of the Emancipation Proclamation, the 1963 March on Washington was steeped in the Lowcountry's Reconstruction-era legacy.[39]

By the time the Gantt Cottage had been completed, Antoinette Norvell had already moved on from the Penn School. Like many Black teachers of her generation, Norvell changed schools several times over the course of her life. In 1911, she would move to Summerville, South Carolina, briefly working for a small rural school funded by the Anna T. Jeanes Foundation. In 1914, she married Simeon R. Cohen, a tailor from Charleston's free-born elite community. At some point over the next half decade, she would move again, this time to Macon County, Alabama. Now widowed, she resided with her sister, a 1906 Hampton graduate, and her brother-in-law, a 1907 Tuskegee graduate. All three family members were employed by Booker T. Washington's Black Belt college. She would remain at Tuskegee for the rest of her career, working as a registrar and dorm mother well into her sixties.[40]

Antoinette Norvell's story highlights the larger world of memory that the Jim Crow generation of teachers entered and how they navigated this educational landscape with their own sense of racial destiny. Despite being acolytes of Samuel Chapman Armstrong and Booker T. Washington, the leaders of the movement for industrial education in the South, Norvell and her teaching cohort had a more complicated relationship than their mentors with the Reconstruction generation. While taking seriously the pedagogical and institution-building aspects of industrial education, they were less committed to the erasure of the Reconstruction generation's political work. Often, in places like the Lowcountry, they found themselves working with leaders, organizations, and institutions that remained deeply committed to a political culture, if not an actual electoral politics, rooted in the Reconstruction generation's vision. While fighting the headwinds of disfranchisement, segregation, and anti-Black violence, the teachers and educators who led the industrial school movement continued to advance the memory of Reconstruction for future generations.

CHAPTER SEVEN

Requiem for Reconstruction
The Great Migration, Interwar African American History, and the Afterlife of the Reconstruction Generation

In 1912, Robert Smalls's health began to fail. A regular attendee at nearly every Republican national convention during his lifetime, he did not travel to Chicago to see the nomination of William Taft. "Whittie, I am not in good health," he told his good friend, Washington, DC, business and civic leader Whitefield McKinlay. "The same troubles that caused me to go the hospital, still hangs over me." Woodrow Wilson was elected that fall, and Smalls was among the many Black federal appointees purged by the Southern-born president—bringing an illustrious two-decade career as US Collector of Customs for the Port of Beaufort to a close. Over the next three years, his health would worsen, and complications from diabetes would require a foot amputation. The once gregarious pillar of the community became withdrawn and sullen. At times, he would yell at children. A double widower, he spent the last months of his life bedridden and under the care of his youngest daughter, Sarah.[1]

On February 23, 1915, Robert Smalls passed away at the age of seventy-five, surrounded by family, in his home at 511 Prince Street in Beaufort. On Friday, February 26, his funeral was held at the First African Baptist Church. It was the largest funeral the town had ever seen. His legacy was honored in several ways: from the pulpit of the church, where preachers extolled his wartime heroics, his commitment to freedchildren's education, and his status as "one of the most notable characters the Negro race has ever produced"; in the grand ceremonial march to his final resting place, led by the local chapters of the Masons, the Odd Fellows, and the Grand Army of the Republic, as well as by the region's Reconstruction-era brass band; and in the hearts of the larger Lowcountry community he had served over the course of his life. As Smalls's body was being viewed for the last time, and the church choir sang "Shall We Meet beyond the River," there was "not a dry eye of the vast crowd that passed," described a reporter for the *Savannah Tribune*.[2]

Robert Smalls's death in many ways marked the beginning of the Reconstruction generation's final chapter. In the national Black press's coverage of Smalls's death, a deep understanding of generational loss permeated the many solemn obituaries. The *New York Age* recognized him as a "national character,"

> **OBITUARY.**
>
> In sad but loving remembrance of our father, Robert Smalls, who departed this life February 23, 1915, at his home, Beaufort, S. C.
>
> Though thou art gone from us thy spirit will still be with us, a peaceful memory of happy days now passed away—an inspiration to high and noble endeavor.
>
> "Life's race well run,
> Life's work well done,
> Life's crown well won."
>
>   S. SMALLS WILLIAMS,
>   E. L. HAMPFIELD,
>   WM. ROBERT SMALLS.
>   Children.

Obituary for Robert Smalls, *The State* (Columbia, SC), February 24, 1916. It appeared in several Southern newspapers to commemorate the anniversary of Robert Smalls's death.

one of the "race's most noted figures," dedicating nearly the entirety of its front page to his life's accomplishments. A year after Smalls passed, C. J. Hardstew, a longtime reporter and writer in the Black press, visited Beaufort to try to capture the legacy Smalls had left in the Lowcountry and in the national Black memory. Hardstew wrote,

> When you talk about Beaufort, it always brings you before you Gen. Robert Smalls, who has since gone to his rest, but his name will ever live.... I consider this Robert Smalls an example for the young people. He was not born with a book under his pillow, nor was he allowed to use one, but in the face of all this he made his way. He went to congress and made his record there. He pleaded for his people and was one of the strong men of America. It was a pleasure to know this.

Once a complicated, and at times divisive figure in local and national politics, Robert Smalls had become a secular saint among the writers and reporters who were sketching a new Black history for the next generation.[3]

Smalls's life embodied the story of the Reconstruction generation, and his death was part of a quiet sunsetting of their moment in the nation's collective memory. As key members of the Reconstruction generation passed away—often with little or no fanfare in the national press—it appeared as though their countermemory would disappear from the national memory of the Civil War era. However, as the nation prepared to enter World War I, and a growing number of Black Southerners began to flee the South for the opportunities available on the other side of the Jim Crow curtain, a renewed push to preserve the history of the Reconstruction generation took place. Responding to both the late emergence of a Lost Cause cultural landscape in the interwar Lowcountry as well as the incrementalism of the growing cohort of Southern white liberals seeking to find a social scientific approach to the region's social problems, a new generation of Black writers, intellectuals, and activists returned to Reconstruction's history at one of the pivotal moments in the twentieth century's long Black freedom struggle. Seeking to rebut the claims of Confederate sympathizers, challenge the historical myopia of their white intellectual would-be allies, and, most important, revive a broader vision of Black social and political life, the "New Negro" movement reached back to Reconstruction's lost legacy and attempted to apply that old world's intellectual architecture to current struggles over civil rights organizing, the Great Migration, and larger debates about the meaning of African American history within the Harlem Renaissance.

With only a handful of members of the Reconstruction generation still living, a new generation of scholars and activists sought to archive their accounts of the postbellum past. These efforts included formal initiatives by nascent historical organizations like the Association for the Study of Negro Life and History (ASNLH). Able to identify living members of the Reconstruction generation, many of whom now resided in the centers of the Great Migration, ASNLH researchers not only restitched the old map of Reconstruction's countermemory but also illuminated a longer history of racial destiny through the lost world of the Reconstruction generation. Challenging the logic of the Jim Crow consensus, activists and intellectuals of the interwar era deployed Reconstruction's countermemory in academic debates, social movement struggles, and day-to-day Northern life. In doing so, they connected the cultural renaissances in places like Harlem and Chicago to the previous generation's political mecca in the Lowcountry—recapturing what racial destiny had once meant and preserving the old guard's legacy within the interwar decade's larger intellectual movement.

The Passing of the Reconstruction Generation and the Rise of the Lost Cause Movement in the Lowcountry

When Robert Smalls passed away, he was among the last surviving members of the Reconstruction generation. In 1907, the sizable cohort of South Carolina's Reconstruction generation left the earthly plane. In April, former Republican governor Daniel Chamberlain passed away; in July, William Whipper passed. By the end of the year, Richard Gleaves, the Northern-born former lieutenant governor who had helped Smalls establish the Republican Party in the Lowcountry, as well as William Elliott, Smalls's longtime Democratic Party rival in Beaufort County, would both be dead. In 1910, Hastings Gantt, Smalls's one-time friend and political ally, would pass away, leaving his remaining landholdings to the Penn School. As one of Smalls's biographers has noted, the passing of the Lowcountry's Reconstruction generation made his death that much more deeply felt because he had "outlived or outlasted the party and the majority of his enemies, rivals, and political partners."[4]

The larger Reconstruction generation's passing was covered with a funereal reverence in the national Black public sphere. On February 22, 1911, Frances Ellen Watkins Harper died in Philadelphia at the age of eighty-seven. Nearly a decade later, Richard T. Greener would die at the age of seventy-eight. In August 1917, *The Crisis*, the official periodical of the National Association for the Advancement of Colored People (NAACP), published a full-page photograph titled "Shadows of Light" that captured three elderly members of the Reconstruction generation. Subtitled "The Last of the 'Old Guard,'" the undated image included M. W. Gibbs, the first elected Black judge in the United States, P. B. S. Pinchback, the first Black governor of a US state, and James Lewis, the first Black customs inspector in the country's history. Lewis and Gibbs passed away in 1914 and 1915—leaving Pinchback the "Sole Survivor" in the photo and one of the last living leaders of the Reconstruction generation. On December 21, 1921, he passed away in Washington, DC. He was buried in Metairie Cemetery in New Orleans, his Reconstruction-era political home.[5]

The passing of the Reconstruction generation coincided with a new chapter in the long arc of sectional reconciliation, a phase that saw a dramatic increase in the scale and scope of the Lost Cause's cultural reach in American life. The first two decades of the twentieth century witnessed the nation's largest spike in public Confederate iconography, with more than 400 monuments built. The United Daughters of the Confederacy (UDC), now at their apex with more than 100,000 members, exercised tremendous power over school boards across the region and ensured that the region's history textbooks provided Southern schoolchildren with an account of the Civil War and Reconstruction that adhered to the central myths of the Confederacy. The 1912 election of Woodrow Wilson not only sent an ardent segregationist to the White House but also highlighted Southern Democrats' successful recapturing of the national party. Just two weeks before Robert Smalls died, D. W. Griffith's *The Birth of a Nation* premiered in Los Angeles. The film would become the landmark cinematic event of the early twentieth century, inventing the cinematic

"The Last of the 'Old Guard,'" *The Crisis*, August 1917

language for the modern Hollywood motion picture and mass-producing the enduring anti-Black portrait of Reconstruction in American popular culture.⁶

The passing of the Reconstruction generation also reshaped the Lowcountry's cultural terrain. In 1910, the Stephen Elliott Chapter of the United Daughters of the Confederacy was established in Beaufort. The organization would play a crucial role in expanding Confederate memory across the region's commemorative landscape. The women of Beaufort's UDC helped expand the celebration of Confederate Memorial Day and played a key role in deemphasizing the celebration of Decoration Day. Following the November 1915 completion of a Marine Corps Recruit Depot, Beaufort County Decoration Day celebrations were segregated, with a Black parade held in the morning and a white parade in the afternoon. By 1918, the UDC would oversee the holiday and attendance from Black out-of-town visitors plummeted—a move that infuriated local Black leaders. "The plan of having two memorial services on

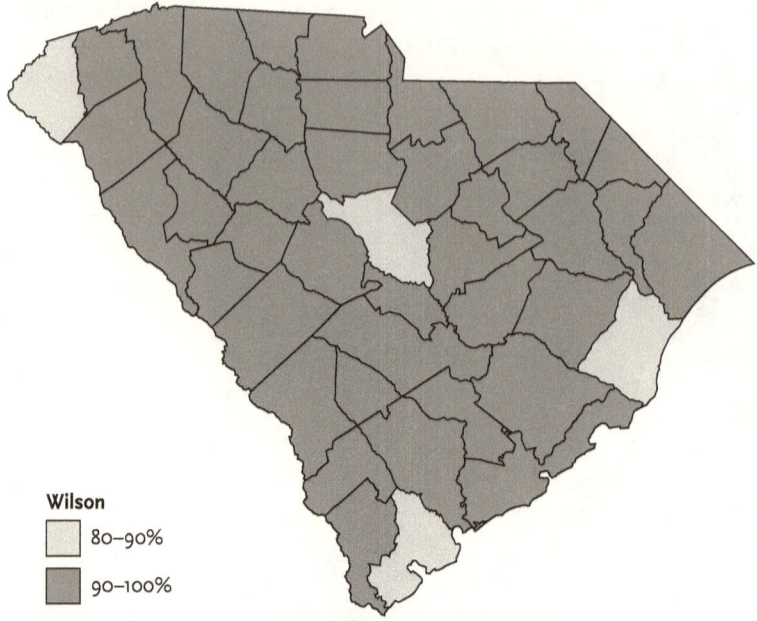

1912 presidential election results in South Carolina by county. All the counties were won by Democratic presidential candidate Woodrow Wilson. Neither Republican presidential candidate William Taft nor Progressive Party candidate Theodore Roosevelt won a single county in South Carolina during the 1912 presidential election. In January 1912, the South Carolina Legislature created a new Lowcountry county, Jasper, carved from portions of Beaufort and Hampton Counties.

this day—one of the colored people and one for the white people in the same cemetery should be frowned down and condemned by all who claim to have honor and respect for the memory of these dead heroes, and who lay claim to love of country," argued longtime Republican leader Julius Washington. In 1917, the organization funded a trip to Savannah for viewing of *The Birth of a Nation*. By the end of the decade, a local chapter of the Ku Klux Klan had begun to flourish in the South Carolina Lowcountry—a region that had repeatedly rebuffed the Reconstruction-era Klan.[7]

For some of South Carolina's demagogues, even the muted persistence of Reconstruction-era memory in the Lowcountry provided the perfect target for shoring up their white supremacist bona fides. Governor Cole Blease, an Upcountry Democrat who sought to inherit his mentor Benjamin Tillman's political enemies, regularly returned to the old trope of Beaufort as a bastion of Black rule. In 1914, he attacked Beaufort County's public school board, on which white Northerners and the Black South Carolinians held a majority of the seats, for not allowing white schoolchildren to celebrate the birthday of "our Great Chieftain," Robert E. Lee.[8]

Blease also took considerable glee in targeting Beaufort County senator Niels Christensen Jr.'s family history. Pointing out that Christensen's father had been a "captain of negro companies in the Union army, who led charges with negro troops against the white soldiers of the Southern Confederacy," and that his mother was a Northern-born abolitionist who now ran a school with a Black man—Booker T. Washington—on its board, Blease repeated earlier attacks on the Lowcountry and perceptively recognized that Lost Cause polemics continued to offer the surest route for a broad-based white populism in the state. Echoing Benjamin Tillman, Blease returned to the old well of "Negro domination" in a moment when the state's white voters no longer had any viable political alternatives.[9]

These cultural and political attacks ultimately sounded the death knell for the Lowcountry's Republican Party. Following Robert Smalls's death, both the town council and school board in Beaufort became all-white. When Black voters were able to sway some local races in 1912 and 1914 by voting their preferred white candidates into local office, the Lowcountry's Democratic leaders began to advocate for a local primary election restricted to registered Democratic Party members. This all-white primary would prevent the county's remaining Black Republican Party voters from taking advantage of the divisions among the county's white voters, thus securing Democratic Party control—and white supremacy—in the region.[10]

World War I, the Great Migration, and the Historical Challenge to Southern Liberalism

The growing visibility of Confederate memory in the early-twentieth century Lowcountry was accompanied by the region's specific chapter of the Great Migration. A seismic demographic upheaval with roots in the 1893 Sea Island storm, World War I amplified the larger region-wide exodus. By the interwar period, the collapse of global cotton prices, which made all rungs on the South's agricultural ladder more precarious, placed the Lowcountry's particular network of smallholding farms in existential jeopardy. Black soldiers returning home from the European war were harshly reminded of how their patriotic sacrifice was not enough to have their basic citizenship rights fully protected. The urban North's promise of mass production, mass consumption, and mass culture offered a sharp contrast to the Jim Crow South's fealty to an imagined organic social order. In response to these changes, the generation born after the 1895 constitutional convention voted with their feet; by beginning of the Great Depression, South Carolina would have a white majority for the first time in its state history.[11]

The Great Migration presented a difficult problem for reform-minded Southerners who believed that the region's great twentieth-century problems—rural poverty and de facto segregation—could be defeated in their lifetime. Faced with defenders of the Jim Crow regime on one side and fleeing Black Southerners the region on the other, white Southern liberals struggled to find models of interracial cooperation that could serve as a middle ground for a moderate, broad-based politics. In 1928, a team of social scientists on the faculty of the University of North Carolina appeared to find such a community: the Lowcountry's St. Helena Island. The home of the now Hampton-affiliated Penn School, St. Helena Island offered a conservative counterpoint against the mass-society freedoms available to those who boarded a north-bound Atlantic Coast Line train.[12]

Unable to synthesize the larger demands for racial justice made by the region's interwar civil rights movements, the Chapel Hill social scientists unintentionally provided a moment of reckoning for Southern liberalism. The silences within their study not only erased the ongoing activism of the civil rights organizations making inroads into the interwar Lowcountry but also ignored the historically grounded work of Black social scientists who were seeking to use their scholarship to confront the modern challenges of their era. Part of a long battle over the sectional reconciliation in American cultural and intellectual life, the struggle to understand the Lowcountry's changing demography highlights how Reconstruction's countermemory was increasingly fading in regional and national discussions about South Carolina's Black population.[13]

The US entrance into World War I marked the beginning of this larger shift of demographic and cultural forces. Like much of Black America, Black residents of the Lowcountry expressed a mixed emotions toward the nation's entry into the European war. On the one hand, a deep sense of patriotism, rooted in both the afterlife of Union memory and the robust network of Black veterans and their families, made the Lowcountry fertile ground for the military's recruiting efforts. By early 1918, one in five Black men from Beaufort County had been drafted into the war effort—one of the highest rates conscription rates in the state. Thirty-one men were killed in combat or died from disease during the war effort. Those drafted into the war effort were often given massive, community-wide send-offs; when they returned home, Black World War I soldiers were celebrated and featured prominently in local Emancipation

Day and Decoration Day parades. Local Black leaders played a major role in recruiting young men into the war effort. At a patriotic rally in the town's Odd Fellows temple, a large crowd heard several former Republican leaders, ministers, and educators speak about "the loyalty of the Negro," "the Negro as a soldier," and "the part that the Negro played in 61 to 65." Joshua Blanton, a Hampton-trained Penn School teacher, became a song leader for Black soldiers on behalf of the Young Men's Christian Association (YMCA) and traveled around the country to boost morale among Black regiments. On St. Helena Island, the Penn School doubled as a center for the US Food Administration, and the school's leaders held several rallies for the islanders to raise awareness about food rationing and drum up support for Liberty bonds.[14]

On the other hand, the multipronged attacks on the Fourteenth and Fifteenth Amendments made the Lowcountry's Black leadership class approach the war effort with a clear-eyed realism. At the April 10, 1917, war rally, Beaufort's Black citizens put forth a series of resolutions making their both their loyalty and trepidations clear: "Resolved by the colored citizens of Beaufort in mass meeting assembled: That we, as loyal citizens of the United States, in spite of the discriminations, injustices and lack of protection under the laws, both local and national, feel that we are still citizens of this great country, whose flag is as much our flag as it is the flag of every other citizen."[15]

While often willing to bite his tongue and echo the accommodationist platitudes of Hampton's leadership, Penn School teacher Joshua Blanton was rattled by a white Southern leader's tirade against a Black crowd in New Orleans celebrating its success in raising funds for Liberty bonds. "You n——s are wondering how you are going to be treated after the war," the man sneered. "Well, I'll tell you. You are going to be treated exactly like you were before the war; this is a white man's country." In 1919, Blanton would speak out against white supremacy and criticize the staging of the Allied victory parade in Paris for overlooking the contributions of Black soldiers to the war effort. As Chad L. Williams has demonstrated, World War I served as a crucible for Black America's leadership class, and strategic calls to "close the ranks" often became untenable as instances of discrimination and segregation in the armed forces, and later violence against veterans in the South, highlighted the need for more direct civil rights action.[16]

Sensing that the political tide in the region was beginning to shift, the NAACP launched an ambitious Southern membership drive. During the war, the organization's membership increased tenfold, from 9,000 to 90,000 members. South Carolina and the greater Lowcountry served as a fulcrum of this Southern expansion. In 1917, new chapters were established in Charleston,

Columbia, and Savannah, Georgia. In the following two years, chapters were established in Aiken, Beaufort, Orangeburg, and Sumter. These new chapters often built on the political foundation laid by the Reconstruction generation—including its surviving members. Julius Washington—a one-time political opponent of Robert Smalls who later worked with him in Beaufort's customhouse—served as the first president of Beaufort's NAACP.[17]

Former Seventh District congressman Thomas Miller helped found a chapter in Charleston, the Lowcountry's largest city. While the Charleston chapter would become one of the most successful and active of the South's early branches, the Beaufort branch struggled. In January 1920, an emergency meeting was held to implore county residents to pay their one-dollar annual dues. "You may not need the aid of the N.A.A.C.P. now, but you don't know how soon," pleaded Beaufort's local leaders. By the end of the year, Beaufort's NAACP branch was listed among the association's "delinquent" local chapters that had not paid its chapter dues.[18]

The interwar Lowcountry also saw the rise of activism by a new generation of the Black radical tradition. On May 10, 1919, Charleston become the site of one of the nation's largest race riots—part of a larger series of racial rebellions that became known as Red Summer. That same year, NAACP president Thomas Miller led a protest to remove white teachers from the city's public schools. Having a living memory of the region's earlier era of Black political power, and the sense of loss at that world's being defeated, Miller accurately read a broader weakness in Jim Crow's edifice that made possible the reclamation of local political power through the language of Black solidarity and collective racial destiny.[19]

This return to a radical vision of racial destiny could most fully be seen in the rise of the Universal Negro Improvement Association (UNIA). Founded by Jamaican immigrant Marcus Garvey and headquartered in Harlem, the UNIA spread across the American South during the interwar years. The Lowcountry's port cities gave rise to some of the South's most active chapters of the UNIA, which found a natural base among working-class Black Southerners who could remember the region's earlier moments of Black nationalism. Steven Hahn has argued that Black Southerners likely saw the UNIA as the successor of earlier grassroots organizations like the Union League. The political geography of UNIA chapters in South Carolina also suggests that sites of Reconstruction's countermemory strongly shaped the networks where the organization could flourish. Of South Carolina's twenty-five UNIA chapters, twenty-one were located in the Lowcountry. In Beaufort, regular UNIA meetings were held at the Central Baptist Church, and leaders from the greater

Lowcountry often visited the Reconstruction-era political hotbed to encourage Black residents to "hold high the banner of Garveyism."[20]

The broader countermemory of Reconstruction was also embedded in the UNIA's accounting of the Black past. In the first iteration of his Black Star line, Marcus Garvey had initially hoped to name one of his ships the SS *Robert Smalls*. John Edward Bruce, the longtime Black newspaper columnist and close friend of Smalls, spent his last years writing for the UNIA's *Negro World* newspaper. Likely under Bruce's influence, the UNIA often attacked Black America's interwar leaders for being poor facsimiles of the "clever politicians" from the "old days." "The trouble with the 1921–22 Negro crop of statemen seems to be that they talk too much, promise too much and write too much," Bruce argued.[21]

More than simple nostalgia, interwar leaders, both Black and white, experienced a sharp turn in Black political culture that was most deeply felt in the mass migration of Black Southerners to the urban North. Responding to the increased wartime economic opportunities, as well as long-standing grievances against the Jim Crow order, nearly 2 million Black Southerners left the region for the cities in the Northeast and Midwest. Between 1900 and 1930, the Black population of Beaufort County dropped from 32,100 to 15,600. Occurring at the same moment that the Reconstruction generation was fading from American life, the demographic gravity of Black America began to shift from rural Black majority regions like the Lowcountry, the Mississippi Delta, and the Alabama Black Belt to the new Black meccas of Chicago's Bronzeville, New York's Harlem, and Detroit's Paradise Valley.[22]

Southern white observers were keenly aware that the Great Migration could reanimate Black political life nationally. At a 1928 Democratic Party rally, one local leader denounced Al Smith, the party's presidential nominee, because "he and Tammany are bringing the Negro back into politics." Eight years later, the same paper once again warned about the rise of Black voters who "have come to be numerous in Northern cities." The paper warned that this reemergence of Black suffrage would not remain in the North. "Once the negroes are voting, the Scalawags will come to life in swarms in South Carolina."[23]

To this end, Southern leaders pursued a cynical, dual-track strategy of denigrating the economic and political promise of the North while still making paeans to a mythic New South where true racial harmony had been achieved. In 1919, South Carolina's commissioner of agriculture claimed that "many who had left in previous years returned disillusioned over life in the North and with a greater appreciation for southern living." Another white Southerner, upon hearing a report of an uptick in return migration at the end of 1925, repeated a standard trope of Southern racial harmony—but added a criticism of the Great Migration: "The South is prosperous, it is the negro's natural home," the writer argued. "He was disappointed in the North in many instances . . . and it is not at all surprising that he is coming back and that he is crowding . . . to the southbound trains."[24]

Many Black leaders saw the Great Migration as misguided and echoed support for Southern life in similar terms as their white counterparts. Benjamin Barnwell, a Penn School teacher and agent of the US Department of Agriculture, echoed the pro-Southern sentiment. "Taking all things into consideration our people are just as well off generally speaking as any group of rural people under similar conditions. They seem contented to remain at home," Barnwell explained to the editor of the *Beaufort Gazette*. Another teacher at the Penn School took a decidedly more pessimistic tone on the Great Migration's impact, estimating that only one-third of all migrants found success in the North. "One third come back damaged," the teacher lamented. "One third come back in their coffins, no good to anybody." While the Hampton-trained teachers continued to push for a more expansive vision of the industrial school movement, the Great Migration served as an existential threat to their Southern-facing view of Black activism.[25]

For a nascent cohort of Southern liberals, the Great Migration served as one of the most important intellectual challenges to their vision of the region's future. Concentrated in organizations like the Commission on Interracial Cooperation (CIC), as well as the University of North Carolina, this cohort of academics, activists, and civic leaders stood at the vanguard of Southern progressivism. Using modern social science to advocate for economic reforms, the South's interwar liberals established alliances with the region's moderate politicians to fight against lynching, expand educational opportunities, and, ultimately, deploy New Deal–era federal programs to address the region's endemic poverty.[26]

Rather than readjust their fundamental assumptions about Southern political power, which largely left the region's structural racial hierarchy unchallenged, these Southern white liberals sought to find Black communities in the region that could be heralded as exemplars of "racial harmony." Funded by major Northern philanthropic foundations like the Laura Spelman Rockefeller Fund, Southern academics produced studies of Mississippi Delta communities like the town of Mound Bayou and Coahoma County. During the Great Depression, sociologist and CIC member Arthur Raper would produce several county-level studies of Georgia's Black Belt. Not dissimilar from the efforts of interwar white folklorists and fiction writers who depicted frozen-in-amber portraits of Black Southern life that often muddied, if not altogether erased, historical change and instead drew an ahistorical line between the antebellum past and twentieth-century present, the Southern social scientists viewed their interwar community studies as a vehicle to emphasize regional consensus and downplay political tensions between Black and white Southerners.[27]

The South Carolina Lowcountry would become an important part of these interwar debates over regional racial harmony. In 1928, T. J. Woofter Jr., a newly appointed sociology professor at the University of North Carolina and a member of the CIC, led a team of researchers to St. Helena Island to conduct a series of studies on the social and cultural world that persisted in Beaufort County. Having examined Black Northern migration from Georgia for the Department of Labor, a topic he would later turn into a dissertation at Columbia University, Woofter was uniquely qualified to tackle the intersection between Black migration and the future of interracial harmony in the South.[28]

Over the course of the six-month community study, Woofter brought several wings of interwar Southern liberalism to St. Helena Island to conduct what would be one of the most sustained and well-funded investigations in Black Southern life. As an incoming professor at the University of North Carolina, Woofter coordinated the project with Howard Odum Jr., then the dean of Southern sociology, and received copious support from UNC's prestigious Institute for Research in Social Science. Pulitzer-prize winning Lowcountry writer Julia Peterkin visited the researchers and helped shape some of the group's findings on Black folklore. In addition, Woofter already had a deep relationship with the Penn School, having befriended the principal, Rossa Cooley, nearly a decade earlier while working on a 1917 study of Black Southern education; family connections also gave him a preexisting relationship with the chair of the Penn School's board of trustees. Woofter's connections to the various wings of the white Southern liberal world gave his work a deep legibility to Northern philanthropists looking to fund "worthwhile" projects on Southern race relations. In total, Woofter and his team of scholars received $30,000, a sum which far exceeded what Black researchers working on similar subjects would receive.[29]

Over the next decade, the team of scholars published four monographs derived from their St. Helena Island data. The first, and most widely read, was Woofter's *Black Yeomanry: Life on St. Helena Island*. Published in 1930, *Black Yeomanry* explored the relationship between St. Helena's high rate of Black landownership and such indicators of social progress as household income, school funding, out-of-wedlock childbirth, and church attendance. That same year, Guy B. Johnson published *Folk Culture on St. Helena Island*. A sociologist and social anthropologist, Johnson offered a revisionist study of the Gullah creole language and folk traditions that challenged the premises of earlier scholars. In addition to offering an extensive catalog of words, stories, and songs, Johnson's book argued that Gullah had an internal logic rooted in the grammar of English. His wife Guion Griffis Johnson published *A Social History of the Sea Islands, with Special Reference to St. Helena Island, South Carolina*, which traced the history of the island's Black community since the Civil War.[30]

The UNC research group's study of the Great Migration would pose the greatest threat to the broader racial-harmony thesis. Clyde Kiser, then a graduate student at Columbia University, published a dissertation and, later, a 1932 book based on his examination of Northern migration from Beaufort County. *Sea Island to City: A Study of St. Helena Islanders in Harlem and Other Urban Centers* offered firsthand accounts from Black Sea Islanders that challenged liberal consensus about the imagined harmony in the region. "In thirty years from now, the Island will be owned by the white people. The only people living there will be the old standbys," lamented one former St. Helena resident. Another young resident put the generational tension more bluntly: "Got tired living on Island. Too lonesome. Go to bed at six o'clock. Everything dead. No dances, no moving picture show, nothing to go to." In summarizing his findings, Kiser admitted that the migrants described greater economic and cultural freedom in the North and that greater levels of self-respect and race consciousness were also part of the migration experience. He nonetheless couched these gains as mixed blessings. Kiser wondered whether the newfound right to vote in the North would be "exercised intelligently," and he suggested that Black Southerners would sell their votes to "local political bosses for a mess of pottage," echoing the familiar Reconstruction-era trope that still survived in the white Southern imagination.[31]

The larger Southern liberal world lauded the works that emerged from the 1928 St. Helena Island research group. T. J. Woofter Jr.'s *Black Yeomanry*, in particular, was perceived to be at the cutting edge of understanding Black Southern life. One Northern writer found *Black Yeomanry* a refreshing change from the "Police Gazette romances of Harlem dives" that dominated works about "the Negro in our midst." Another review enthused that Woofter's book "cannot be too earnestly commended to the attention of all intelligent readers" and "should be in the library of every high school and every organization devoted to any form of social welfare work, throughout the country." Leo Favrot, a field agent for the General Education Board, implored the director of the Southern liberal organization to place a copy of Woofter's book in the hands of all the organization's Southern agents.[32]

Black writers and scholars painted a more dismal portrait of Woofter's work. The *Baltimore Afro-American* criticized *Black Yeomanry*'s inability to confront the damage wrought by segregation. "When everywhere throughout the South average colored schools are found to be below average white schools, it is evident there must be some reason for it," the paper maintained. W. E. B. Du Bois framed the inability to address segregation and racial inequality more damningly. "There is not a single word of really illuminating truth," he deplored. "Woofter's study is little less than a calamity." In a 1931 review of *Black Yeomanry* in the *Journal of Negro History*, Carter Woodson not only criticized the book but also highlighted the cultural investment among Southern white liberals and their Northern benefactors in upholding the color line, which he found partially to blame for the project's inability to confront structural forces that reproduced racial and economic inequality in the Lowcountry. "In the beginning of this survey," Woodson recalled, "it was urged that Negro investigators be placed on this staff to interpret certain phases of the life of their race which only a Negro can understand, but probably because Negroes cannot break bread with white men they were not required to cooperate." For Woodson, Du Bois, and the larger cohort of interwar Black scholars, the well-funded and deeply ahistorical *Black Yeomanry* exposed in sharp relief their struggle to secure funding for rival interpretations of the South's social problems—interpretations that took white supremacy seriously.[33]

Embedded in a larger intellectual world shaped by white elites who had inherited the major myths of sectional reconciliation, interwar social scientists were only able to see the topsoil of racial inequality and not the deep sediment of Redemption's violence and plunder. Historian Mark Ellis has noted that Southern white liberals like Woofter were "seduced by the possibility that an idyllic balance had been struck on St. Helena Island between Black autonomy, cultural purity, and white guardianship." Woofter was aware that white leaders in Beaufort County had never "entirely forgotten" that Black landowners had acquired their land from the region's white elites during the Civil War, but he was also willing to turn to toward the paternalism of Northern philanthropy because "the federal government turned the land over to these people and then stepped aside without seeing the experiment through." Invested in their own myth of the postbellum South, a myth that also viewed the Reconstruction era as a moment of social and moral peril, Southern white liberals emphasized an idealized vision of racial harmony over the hard truth of a full accounting of the postbellum past. Confronting this myth in a 1948 report for the Penn School, Ira De Reid and a team of Black social scientists offered a pointed critique of how Woofter's generation of Southern scholars framed communities like St.

Helena Island. "There are at least two St. Helena Islands," De Reid remarked. "One is part memory and part myth. The other is a stern reality." Separating myth from reality would become the duty of a new generation of scholars who unearthed the Reconstruction generation's rival archive to tell a new version of African American history.[34]

Reconstruction's New History: The Association for the Study of Negro Life and History and the Archiving of Countermemory

At the same moment that Southern liberals were confronting the limits the Great Migration imposed on their vision of racial harmony, a new generation of Black scholars used the intellectual ferment unleashed along the nation's northbound tributaries to recapture the lost history of Reconstruction. Beginning with the 1915 foundation of the Association for the Study of Negro Life and History in Chicago's Wabash Avenue branch of the YMCA, to the quest to track down surviving members of the Reconstruction generation in Northern cities, the scholars who built the architecture of modern African American history used the Great Migration to tell the most expansive and fully realized history of the era's Black officeholders.[35]

Certainly, some of the intellectual labor of challenging the rising tide of the Lost Cause had already begun before the Great Migration. The semicentennial of the Civil War saw the publication of a series of accounts that defended both Unionist and emancipationist interpretations of the war's larger meaning. In 1912, Rupert Holland, the nephew of former Penn School teacher Laura Towne, published his aunt's diary, which covered the abolitionist's wartime experience with the Port Royal Experiment, her lifelong commitment to Black education in the Lowcountry, and her unflagging support for radical Reconstruction. The following year, John Lynch, former congressman for Mississippi's Reconstruction-era Black district, published *The Facts of Reconstruction*, which offered a conservative rebuttal to the charge that the Reconstruction-era state governments were sites of unrestrained Black political power. In 1913, the Crisis Publishing Company, producer of the NAACP's monthly periodical, published a memoir by Maud Cuney Hare, daughter of Reconstruction-era Texas politician Norris Wright Cuney.[36]

The Great Migration, however, radically changed how historians of the African American experience collected archival documents and produced accounts of the postbellum past. In Chicago's Southside, a new world of urban cultural institutions anchored Reconstruction's interwar Black countermemory. As Davarian Baldwin has demonstrated, the Great Migration forever transformed the means of Black cultural production. The rise of a "New Negro modernity" in the city's interwar Black institutions opened a new chapter in Black history. The Wabash Avenue YMCA, a hub for the city's old settlers to impart lessons of racial uplift to the city's incoming Southern migrants, provided space for Carter Woodson to deliver lessons in African American history. Robert Abbott, a Lowcountry native and Hampton graduate, would use the pages of the *Chicago Defender* to both challenge the paternalist regional myths offered in the Southern press and provide his national readers with a rival history of postbellum Black life. In 1920, Chicago filmmaker Oscar Micheaux premiered his second feature film, *Within Our Gates*, which offered a pointed cinematic counterargument to *Birth of a Nation*.[37]

In addition, several members of the Reconstruction generation also relocated to Chicago after the Black South's political collapse. Neander DePriest, the father of future Southside congressman Oscar DePriest, once saved the life of his friend Congressman James T. Rapier during a Redemption-era mob attack and later moved his family from Alabama to Chicago because his affiliation with the Republican Party made him a target for political violence. In 1905, George Washington Murray, the last congressman to represent South Carolina's Black Seventh District, fled the Palmetto State for Chicago following a dubious forgery conviction. In 1912, John Lynch, former congressman for Mississippi's Reconstruction-era Sixth District, joined the larger wave of Black Mississippians seeking refuge and opportunity in the Windy City. Arriving before the interwar moment, members of Chicago's Reconstruction generation occupied important positions in the city's "old settler" leadership class, giving them greater power to shape the contours of the growing, Great Migration–era world of Black associational and cultural life.[38]

The cultural and social networks that produced the ASNLH contained a hidden archive of the earlier era's countermemory—the surviving members of the Reconstruction generation. Led by Monroe Work, a leading social scientist at Tuskegee and editor of the *Negro Yearbook*, the *Journal of Negro History* created the first archive of the previous century's Black officeholders. "No systematic effort has hitherto been made to save the records of the Negro during the Reconstruction period," Work lamented. "American public opinion has been so prejudiced against the Negroes because of their elevation to prominence in southern politics that it has been considered sufficient to destroy their regime and forget it." Having received $4,000 from the Laura Spelman Rockefeller Fund to begin collecting sources, Woodson and leaders of the ASNLH recognized that gathering the necessary primary source material to produce a fair and full portrait of the Reconstruction era would be an uphill challenge.

"The investigator... did not go to all the nooks and corners of the country," Woodson explained. "Neither time nor the means at his disposal would permit such an exhaustive effort.... Hundreds of distant places where such valuable documents do exist could not be touched at all."[39]

The call issued in the *Journal of Negro History* proved to be a turning point in the collection effort. An 1874 scrapbook once owned by William A. Hayne, a member of Charleston's free-born Black elite who served in the South Carolina General Assembly, was sent to Monroe Work because of the initial call for Reconstruction-era materials. Helen James Chisholm, a Hampton graduate who had once taught at the Penn School, offered a rich portrait of the descendants of the Lowcountry's lost generation. While she now resided in Connecticut, Chisholm remained in contact with Sarah Voorhees Smalls Williams, "who still lives in the paternal home in Beaufort, where are the books and personal possessions of her distinguished father." Susan and Olive Rainey, the wife and daughter of former congressman Joseph Rainey, now lived in Springfield, Massachusetts. She cautioned that while Mamie Hayne, the daughter of Henry E. Hayne, the first Black person to serve as secretary of state in South Carolina, was a close friend who maintained friendships with many members of her father's generation, Henry Hayne's white-passing brothers would be more difficult to locate because "they do not identify themselves with the Negro race."[40]

In the dozens of letters sent to the journal emerged a deep sense of loss over the fading of the Reconstruction generation. "There is a vast amount of fact reposing only in the memories of elderly people now living that should be rescued and recorded while they live, lest it is lost forever," remarked one respondent. Henry Wallace, who had worked in a Columbia, South Carolina, post office during Reconstruction, and had a brother who was a page in the South Carolina statehouse, expressed keen awareness that he was among the last generation of Black Americans with a living memory of Reconstruction. "There are very few of us left now to tell the tale, and that in a very unsatisfactory way." Published over the course of several issues of the *Journal of Negro History*, the "Letters on Reconstruction Records" series saw the children and grandchildren of nineteenth-century officeholders attempt to stitch together the lost world of their Reconstruction-generation elders.[41]

Those who responded to Monroe Work's archival project expressed their desire to participate in a retelling of the Reconstruction era in the language of generational duty. In a separate letter, Helen James Chisholm voiced a similar concern about the generational shift in memory. "I have long felt that the last opportunity to collect data concerning this interesting period in our history, is while this present generation lives," she wrote. "The next generation will have no interest in it." A Hampton alumna whose teaching career in the industrial school movement had allowed her to see the afterlife of slavery in both the Lowcountry and in Hawaii, James would later earn a graduate degree in history, economics, and sociology at Atlanta University, where she studied with W. E. B. Du Bois. Similarly, John W. Cromwell, the former president of the Bethel Literary and Historical Society, put the point more sharply in a letter to John Mitchell Jr., the editor of the *Richmond Planet*, asking him to use the pages of the prominent Black newspaper to assist the *Journal of Negro History*'s archive-building project. "Will you for the sake of history allow this communication in your columns?" Cromwell asked. For Cromwell, Black periodicals like the *Richmond Planet* had a critical role in the larger struggle to actively produce a "racial history" and not allow "the imputation by our silence" in the ongoing historical debates over the meaning of the Reconstruction era.[42]

These source-collecting efforts seeded the desired fruit-bearing history. Alrutheus Ambush Taylor, the ASNLH's lead researcher during its early years and one of Carter Woodson's first protégés, published *The Negro in South Carolina during Reconstruction*, the first monograph by a Black historian on the Reconstruction era. Taylor's book was a watershed not only for the ASNLH but also the broader field of African American history. In addition to offering the first examination of Black congressmen based on the printed congressional record, it provided an unprecedented examination of the social and economic matters of the era. In 1924, NAACP president Walter F. White praised Taylor's intellectual achievement but also lamented that the book would "probably be completely ignored by the white South and North." He did hold out hope that Taylor's history of Reconstruction could be used to challenge "the stories . . . so familiar to the followers of the Rev. Thomas Dixon and D. W. Griffith." A year later a review in *The Crisis* remarked, "Students and teachers will welcome so trustworthy a work in this field, for much of the printed matter generally used in the schools and colleges of this country in teaching the history of the Reconstruction period is junk—absolute junk!"[43]

That same year, Taylor invited Thomas Miller, one of the nineteenth century's last living Black congressmen to sit on a panel at the ASNLH's annual meeting. Joined by NAACP leader James Weldon Johnson, the three men connected the history of Reconstruction to the interwar struggle for civil rights. Miller would spend much of his later years traveling the country to preserve the legacy of the Reconstruction era. On July 30, 1927, Miller gave a speech in Charleston where he argued that the state needed to build a monument to honor his friend and mentor, the war hero Robert Smalls. At a 1930 event in Chicago, he was joined John Lynch, his sole surviving political contemporary from the Reconstruction era. Oscar DePriest, in his first term as congressman for Illinois's First Congressional District, joined Miller and Lynch, drawing a clear line between his status as the first Black person to serve in Congress since Reconstruction and the last two living members of the Reconstruction generation.[44]

The pioneering work of Woodson, Taylor, and the ASNLH would create the scholarly scaffolding for W. E. B. Du Bois's seismic reinterpretation of the Reconstruction era. In 1924, Du Bois published *The Gift of Black Folk: The Negroes in the Making of America*, which included the essay "The Reconstruction of Freedom." In his first return to the subject of Reconstruction since his 1910 *American Historical Review* article, Du Bois significantly revised his argument about the Reconstruction era's meaning. His 1924 essay now included the first iteration of his then-provocative theses about self-emancipation and Reconstruction-as-turning-point in the world-historical march toward democracy: "The North being unable to free the slave, let him free himself. And he did, and this was his greatest gift to this nation."[45]

"The Reconstruction of Freedom" also offered a more richly textured map of emancipation and Reconstruction than his previous work on the era, drawing out the Lowcountry's specific role in the drama. "The Freedmen were massed in large numbers at Fortress Monroe, Va., Washington, D.C., Beaufort and Port Royal, S.C., New Orleans, La., Vicksburg, and Corinth, Miss., Columbus, Ky., Cairo, Ill., and elsewhere." In addition, in emphasizing the importance of Sherman's Field Order Number 15, a document that Du Bois viewed as crucial for understanding the thwarted revolutionary promise of the war effort, he drew close attention to the language of the military document, which highlighted the role the Lowcountry's major population centers would play in shaping new patterns of postbellum Black settlement and landownership. Finally, in his measured reinterpretation of Black officeholders, Du Bois highlights how Beaufort, South Carolina, had "retained Negroes as sheriffs and school officials." This increased awareness of the Reconstruction generation's geographic footprint likely came from his time as editor of *The Crisis*, which regularly reported on its recruitment drives in former centers of radical Reconstruction and tried to honor the legacy of the generation's surviving members.[46]

Du Bois's 1924 essay also included significant revisions to his thinking on Black officeholders and the legacy of the Reconstruction generation. Where Du Bois only briefly mentioned a handful of Black officeholders by name in his 1910 article, "The Reconstruction of Freedom" provided a more expansive and admiring view of the figures who held office after the Civil War. He enumerated and profiled the twenty-two men who served in Congress during the long

Reconstruction era, underscoring the high levels of educational and career success that many of these figures had attained before entering politics. "The colored men who took seats in both Senate and House did not appear ignorant or helpless," Du Bois observed. "They were as a rule studios, earnest, ambitious men whose public conduct ... would be honorable to any race of men."[47]

Much of this new synthesis depended on earlier generations of Black historical practice and countermemory. Du Bois drew his data on the twenty-two known congressman from prior research done for the *Journal of Negro History*. The text for an 1895 speech given by Thomas Miller at South Carolina's constitutional convention came from an 1899 paper delivered before the American Negro Academy—with the original document likely being the pamphlet published by Thomas Miller's daughter Mary J. Miller. Du Bois's most prominent biographer observed that Du Bois's 1935 magnum opus *Black Reconstruction* was "the particular beneficiary" of the work of Alrutheus Ambush Taylor. Indeed, in the aftermath of *Black Reconstruction*'s release, several scholars who had begun their careers at the Association for the Study of Negro Life and History privately grumbled that while Du Bois's book was important, Du Bois had only offered an "new interpretation of old facts"—facts that they had established by archiving Reconstruction's countermemory.[48]

The Cultural Afterlife of the Reconstruction Generation in the Interwar North

The memory of the Reconstruction generation not only persisted in the Great Migration's Northern intellectual institutions but also seeped into the broader cultural life of the Harlem Renaissance. Langston Hughes quietly carried the name of his grandfather, James Mercer Langston, whose brother was the first Black man elected to the US Congress from Virginia. In a 1951 essay for John H. Johnson's *Negro Digest*, Hughes would pull from family memory to depict a vision of Reconstruction-era Washington where "Reconstruction congressmen of color drove from their Washington mansions to the Capitol in the handsomest rigs money could buy behind the finest horses available." Drawing a direct parallel between interwar Harlem and late nineteenth-century Washington, DC, Hughes presented a long history of striving and social mobility—in many ways the afterlife of the vision of racial destiny held by his great uncle's generation—connecting the horse-drawn carriages of yesteryear to the luxury automobiles that Harlem's elites drove during the Roaring Twenties.[49]

The Great Migration unearthed the Lowcountry's specific countermemory in other, more unexpected ways. The Penn School Club, an organization founded by graduates of the famous Lowcountry school who had moved to Harlem, met monthly in the Urban League's 136th Street building. In the process of submitting revisions to the *Journal of Negro History*'s archival project for childhood details that he had initially misremembered, the elderly Henry Wallace recounted a chance encounter with Leigh Whipper, the son of the Reconstruction-era judge and legislator. Neighbors in Harlem, Whipper and Wallace reminisced over nineteenth-century South Carolina politics and the younger man shared key details about his father's life. One of the nation's most prominent Black stage actors, Leigh Whipper had previously used his childhood memory of Beaufort to challenge DuBose Heyward's rendering of the Lowcountry in *Porgy*, the stage play that would eventually become the more well-known opera, *Porgy and Bess*. "One day, Leigh Whipper . . . came to us and introduced himself as a fellow Charlestonian," Heyward explained. "His father had been a judge in South Carolina during the Black Republican Administration following the Civil War."[50]

Over the course of the interwar period, more and more of the pillars of the Black intellectual world migrated to Harlem. *The Crisis*, the *New York Age*, *Opportunity*, *The Messenger*, and the *Negro World* all had their headquarters in the uptown neighborhood. By the 1920s, the 135th Street Branch of the New York Public Library had become the de facto intellectual center of the Harlem Renaissance. Hosting literary gatherings, lectures, and theatrical productions, it captured the spirit that had been present in the lyceums of the late nineteenth century. When the Afro–Puerto Rican bibliophile Arturo Schomburg transferred his collection of more than 4,000 books to the library, the 135th Street Branch became the nation's most important public resource for the study of the African diaspora.[51]

Providing a capstone for this transformative cultural moment, the painter Aaron Douglas was commissioned to paint a four-part series of murals for the 135th Street Branch library as part of a Public Works Administration project. Already well known in Harlem's intellectual and artistic circles, Douglas had developed a modernist style that captured the forward-looking spirit of the New Negro movement. The second panel, "From Slavery to Reconstruction," captured the ongoing importance of Reconstruction as a site of countermemory. Completed the year before W. E. B. Du Bois published *Black Reconstruction*, Douglas was likely aware of Reconstruction's importance not only from private and public discussions with the senior scholar as he completed his book but also from the broader intellectual world, where discussions of the Black past required at least some awareness of Reconstruction's legacy.[52]

Aaron Douglas, "From Slavery to Reconstruction," panel 2 of *Aspects of Negro Life*, 1934. Art and Artifacts Division, Schomburg Center for Research in Black Culture, New York Public Library, New York.

"From Slavery to Reconstruction" distills the countermemory of Reconstruction to its essential themes. Using a muted color palette, Douglas stages the march toward freedom as nightscape—emphasizing this period as a moment of uncertainty. Capturing the era's storm and stress, Douglas's Art Deco mural counterbalances the menacing silhouettes of night-riding Klansmen on the images left side of the painting with faintly outlined Union soldiers on the right side of the image and in the distance. The image's central figure, likely meant to be a Reconstruction-era politician, stands on a pedestal holding a haloed ballot and pointing to a city on a hill in the distance. Flanked on both sides by enslaved men laboring in a cotton field, the politician's centrality to a broader Reconstruction-era Black world recalls the visual tropes of racial destiny that first appeared in *Heroes of the Colored Race*. Unlike the earlier image, Douglas's mural captures a Reconstruction story where the hagiographic elements have either disappeared or been dampened and the vicissitudes of the past era are more present. Offering a hopeful endpoint, an urban mecca just beyond the valley of the shadow, Douglas crystallized the past generation's historical vision within the interwar Black public sphere.

Even counterfeit memories of Reconstruction provided a usable past. Edwin Smalls, a Charlestonian who moved to Harlem in 1917, operated one of the preeminent nightclubs of the Harlem Renaissance. Opened in 1925, Small's Paradise would become a hub for Black night life in New York, eschewing the de facto policy of segregation that led many of the uptown clubs to only

Postcard of the Paradise Room in Smalls Paradise (also called Small's Paradise), ca. 1940. The image of Edwin Smalls is in the upper right-hand corner. Eagle Post Card View Company.

admit white patrons. "Small's Paradise is known the world over and many of the greatest names in show business owe to it their start," remarked one Southern newspaper. A self-made man who had been an elevator operator and the proprietor of a billiard hall before making his mark as the king of the city's interwar Black cabaret world, Smalls used his name and background to connect his own bootstrap story with that of another self-made Lowcountry figure. Claiming to be the grandson of Robert Smalls, Edwin Smalls used the legacy of the Reconstruction-era hero to frame himself and his nightclub in a long, proud tradition that would have been visible to his Black patrons.[53]

This imagined legacy was clearly a fabrication. Born in 1882, Edwin Smalls could have been old enough to be the child of one of Robert Smalls's two daughters, but neither Elizabeth Smalls Bampfield nor Sarah Smalls Williams lived in Charleston. No census, newspaper, or manuscript records identify a male Smalls descendent named Edwin. Most likely, Edwin Smalls recognized that the story possessed enough veneer of truth that his mythic past would not be betrayed in the dim nightclub lights. Part of Harlem's larger cosmopolitan milieu, Smalls's club reminded his Great Migration patrons that their affluent cultural moment had a much longer history.[54]

As Reconstruction's countermemory became a larger part of the twentieth century's new Black cultural centers, it slowly receded from some of the old sites of racial destiny. During World War I, the Bethel Literary and Historical Society would reorganize itself, dropping the "Society" from its name and reconvening as the Bethel Literary and Historical Association. Membership began to flag and the once-robust attendance for the organization's weekly lectures began to drop. An April 1919 visit from W. E. B. Du Bois brought some of the old excitement, with one observer noting, "It has been years since such an immense throng crowded into the auditorium of the Metropolitan AME Church to witness a session of the famous Bethel Literary." By the 1920s, records and reports of the association's meetings became even more sparse, and it appears that by the eve of the Great Depression Bethel Literary had ceased to exist. Any future mention of the once-august organization in the Black press would appear in an obituary of one of the group's former leaders.[55]

The decline of the Bethel Literary and Historical Society was in many ways the final refrain in the Reconstruction generation's long requiem. As the last remaining members of the Reconstruction generation began to pass away during World War I, a nascent cohort of historians took note of what was in danger of being lost. Moreover, as Black Americans left the South in large numbers and the myth of the Lost Cause became the dominant mode of understanding the legacy of the Civil War era, the stories of Reconstruction's political generation, and the political worlds that they built, were increasingly forgotten and erased.

During the interwar years, the fight over the Reconstruction generation's legacy was waged with a new intensity. As its last surviving members began to pass away, a corresponding rise in Lost Cause mythology began to descend across the former hub of Black political power, further diminishing the legacy of Reconstruction in the region. With the US entrance into World War I, a number of social and cultural forces were unleashed that forced white Southerners, on all sides of the political spectrum, to confront the limits of the New South mythos that sought to erase Reconstruction-era political conflict and instead painted the region as a site of long-standing racial harmony. Ultimately, the legacy of the Lowcountry's Reconstruction generation persisted in the interwar civil rights organizations, the early efforts to produce African American history, and through the institutions and ideas that Southern migrants transplanted in Northern cities. While the Reconstruction generation saw their political work undone and erased in their twilight years, the generation who followed them carried their legacy forward into the interwar decades and connected the countermemory of the Lowcountry's lost political generation to the emerging twentieth-century Black freedom struggle.

Epilogue

On March 21, 1940, the student chorus of Robert Smalls High School was scheduled to visit the South Carolina statehouse in Columbia to sing a series of spirituals before the legislature. One of the crown jewels of the fifteen-year-old interwar high school, the choir had traveled the across the country, performing with the likes of Paul Robeson, Marian Anderson, Lionel Hampton, and the Clara Ward Singers. Trained in classical, religious, and secular music, the Robert Smalls High School choir "could sing an anthem, an aria or a popular song, as well as a negro spiritual." Invited by Calhoun Thomas, one of Beaufort County's representatives in the statehouse, Robert Smalls High School's ambitious principal W. Kent Alston was "glad" to sing before the legislators and likely viewed this as an opportunity to showcase the school and its students before a larger audience.[1]

What should have been an uneventful ceremonial affair, however, became mired in a clash of conflicting Southern memories of the Reconstruction era. William Rufus Bradford, a representative from York County in the state's Upcountry, found the invitation of students representing a school named after a Reconstruction-era Black hero an affront to the myth of the Lost Cause. "When we write history, we should write it correctly," he warned. Quoting Benjamin Tillman's nineteenth-century attacks on Smalls, Bradford claimed that the Civil War hero had used the bias of the federal government to unseat his white congressional opponent, and had been part of a political movement that made the Lowcountry unsafe for white people. "If Smalls was not a consummate rascal, there never was one," he charged. The evocation of Reconstruction's memory spurred a larger debate about the legacy of Reconstruction and the current anxiety in the statehouse about an antilynching bill being debated in the US Congress. While some of the state's representatives believed that the invitation for Robert Smalls High School chorus should be rescinded, Representative Calhoun Thomas cautioned that such a move would allow "the negro press [or] leftist organizations" to draw national attention to the state's Jim Crow order and potentially invite further federal interference in Southern politics.[2]

In the decades that followed his passing, Robert Smalls continued to embody a countermemory of Reconstruction through the high school that bore his name. Founded in 1925, Robert Smalls High School was the product of a long struggle to build a Black public school in Beaufort County. The Reconstruction-era building that had been purchased by Smalls and operated by a Black school board during the late nineteenth century had now fallen into disrepair as a result of Jim Crow–era underfunding. The new Robert Smalls High School, a product of grassroots fundraising and political mobilizing, was not only "modern in every way" but also provided the region's Black public-school students their first opportunity to take classes beyond the middle-school level. The new high school offered advanced course work, upper-school grades for teenaged students, and a state-recognized high school diploma.[3]

This was no small feat. When Robert Smalls High School opened, Black high schools were an almost imperceptibly small component of the Southern educational world. Before World War I, fewer than 3 percent of eligible Black students had been enrolled in high school. Black communities in the rural South depended almost entirely on privately funded Rosenwald schools, which often had little more than one room to educate a wide range of students. Most major Southern cities would lack a Black public high school until well into the interwar period. While Black secondary schools were still deeply unequal in terms of funding and access, educational leaders in the urban South slowly saw the need for them—due, in large part, to the inroads that the NAACP had made in the region. Working in conjunction with white Southern liberals, many of whom saw the expansion of Black public education as a worthwhile and important aspect in the larger fight against economic inequality in the region, local Black leaders in major Southern cities demanded public schools that could offer high-achieving Black students the chance to receive a high school diploma.[4]

The first generation of public schools often bore the name of the Black leader most likely to receive support from moderate and conservative white people: Booker T. Washington. In 1915, the first school named after Booker T. Washington was established in Norfolk, Virginia. The following year, a Booker T. Washington High School would open in Columbia, South Carolina. Between 1919 and 1921, the Atlanta chapter of the NAACP led a successful voter registration campaign that created grassroots support for new bonds to establish new Black schools in the city. Opened in 1924, Atlanta's Booker T. Washington High School would become the first Black public high school in the state of Georgia. By the end of World War II, seventeen Black high schools had been named after the Tuskegee educator.[5]

Less documented, however, was the rise of public schools named after Reconstruction-era figures. In 1893, a Black high school named after John Mercer Langston opened in Johnson City, Tennessee. In 1932, another Langston High School was established in Danville, Virginia. In 1912, James Hill, the last Black man to serve in the Mississippi state legislature, established an elementary school for Black children in Jackson, Mississippi, on Lynch Street—named after former congressman John R. Lynch. In 1928, Cardozo Senior High was founded in Northwest Washington, DC. Named after Francis Cardozo, the Charleston-born politician who spent his post-Reconstruction life as an educator in Washington's Black schools, Cardozo High School was a crown jewel in the city's preintegration Black world. These schools were established in communities where a countermemory of the Reconstruction era persisted, and they remained an important part of the deeper lessons that parents, teachers, and school leaders sought to impart to students.[6]

The students who attended these schools were given a more robust vision of Reconstruction's countermemory than those who passed through the region's early twentieth-century industrial schools. In his 1945 memoir *Black Boy*, Richard Wright remarked on how attending the Jim Hill School in the 1920s changed his life. "Until I entered Jim Hill Public school, I had had but one year of unbroken study.... Though I was not aware of it, the next four years were to be the only opportunity for formal study in my life." James E. Mayo, a Cardozo graduate, played a pivotal role in shaping Black cultural life in Washington during the 1960s and 1970s.[7]

Robert Smalls High School was a part of this important but often-overlooked strand of twentieth-century countermemory. Initially led by Daniel W. Bythewood, a longtime local pastor and political leader, the school quickly became the hub of the Jim Crow–era Black Lowcountry. Graduations and pageants brought community leaders as keynote speakers and invited guests. Unlike the region's industrial schools, Robert Smalls High School supported a rich set of extracurricular options for its students. In addition to its nationally known choir, Robert Smalls also boasted a prestigious marching band, an active theater repertoire, and a talented debate society. A rich sporting culture took hold at Robert Smalls High School and the "Generals" football team became the pride of Beaufort, playing other Black high schools across the state and finishing its season competing in the "Oyster Bowl Classic," a New Year's Day rivalry game meant to capture the spirit of the high-stakes contests that became popular in Black college football in the immediate aftermath of World War II.[8]

Robert Smalls High School marching band, 1940s. Winifred Kent Alston Papers, Avery Research Center, College of Charleston, South Carolina.

The school took a giant step forward in national prominence under the leadership of W. Kent Alston. A graduate of South Carolina State College in Orangeburg, Alston promised to make Robert Smalls High School "the Biggest Little School East of the Mississippi."

Under his leadership, student groups traveled far and wide, participating in parades and contests in nearby Southern cities, as well as the nation's capital. Alston also managed to bring mid-twentieth-century Black America's most prominent figures to Robert Smalls High School. Mary McLeod Bethune, Benjamin Mays, and Mordecai Johnson all delivered keynote addresses during his tenure as principal. Less than two months after the school chorus sang before the state legislature, Zora Neale Hurston gave an address to students and faculty based on her Southern folklore research. A makeshift boxing ring was built on the school's football field to host a boxing exhibition between Joe Louis and a local amateur. A ceaseless striver who refused to take no for an answer, Alston was likely assisted by the cultural gravity of the school's name—one that held an outsized place in Black collective memory.[9]

Perhaps no figure reflected the long afterlife of Reconstruction's countermemory more than Sara Dunlap Jackson. Born in interwar Columbia, South Carolina, Jackson graduated from Booker T. Washington High in 1938. Upon graduating from Johnson C. Smith University, she took a job teaching at

Archivist Sara Dunlap Jackson, 1955. Public Relations Photographs Relating to National Archives Personnel, Facilities, and Events, 1939–1968, RG 64, National Archives II, College Park, Maryland.

Robert Smalls High School under Principal W. Kent Alston. Shortly after the end of World War II, Jackson left the Lowcountry for Washington, DC, finding that the nation's capital offered greater opportunities and financial security than teaching in one of the state's most underfunded school districts. Taking a position at the National Archives, Jackson would play a crucial role in shepherding a generation of scholars through the then mostly unused and unprocessed records of the Freedmen's Bureau.[10]

The organization of these records, which became the foundation for the groundbreaking Freedmen and Southern Society Project, as well as much of the scholarship on Reconstruction produced in the post–civil rights era, would have been impossible without Jackson. "It is no exaggeration to say that history rests, to a considerable measure, on the work of Sara Jackson," memorialized Ira Berlin, one of the historians who helped found the Freedmen and Southern Society Project. "The young historians and archivists who were taught by Sara Jackson—her boys and her girls—and I proudly number myself among them—learned many things, and not all of them came out of a Hollinger box."[11]

Sara Jackson arrived in Washington from a world that had been built by the Reconstruction generation. She grew up in the shadow of the statehouse where Robert Elliott and William Whipper led the Republican Party, the salon where the Rollin sisters curated Reconstruction's political culture, and the cemetery that honored some of the era's martyrs. She began her teaching career at a Lowcountry school named after Robert Smalls, the champion of the most important political center in the Reconstruction-era South. In her archival labor and legacy, their memory, and the memory of their generation, would live on.

Acknowledgments

In many ways, this book is a history of debt. In trying to examine the world of the Reconstruction generation, especially the world that they inherited and the dreams they tried to pass along their successors, I have gained my series of obligations to those who came before me and paved the intellectual toll roads that I know travel. These debts are not the burdens of future bankruptcy—hopefully—but the ties of mentorship, academic friendship, and deep mutuality. I am honored to offer a small repayment here for those who helped me make this book possible.

I want to begin by acknowledging my undergraduate mentors at Williams College: Gretchen Long, for making African American history feel like a place of excitement and discovery; Tess Chakkalakal and David L. Smith, for showing the highest frequency version of the Black intellectual tradition; and Kenda Mutongi and Shanti Singh, for providing a wayward Americanist the guidance and mentorship on a senior thesis on African history. Finally, a deep thank you to Molly Magavern for seeing academic potential early in me and guiding me into the Mellon Mays Undergraduate Fellowship.

The MMUF changed the arc of my life. The broader MMUF world made this profession feel habitable. It showed me that academic history was not only a possible career path but worth pursuing in the face of the professoriate's past barriers and current obstacles. It also showed me that academic history could be a place of intellectual flourishing and rich sociality. Thank you to Cally Waite for stewarding the world of Mellon Graduate Initiatives and sustaining the network of conferences, writing retreats, and professional workshops that brought multiple generations of scholars, from early-stage graduate students to tenured faculty. It is impossible to fully detail how meaningful the support from Mellon has been for me.

I began my journey into African American history as a high school teacher in Mississippi. My time in Jackson brought an invaluable assemblage of great mentors and friends who made me a better thinker, a better teacher, and a better human being. Thank you to my friends in the Mississippi Teacher Corps, the faculty and staff at Jim Hill High School, and, most important, the students and athletes I worked with at Jim Hill and Powell. You understand American history in ways that few will ever comprehend.

At the University of Maryland, I received the best possible academic training at the University of Maryland. Leslie Rowland, thank you for your high expectations, endless patience, and deep commitment to graduate mentoring. You have been a true model of the historian's craft and I am better scholar because of your guidance. Elsa Barkley Brown, your presence has meant the world to me, and I am deeply thankful that you were a part of my journey to the PhD. Chris Bonner, David Freund, and Edlie Wong provided invaluable feedback on my dissertation, and I am deeply grateful to have had you on my committee. Finally, I am deeply honored to have had Ira Berlin as a mentor, dissertation committee member, and all-around North Star during my time at Maryland. Your humor, your generosity, and your brilliance made Francis Scott Key Hall a special place to study the past.

To my former colleagues at the University of Pittsburgh and at St. John's University, Robin Brooks, Michell Chresfield, Vincent Leung, and Molly Warsh, thank you for making my short time in Pittsburgh memorable; Dohra Ahmad, Natalie Byfield, Raj Chetty, Jeremy Cruz, Philip Misevich, Susie Pak, Bobby Riveira, Anthony Rodriguez, Nerina Rustomji, LaToya Sawyer, Lequez Spearman, Konrad Tuscherer, and Lara Vapnek, thank you for making my time in Queens intellectually rich.

I am deeply thankful to all of my colleagues at the University of Tennessee for making Knoxville a more hospitable and hopeful place, especially for the friendship of Luke Harlow, who despite his misguided appreciation for all things Philadelphia has a compass that always points in the right direction. I cannot thank Latoya Eaves, Beau Gaitors, Larry Perry, Deadric Williams, and Brandon Winford enough for being expert community builders and bread breakers.

This book would not be possible without the expertise and labor of a considerable number of archivists. To the various staff members at the Library of Congress, National Archives II, the South Carolina Department of Archives and History, the Southern Historical Collection at the Wilson Library, the Rockefeller Archives Center, the Beaufort County Historical Collection, the Avery Center, and the Schomburg Library, thank you. And to Chris Barr, Rich Condon, and Olivia Williams, thank you for your work in preserving Reconstruction's legacy and orchestrating the world of documents at the National Park Service in Beaufort. Your efforts are the only way that any of this happens.

Several organizations and institutions have provided critical support for this project over its long journey. I would like to express my deep gratitude to the Social Science Research Council, the Woodrow Wilson Foundation, the University of Maryland's College of Arts and Sciences, St. Johns University's College of Arts and Sciences, and the Denbo Center for the Humanities and Arts for providing, time, space, and resources to complete this book.

The Institute for Responsible Citizenship has been my deepest place of community over the past two decades. Bill Keyes, thank you for bringing me into the brotherhood and continuing to believe in me. Dr. W. B. Allen, thank you for your years of crafting a rigorous and deeply humanistic classroom. Thank you for entrusting that responsibility to me. To my brothers in the program, Chris Binns, Calvin Hadley, Elijah Heyward, Julian Hill, Stefan Lallinger, Christien Oliver, and Chuck Redmond, you all made the DC years a truly great era. To all the Washington scholars I have taught over the years, thank you for making me a better teacher.

Shanna Greene Benjamin, Amy Murrell Taylor, Nicole Myers Turner, Elizabeth Todd-Breiland, and Kidada Williams have all read previous iterations of material from this book. Thank you so much for your support and your generosity. A special thank you to Greg Downs and Kate Masur for all of your mentorship over the years. The world that you have built at the *Journal of the Civil War* is capacious in the best way, and I'm honored to play a small part in shaping the house that you built.

To all my friends near and far—Chimaobi Amutah, Ashley Brown, Sam Brown, Aimee Chambers, Jaris Cole, Thomas Cuffie, Jeff Delaney, Brian Doyle, Burgess Everett, Kali Gairy, Justin Hudson, Ifiok Inyang, Aaron Jenkins, Deyon Johnson, Illunga Kalala, the Knoxville BBQ Crew, Dana Leary, Asia Leeds, Leroy Lindsay, Charles Lomax, LaKenya Middlebrook, Kody Manke-Miller, Brandon Mirach, Kellen Williams Jamaal Mobley, Paul

Ricketts, Latesha Smith, Noah Susskind—you have all given me true abundance in friendship. Finally, to Seulghee Lee, it's been a genuine joy to count you as a friend through the arc of this journey.

My family has seen this book through all its ups and downs. To my brothers Samuel and William I am so proud of both of you—I am rooting for you two with all my heart. To Joyce, thank you for all that you do. To Aunt Nadine and Aunt Gina—thank you for always checking in on me and keeping me connected and grounded. To my cousins Marlena and Nia and Tricia—thank you for blazing the path first and showing the way. To Lauren and William Colson, you all are my oldest friends and will always be family. Libby, I am amazed at the life that you have built and draw inspiration from your courage and clarity. You, and Jose, and Calie remind me of all that is good in the world. Allison, you have always been a North Star, and I am lucky to be your brother. Dad, thank you for always believing in me. I am always honored to be your son and try every day to make you proud. Mom, thank you for giving me a love of books, for history, and a sense of what is good and just. I cannot thank you enough for all the ways that you have poured into me and helped me see the world with open eyes and an open heart.

Notes

Introduction

1. "The Bethel Literary," *Washington Bee*, January 27, 1883; Cromwell, *History of the Bethel Literary and Historical Association*, 10; Holt, *Black over White*, 76, 150, 185–89, 198; chap. 5; Pike, *Prostrate State*, 199; Department of Commerce and Labor, Bureau of the Census, Official Registrar of the United States, Containing a List of the Officers and Employees in the Civil, Military, and Naval Service, vol. 1 (1883).

2. "Reconstruction," *National Republican* (Washington, DC), January 27, 1883; "Bethel Literary."

3. Holt, *Black over White*, 185–86; Ione, *Pride of Family*, 196; "Reconstruction."

4. Cromwell, *History of the Bethel Literary and Historical Association*, 10; Holt, *Black over White*, 208–10; Parry, "Radical Experiment of South Carolina"; "Bethel Literary."

5. Rose, *Rehearsal for Reconstruction*.

6. Scholars of the Civil War and African American history have long used "generation" as a framework for understanding the Black past. See Berlin, *Many Thousands Gone*; Gronningsater, *Rising Generation*; and Lewis, *Shadows of Youth*. On recent uses of "generation" to understand twenty-first-century Black life, see Alexander, *Trayvon Generation*; and Reed, *South*.

7. On political generations, see Braungart and Braungart, "Life-Course and Generational Politics." Recently, Van Gosse and Kate Masur have highlighted the various ways that Black Americans voted, held office, and shaped previously unexplored movements in the North and Midwest for political and civil rights during the early national and antebellum periods. Gosse, *First Reconstruction*; Masur, *Until Justice Be Done*.

8. On the memory work of white Southerners and academic historians in creating silences in the history of Reconstruction, see Blight, *Race and Reunion*; Brundage, *Southern Past*; and Lowery and Smith, *Dunning School*. For an account that frames the interwar Lost Generation in the context of its broader cultural milieu, see Cohen, *Last Call at the Hotel Imperial*.

9. Blight, *Race and Reunion*, 53; Penn, *Afro-American Press*, 186. Penn cites an undated Ida B. Wells quote that was initially published in the *Detroit Plaindealer* under her pseudonym "Iola." On the broader discussion of confronting the funereal in Black life, see Manigault-Bryant, *Talking to the Dead*; Roediger, "And Die in Dixie"; and Sharpe, *In the Wake*. In thinking about melancholy as a generation-defining framework, I also draw on the rich literature on emotional history. For a short overview, see Matt, *Cultural History of the Emotions*; Stearns, *American Cool*; and Woods, *Emotional and Sectional Conflict*.

10. Over the course of this book, the definition for the term "countermemory" most closely corresponds with the following framing by George Lipsitz: "Unlike historical narratives that begin with the totality of human existence and then locate specific actions and events within that totality, counter-memory starts with the particular and the specific and then builds outward toward a total story. Counter-memory looks to the past for the hidden histories excluded from dominant narratives. But unlike myths that seek to detach events

and actions from the fabric of any larger history, counter-memory forces revision of existing histories by supplying new perspectives about the past." Lipsitz, "History, Myth, and Counter-memory," 213.

11. On the cultural struggle over sectional reconciliation, see Blight, *Race and Reunion*, 98–139; Janney, *Remembering the Civil War*; Prince, *Stories of the South*; and Silber, *Romance of Reunion*. For the major themes of the sectional reconciliation historiography, see Silber, "Reunion and Reconciliation."

12. On the battles over race and memory in the late nineteenth century, see Blight, *Race and Reunion*; Brundage, *Southern Past*; Gannon, *Won Cause*; Blair, *Cities of the Dead*; Kachun, *Festivals of Freedom*; and Clark, *Defining Moments*. The historical work focusing solely on Reconstruction's legacy in American memory remains painfully small. Key works include Baker, *What Reconstruction Meant*; Baker and Emberton, *Remembering Reconstruction*; and West, "Remembering Reconstruction in Its Twilight."

13. Harper, "Democratic Return to Power"; Du Bois, *Souls of Black Folk*, 38–39.

14. Hall, *Faithful Account of the Race*, chap. 5.

15. Gates, *Stony the Road*, 185–96. On racial destiny, see Mitchell, *Righteous Propagation*; Johnson, *No Future in This Country*; and Brundage, "Working in the 'Kingdom of Culture.'" On linked fate, see Dawson, *Behind the Mule*.

16. On structures of feeling, see Williams, *Marxism and Literature*, 128–35; and Sharma and Tygstrup, *Structures of Feeling*. On works of US history that model a sensitivity to a structure of feeling, see Ayers, *Promise of the New South*; Peiss, *Cheap Amusements*; and Hartman, *Wayward Lives, Beautiful Experiments*. In her cultural history of James Weldon Johnson's hymn, "Life Every Voice and Sing," Imani Perry has provided the fullest and most textured examination of this generational maker's mark. Perry, *May We Forever Stand*, chap 1.

17. On the postbellum talented tenth and elite capture, see Blakely, "Richard Greener and the 'Talent Tenth's' Dilemma"; and Táíwò, *Elite Capture*, chap. 2.

18. On the role of gender in shaping the postbellum Black public sphere, see Barkley Brown, "Negotiating and Transforming the Public Sphere"; Jones, *All Bound Up Together*, chap. 6; and Mitchell, *Righteous Propagation*.

19. On the limits of countermemory in understanding the production of Black history, see Glymph, "Liberty Dearly Bought"; Green, *Unforgettable Sacrifice*.

20. Trouillot, *Silencing the Past*. On the struggle over the assemblage of historical fact and the late nineteenth-century historical archive in the United States, Lewis, *Unseen Truth*.

21. On wartime reconstruction in the South Carolina Lowcountry, see Rose, *Rehearsal for Reconstruction*; Saville, *Work of Reconstruction*; and Williamson, *After Slavery*.

22. Nora, "Between Memory and History," 23; Sinha, *Rise and Fall*. On the field of memory studies more broadly, see Halbwachs, *On Collective Memory*; Lipsitz, *Time Passages*; Hobsbawm and Ranger, *Invention of Tradition*; and Trouillot, *Silencing the Past*. The literature on the Lowcountry during the Civil War era would be impossible to fully recount here. For a brief overview, see Rose, *Rehearsal for Reconstruction*; Saville, *Work of Reconstruction*; Schwalm, *Hard Fight for We*; Wise et al., *Rebellion, Reconstruction, and Redemption*; and Miller, *Gullah Statesman*.

23. For an example of the anti-Black accounts of South Carolina in the Northern press, see Pike, *Prostrate State*.

24. Anderson, *Imagined Communities*. On the postbellum Black press, see Barkley Brown, "Negotiating and Transforming the Public Sphere"; Penn, *Afro-American Press*; Gardner, *Black Print Unbound*; Suggs, *Black Press in the South*; and Alexander, "T. Thomas Fortune."

25. On the quantitative turn in Gilded Age Black life, see Womack, *Matter of Black Living*.

26. On Black geographies in the postbellum South, see Anderson, *Race and Politics in North Carolina*; Barkley Brown and Kimball, "Mapping the Terrain of Black Richmond"; Behrend, *Reconstructing Democracy*; Woods, *Development Arrested*; and Davis, *Emancipation Circuit*.

27. Moses, *Golden Age of Black Nationalism*.

28. For works that examine Black counterpublic life during the Jim Crow era, see Hartman, *Wayward Lives*; Haley, *No Mercy Here*; Harris, *Sex Workers, Psychics and Numbers Runners*; and Roane, "Plotting the Black Commons." For a more theoretical examination of the cultural politics of Black undergrounds, see Moten and Harney, *Undercommons*; and Hall et al., "Subcultures, Cultures and Class."

29. On the production of Jim Crow–era Black countermemory, see Brundage, *Southern Past*, 138–82; Holloway, *Jim Crow Wisdom*; Perry, *May We Forever Stand*; Prince, *Ballad of Robert Charles*; Behrend, "Facts, Memories, and History."

Chapter 1

1. Gatewood, "'Remarkable Misses Rollin,'" 176; Ione, *Pride of Family*, 130. On Charleston's antebellum free black population, see Berlin, *Slaves without Masters*; and Powers, *Black Charlestonians*. On Philadelphia's Institute for Colored Youth and the city's antebellum Black elite, see Favors, *Shelter in a Time of Storm*, chap. 1; and Greenidge, *Grimkes*, chaps. 1, 3, 7.

2. Stevenson, *Journals of Charlotte Forten Grimké*; Wright, *Centennial Encyclopedia*, 111; Fields-Black, *Combee*; "Martin R. Delany Counsels Freedmen: Address to Freedmen on St. Helena Island," July 28, 1865, Records Group 105, Letters Received, Assistant Commissioner, South Carolina, National Archives and Records Administration, Washington, DC.

3. "Diary of Frances Anne Rollin, 1868," Smithsonian Digital Volunteers: Transcription Center, 2025, https://transcription.si.edu/project/28477; Ione, *Pride of Family*, 108–11. On Boston's Black elite world, see Kantrowitz, *More than Freedom*.

4. Rollin, *Life and Public Services*, 229; Rollin, *Life and Public Services*, 7. On Frances Rollin's role in shaping a Black history of the Civil War era, see Lande, "Black Badge of Courage."

5. Rollin, *Life and Public Services*, 299.

6. Freedpeople's struggles over family autonomy and their place within the new free labor regime have long occupied a central place in the histories of emancipation and Reconstruction. For a brief overview of the historiography, see Berlin et al., *Slaves No More*; Foner, *Reconstruction*; Saville, *Work of Reconstruction*; Schwalm, *Hard Fight for We*; Williams, *Help Me to Find My People*; Penningroth, *Claims of Kinfolk*; and Hunter, *Bound in Wedlock*.

7. On Black abolitionist world-building, see Berlin, *Long Emancipation*; Foreman, *Colored Conventions Movement*; Rael, *Black Protest and Black Identity*; Kantrowitz, *More than Freedom*; Gronningsater, *Rising Generation*; and Bonner, *Remaking the Republic*. On the Port Royal Experiment, see Rose, *Rehearsal for Reconstruction*; and Ochiai, "Port Royal Experiment Revisited."

8. Jones, *All Bound Up Together*.

9. Berlin et al., *Wartime Genesis of Free Labor*; Camp, *Closer to Freedom*. On wartime Black geographies, see Taylor, *Embattled Freedom*; and Cooper, "'Away I Goin' to Find My Mamma.'" On the legacy of Stephanie Camp's work in African American history broadly and the recent literature on slavery in particular, see Bonner, "Possessed."

10. On South Carolina's colonial slave society and the intellectual world of its antebellum elite, see Wood, *Black Majority*; Morgan, *Slave Counterpoint*; Berlin, *Many Thousands Gone*; Carney, *Black Rice*; Faust, *James Henry Hammond*; O'Brien and Moltke-Hansen, *Intellectual Life in Antebellum Charleston*; Fraser, *Charleston! Charleston!*; and McCurry, *Masters of Small Worlds*.

11. Sternhell, *Routes of War*, 96; Pierce, *Negroes at Port Royal*; Taylor, *Embattled Freedom*, chap. 2.

12. Taylor, *Embattled Freedom*, chaps. 1–5; Berlin et al., *Slaves No More*, 38–40.

13. Rose, *Rehearsal for Reconstruction*; Williams, *Self-Taught*, 35–36, 39. On the range of antislavery thought in the nineteenth-century United States, see Oakes, *Freedom National*; and Jones, *Vanguard*, 108–9.

14. Higginson, *Army Life in a Black Regiment*, chap. 1; Berlin et al., *Slaves No More*, 187–234; Willis, *Black Civil War Soldier*; Fields-Black, *Combee*.

15. Miller, *Gullah Statesman*, 23.

16. By 1880, Beaufort County contained nearly 4,000 family-owned farms, one of the highest rates of Black landownership in the country. Schweninger, *Black Property Owners*; Wise et al., *Rebellion, Reconstruction, and Redemption*, 497–98. For a stunning new synthesis on the meaning of Sherman's March in reshaping the Lowcountry's social and cultural geography, see Parten, *Somewhere toward Freedom*.

17. On the Freedmen's Bureau and its work in South Carolina, Abbott, *Freedmen's Bureau in South Carolina*; Foner, *Nothing but Freedom*, chap. 3. See also Lowe, "Freedman's Bureau"; Saville, *Work of Reconstruction*, chaps. 4–5; and Schwalm, "'Sweet Dreams of Freedom.'"

18. Capt. Charles C. Soule to Maj. Gen. O. O. Howard, [June 12, 1865], enclosing an address "To the Freed People of Orangeburg District"; and Maj. Gen. O. O. Howard to Capt. Charles C. Soule, [June 21, 1865], S-17 1865, Letters Received, Series 15, Washington Headquarters, Bureau of Refugees, Freedmen, & Abandoned Lands, Records Group 105, National Archives and Records Administration, Washington, DC; Saville, *Work of Reconstruction*, 79–85.

19. James Lynch, "Letter from South Carolina," *Christian Recorder*, January 16, 1864.

20. Letter from J. J. Wright, *Christian Recorder*, September 23, 1865; Sarah Bram and Jennie Lynch, "A Great Movement in South Carolina," *Anglo-African*, August 26, 1865.

21. Schwarz, "Reluctant Judge"; Gatewood, "Remarkable Misses Rollin," 177; 1st Lt. Edward M. Stoeber to Brev. Maj. S. M. Taylor, 24 July 1865, in Hahn et al., *Land and Labor*, 254–59. For another account of Delany's speech, see Memorandum by 2d Lieut. Alexander Whyte Jr., July 23, 1865, in Berlin et al., *Black Military Experience*, 739–41; and Holt, *Black over White*, 73–76. On the Freedmen's Bureau in South Carolina, see Abbott, *Freedmen's Bureau*.

22. Strickland, *Unequal Freedoms*; US Census Bureau, "Population of Civil Divisions Less Than Counties. Table III—State of South Carolina," in *1870 Census*, vol. 1, *The Statistics of the Population of the United States*, 258, www2.census.gov/library/publications/decennial/1870/population/1870a-25.pdf; Blassingame, "Before the Ghetto," 474. On free Black communities in the antebellum Lowcountry, see Berlin, *Slaves without Masters*; and Powers, *Black Charlestonians*.

23. "Population of South Carolina," 258–60. On the role that the Lowcountry's racial demographics played in the postbellum political order, see Foner, *Nothing but Freedom*.

24. Walker, "A.M.E. Church," 10–12; Kachun, "Interrogating the Silences," 651. On the broader importance of the AME Church during the Civil War era, see Dickerson, *African Methodist Episcopal Church*, 108–56.

25. Gardner, "Remembered (Black) Readers," 233, 236. On the making of the postbellum circuit of Black political thought, see Davis, *Emancipation Circuit*.

26. Gardner, "Remembered (Black) Readers," 240; Jane M. Lynch, "Letter from a Teacher of Freedmen's School in S.C.: Christmas and New Year's in South Carolina," *Christian Recorder*, February 7, 1866. On the limits of the AME Church's missionary work, see Davidson, *Dominican Crossroads*.

27. "Worthy of Attention," *Christian Recorder*, March 9, 1867; "The Political Meeting at Beaufort, S.C.," *Christian Recorder*, May 4, 1867. On the rise of the Republican Party in the Lowcountry, see Miller, *Gullah Statesman*; Gelston, "Radical versus Straight-Out"; and Kelly, "Black Laborers."

28. "Address," *New National Era*, November 2, 1871.

29. Barkley Brown, "Negotiating and Transforming the Public Sphere"; Hahn, *Nation under Our Feet*.

30. Gatewood, "'Remarkable Misses Rollin'"; *New York Sun*, March 29, 1871.

31. Masur, *Example for All the Land*, 159–60; Turner, *Soul Liberty*; Cheek and Cheek, *John Mercer Langston*; Wolfe, "Idol of the Negroes"; Bollinger, "North Comes South"; Asch and Musgrove, *Chocolate City*, 168.

32. Underwood and Burke, *At Freedom's Door*, 73.

33. "The Good Cause Progressing," *Christian Recorder*, August 3, 1867; Burke, *All for Civil Rights*, 224–25.

34. William Elliott III, "Reminisce" (n.p., 1941), 86, in Elliott Family Papers, South Caroliniana Library, University of South Carolina, Columbia; Pike, *Prostrate State*; Simkins and Woody, *South Carolina during Reconstruction*. For an example of the cultural afterlife of the Lowcountry's Reconstruction-era Black attorneys, see the Simon Frasier character in DuBose Heyward's *Porgy*.

35. Coulter, "Aaron Alpeoria Bradley," part 2, 170–71.

36. "Republican State Convention of South Carolina—Colored President," *Christian Recorder*, May 18, 1867; "Colored Lawyer from Pennsylvania," *Christian Recorder*, March 23, 1867; "Oliver Otis Howard," *New National Era*, February 9, 1871.

37. On the Civil War–era Black press, see Fagan, *Black Newspaper*; Gardner, *Black Print Unbound*; Spires, *Practice of Citizenship*; and Jackson, "'Cultural Stronghold'"; Letter from J. W. Wright, *Christian Recorder*, September 23, 1865; "The Republican State Convention of South Carolina—Colored President," *Christian Recorder*, May 18, 1867.

38. *New National Era*, December 7, 1871; Jennie Lynch, "Letter from a Teacher of Freedmen's School in S.C.," *Christian Recorder*, February 7, 1866; Letter from J. W. Wright, *Christian Recorder*, September 23, 1865. On Ethiopianism, see Moses, *Golden Age of Black Nationalism*.

39. Brock, "Thomas W. Cardozo"; Wynes, "T. McCants Stewart," 311–17; McKivigan, "Stalwart Douglass."

40. "Condition of the Freedman," *Morning Republican* (Little Rock, AR), August 10, 1871; "Revolutions Going Backward," *Weekly Louisianian* (New Orleans), May 18, 1872. On Robert Brown Elliott and his nineteenth-century political celebrity, see Lamson, *Glorious Failure*, 117–32.

41. "Revolutions Going Backward"; "Plain Talk from a Black Congressman," *Weekly Louisianian* (New Orleans), March 28, 1874.

42. On the conservative turn in the Northern press's coverage of Reconstruction in South Carolina, see Richardson, *Death of Reconstruction*; Prince, *Stories of the South*; and Summers, *Press Gang*.

43. "Letter to Major Delany (from Douglass)," *New National Era*, August 31, 1871.

44. Edwards, *Savings and Trust*, chap. 7; "South Carolina," *New National Era*, August 6, 1874; Lamson, *Glorious Failure*, 205.

Chapter 2

1. "Rikers Island–Trained USCT Regiments' Chaplains," New York Correction History Society, accessed June 28, 2025, www.correctionhistory.org/html/chronicl/cw-usct/2rikersusctchaplains.html.

2. Taylor, *Negro in South Carolina*, 383; Holt, *Black over White*, 131–34; Du Bois, *Black Reconstruction*, chap. 7.

3. On Benjamin Randolph's assassination, see Zuczek, *State of Rebellion*, 54–57, 60.

4. Downs, *After Appomattox*, 2–10, 179–236.

5. Williams, *They Left Great Marks on Me*. More recently, scholars have begun to take seriously the invisible marks of violence and trauma in the lives of freedpeople and their families. See Emberton, *To Walk About in Freedom*; and Williams, *I Saw Death Coming*.

6. On the idea of rival geography in African American history, see Camp, *Closer to Freedom*; and Johnson, *Slavery's Metropolis*.

7. Elias Hill, "KKK Testimony," July 25, 1871, in *Report of the Joint Select Committee to Inquire into the Condition of Affairs in the Late Insurrectionary States* (Washington, DC, 1872), 5:1406–16. On the Upcountry Klan and the Ku Klux Klan trials, see Parsons, *Ku-Klux*; Williams, *They Left Great Marks on Me*; Williams, *Great South Carolina Ku Klux Klan Trials*; and Zuczek, *State of Rebellion*.

8. *Journal of the House of Representatives of the State of South Carolina*, 14.

9. *Journal of the House of Representatives of the State of South Carolina*, 15–16, 44–45.

10. Baker, *This Mob Will Surely Take My Life*. On struggles within South Carolina's Republican Party, see Holt, *Black over White*; and Kelly, "Black Laborers."

11. Holt, *Black over White*, 116.

12. Foner, *Freedom's Lawmakers*, 87; Levine, *Martin Delany*, 224–48; *New York Times*, February 21, 1874; Painter, "Martin R. Delany."

13. Kantrowitz, "One Man's Mob Is Another Man's Militia," 68–71; "War Clouds in South Carolina," *New York Herald*, May 4, 1871. On the political and social role of South Carolina's Black militias, see Emberton, *Beyond Redemption*, 136–67; and Proctor, "'From the Cradle to the Grave.'"

14. *Reports and Resolutions of the General Assembly*; Miller, *Gullah Statesman*, 160–64.

15. "Escaped from His Bond," *Charleston Daily News*, January 2, 1872.

"Emancipation Day," *Charleston Daily News*, January 2, 1872.

16. Duncan, *Freedom's Shore*, 23–25, 67–68; "Emancipation Day: Grand Celebration in Beaufort," *The Crescent* (Beaufort, SC), January 4, 1872.

17. "War Clouds in South Carolina," *New York Herald*, May 4, 1871; "A False Alarm," *Charleston Daily Courier*, May 8, 1871; Kantrowitz, "One Man's Mob Is Another Man's Militia," 67. On broader legacy of Reconstruction-era violence, see Emberton, *Beyond Redemption*.

18. "Emancipation Day: Grand Celebration in Beaufort," *The Republican* (Beaufort, SC), January 4, 1872.

19. Holt, *Black over White*, 194.

20. "From South Carolina," *New National Era*, August 13, 1874.

21. Allen, *Governor Chamberlain's Administration*, 193–94, 228; "Will Vote for Chamberlain if Nominated, but Condemn His Action on Whipper Judgeship," *Port Royal Standard (SC) and Commercial*, August 3, 1876.

22. Allen, *Governor Chamberlain's Administration*, 198. On the Hamburg Massacre, see Harris et al., "After Slavery."

23. *An Address to the People of the United States*; Baker, *What Reconstruction Meant*, 19.

24. Allen, *Governor Chamberlain's Administration*, 68–69.

25. Kelly, "Black Laborers," 395; "Gov. Chamberlain at Beaufort," *Port Royal (SC) Standard and Commercial*, July 20, 1876.

26. "The Meaning of Hamburg," *Portland (ME) Daily Press*, July 26, 1876.

27. "The Black Reign of Terror," *Charleston News and Courier*, September 15, 1876; Hahn, *Nation under Our Feet*, 348; Robert Smalls to Daniel Chamberlain, August 24, 1876, Daniel Chamberlain Papers, South Carolina Department of Archives and History, Columbia.

28. "Freedmen's Savings and Trust Company," *New Era* (Washington, DC), May 10, 1870. On the Freedmen's Bank, see Baradaran, *Color of Money*; Edwards, *Savings and Trust*; Stein and Yannelis, "Financial Inclusion"; and Davis, "Bankless in Beaufort."

29. *Charleston News and Courier*, October 14, 1876.

30. *The Crescent* (Beaufort, SC), April 7, 1875.

31. Holt, *By One Vote*; "The 'Palmetto' of the Future," *Charleston News and Courier*, January 3, 1878.

32. *Beaufort (SC) Tribune and Port Royal Commercial*, October 25, 1877. On the antebellum history of Beaufort County's white yeomen, especially how they came to support the Democratic Party, see McCurry, *Masters of Small Worlds*.

33. "The Campaign in Hampton," *Charleston News and Courier*, October 22, 1878; "Hampton County," *Charleston News and Courier*, September 4, 1878; "South Carolina News," *Winnsboro (SC) News and Herald*, March 19, 1878; "Good for Gillisonville," *Charleston News and Courier*, October 28, 1878.

34. "Good for Gillisonville," *Charleston News and Courier*, October 28, 1878.

35. *Charleston News and Courier*, October 30, 1878; "Hampton County," *Charleston News and Courier*, September 4, 1878.

36. "Matters in the State: Smalls Talks of Withdrawing from the Race for Congress," *Charleston News and Courier*, October 30, 1878.

37. Holland, *Letters and Diary of Laura Towne*, 291; "Matters in the State."

38. Holland, *Letters and Diary of Laura Towne*, 291; "Work of the Red-Shirted White Liners," *Juniata (PA) Sentinel and Republican*, November 27, 1878.

39. Holland, *Letters and Diary of Laura Towne*, 291.

40. "South Carolina News," *Yorkville (SC) Enquirer*, October 10, 1878; "The Great Day at Lawtonville," *Charleston News and Courier*, October 22, 1878; "Matters in the State," *Charleston News and Courier*, October 30, 1878. On the cultural power of the color blue in African American history, see Perry, *Black in Blues*.

41. As scholars of postemancipation Black women's history have demonstrated, self-fashioning and the "will to adorn" constituted a critical part of the transition from slavery to freedom. See Glymph, *Out of the House of Bondage*, chap. 7.

42. "Small's Defeat," *National Republican* (Washington, DC), November 15, 1878; "By Foul Means if Not by Fair," *New York Times*, August 19, 1878; "Small's Defeat," *National Republican* (Washington, DC), November 15, 1878.

43. "Southern Crimes: Report of the Teller Committee," *Scranton (PA) Tribune*, February 28, 1879; "The South: Removals Hinted At," *Chicago Tribune*, December 28, 1878. On the Teller Committee, see Williams, *They Left Great Marks on Me*, 65–66, 68.

44. Painter, "Soul Murder and Slavery," chap. 1; "Ex-Governor Chamberlain on Negro Rule," *Union (SC) Times*, September 16, 1904; Egerton, "Terrorized African-Americans Found Their Champion." Robert Smalls likely arrived at the 50,000 figure from his friend John Edward Bruce, who quoted the same number of Reconstruction-era deaths in an 1891 article. Crowder, *John Edward Bruce*, 73–74.

45. "Randolph Cemetery," National Park Service, last updated June 23, 2022, www.nps.gov/places/randolph-cemetery.htm.

Chapter 3

1. "The Negro's Paradise," *Weekly Louisianian* (New Orleans), January 10, 1880. On Hayes's struggles and Grant's third presidential campaign, see Waugh, *U.S. Grant*, 155–66.

2. "Grant's Flying Trip through the South: How the People Act and What They Say," *Daily Inter Ocean*, January 15, 1880; "Grant at Beaufort," *New York Times*, January 10, 1880.

3. "Grant's Flying Trip through the South." On the response of Black voters in the South to Hayes's administration, see Logan, *Betrayal of the Negro*.

4. "Grant's Flying Trip through the South."

5. Blight, *Frederick Douglass*, 614.

6. "1880 Presidential General Election Results: South Carolina," Dave Leip's Atlas of U.S. Elections, accessed June 28, 2025, https://uselectionatlas.org.

7. Kantrowitz, *Ben Tillman*, 103.

8. Kantrowitz, *Ben Tillman*, 100. On the Greenback Party in the New South, see Ali, *In the Lion's Mouth*, 1–77; Ayers, *Promise of the New South*, 214–48; Hild, *Greenbackers, Knights of Labor, and Populists*, chap. 2; Kantrowitz, *Ben Tillman*, 110–55; Tindall, *South Carolina Negroes*, 41–53; and Woodward, *Origins of the New South*, 81–85.

9. "The Republican Circus," *Anderson (SC) Intelligencer*, September 21, 1882. On J. Hendrix McClane, see Kantrowitz, *Benjamin Tillman*, chap. 5.

10. "The Lone Greenbackers," *Palmetto Post* (Port Royal, SC), September 14, 1882. On the larger rise of third-party challenges in the late nineteenth-century South, see Kantrowitz, *Ben Tillman*, 98–109; Dailey, *Before Jim Crow*; Hahn, *Roots of Southern Populism*; and Turner, *Soul Liberty*.

11. On the 1882 election law, see Gelston, "Radical versus Straight-Out," 232–34. See also Ayers, *Promise of the New South*, 50–51, 286–87; and Tindall, *South Carolina Negroes*, 68–78.

12. "The Stock Law," *Orangeburg (SC) Times and Democrat*, February 16, 1882; Kantrowitz, *Ben Tillman*, 90–98; Hahn, *Nation under Our Feet*, 389–91.

13. Painter, *Exodusters*, chap. 9; "Flight from South Carolina: Real Causes of the Exodus of the Colored People," *New York Times*, January 12, 1882. Postbellum emigration to the Lowcountry ran counter to the larger patterns of late nineteenth-century Black movement, which saw freedpeople and their descendants move to the region's new urban centers such as Atlanta, fast-growing frontiers such as the Mississippi Delta and Appalachian coal country; or, most notably, the Trans-Mississippi West. On postbellum Black migration, see Ayers,

Southern Journey; Cohen, *At Freedom's Edge*; Mitchell, *Righteous Propagation*; and Field, *Growing Up with the Country*.

14. *Lexington (NC) Dispatch*, January 11, 1882; "A New Phase of the Exodus," *Charleston News and Courier*, January 6, 1882.

15. Cooper, *Conservative Regime*, 130.

16. South Carolina, *Journal of the Senate*, 1169–70. On the role maps played in the postbellum United States, see Lewis, *Unseen Truth*, chap. 4; Schulten, *Mapping the Nation*, chap. 5.

17. "Gerrymandering," *Pittsfield (MA) Sun*, August 24, 1843; "Gerrymandering in Florida," *Macon (GA) Weekly Telegraph*, November 1, 1867; Kousser, *Shaping of Southern Politics*. chap. 2.

18. Kousser, *Colorblind Injustice*, 26–32.

19. "Confessions of a Tribune Correspondent," *Macon (GA) Telegraph*, May 1881; "Southern Republicans," *Daily Inter Ocean*, November 6, 1886.

20. Thomas E. Miller, in *Miller vs. Elliott: Report of the Committee on Elections*, 51st Cong., 1st Sess., June 20, 1890; Cooper, *Conservative Regime*, 103; *Charleston News and Courier*, June 28, 1882; "The South Carolina Gerrymander," *Chicago Daily Tribune*, July 19, 1882. The populations of the seven districts were as follows: First, 118,803; Second, 136,748; Third, 131,569; Fourth, 167,230; Fifth, 121,808; Sixth, 132,383; Seventh, 187,535.

21. "Carolina's New District," *Charleston News and Courier*, July 4, 1882; *Charleston News and Courier*, quoted in *New York Tribune*, July 19, 1882; "The Gerrymandering Gospel," *Charleston News Courier*, June 26, 1882.

22. "The South Carolina Gerrymander," *Chicago Daily Tribune*, July 19, 1882; "Gerrymandering in Illinois," *Charleston News and Courier*, July 25, 1882.

23. "Tillman, of South Carolina, Unseated in Favor of Smalls," *New York Times*, July 20, 1882.

24. *Republican Campaign for 1882*, 61.

25. "Dibble's Gerrymander," *Boston Herald*, September 28, 1882; "Flaws in the Solid South," *New York Times*, July 13, 1882. On Edmund W. M. Mackey, see Reynolds, *Reconstruction in South Carolina*, 79, 262, 410–22.

26. "Rampant Radicalism," *Palmetto Post* (Port Royal, SC), August 24, 1882.

27. Rampant Radicalism, *Palmetto Post* (Port Royal, SC), August 24, 1882; "The Congressional Outlook," *Palmetto Post* (Port Royal, SC), September 7, 1882.

28. "The Black District Fight," *Charleston News and Courier*, September 22, 1882; "The Political Campaign," *Charleston News and Courier*, September 28, 1882; *Charleston News and Courier*, October 9, 1882.

29. *Washington Bee*, June 24, 1882; "Color for Color," *Palmetto Post* (Port Royal, SC), October 19, 1882.

30. "Death of E. W. M. Mackey," *Columbia (SC) Daily Register*, January 29, 1884; "D. A. Straker, South Carolina Topics: The Late Congressman Mackey's Position," *New York Globe*, February 16, 1884.

31. Kantrowitz, *Ben Tillman*, 150–56.

Chapter 4

1. *Newberry (SC) Weekly Herald*, August 21, 1884; *Sumter (SC) Watchman and Southron*, August 26, 1884; Lamson, Glorious Failure, 174–82.

2. T. McCants Stewart, "Gen. R. B. Elliott. Statesman, Jurist and Orator," *New York Globe*, August 16, 1884; "Mr. Douglass on Elliott," *New York Globe*, September 6, 1884.

3. "The Elliott Memorial: Impressive Services Held at the Capital of South Carolina," *New York Globe*, October 11, 1884; "The State Republican Convention," *Yorkville (SC) Enquirer*, October 2, 1884.

4. "The State Republican Convention," *Yorkville (SC) Enquirer*, October 2, 1884; "The Elliott Memorial: Impressive Services Held at the Capital of South Carolina," *New York Globe*, October 11, 1884; Adeleke, *Without Regard to Race*, 174–78; Coulter, "Aaron Alpeoria Bradley," part 3, 301–2; "What Our Editors Say," *Sumter (SC) Watchman and Southron*, August 26, 1884; Campbell, *Sufferings of the Rev. T. G. Campbell*, 27.

5. *Washington Bee*, September 27, 1884; Lamson, *Glorius Failure*, 280–82; Billingsley, *Yearning to Breathe Free*, 162.

6. Freeman, *Field of Blood*, 106.

7. On the promise and peril of the outsized emphasis on the Black military experience in Unionist Civil War memory, see Emberton, *Beyond Redemption* chap. 4.

8. Miller, *Gullah Statesman*, chap. 3. On the gender politics of the late nineteenth century Black public sphere, see Barkley Brown, "Negotiating and Transforming the Public Sphere"; Higginbotham, *Righteous Discontent*; Mitchell, *Righteous Propagation*.

9. On the broader generational shift toward independent politics within the Gilded Age Black public sphere, see Alexander, "T. Thomas Fortune"; Bergeson-Lockwood, *Race over Party*; and Blakely, "Richard T. Greener."

10. Penn, *Afro-American Press*, 132–33. On the "golden age" of the Black press in the late nineteenth century, see Rathbun, *Rise of the Modern American Negro Press*; and Vogel, *Black Press*; Kelley, "Abolition Democracy's Forgotten Founder"; Alexander, "T. Thomas Fortune"; and Crowder, *John Edward Bruce*.

11. Alexander, "T. Thomas Fortune," 60–62, 71.

12. Penn, *Afro-American Press*, 136.

13. "The VIIth District of South Carolina," *Washington Bee*, August 30, 1884; "The National Capital: Exposure of the Buncombe Resolution in the O'Donnell Case," *New York Globe*, January 19, 1884.

14. *People's Advocate* (Washington, DC), February 23, 1884; *New York Globe*, February 23, 1884. On D. A. Straker, see Blair, *Cities of the Dead*, 150–51; Burke, *All for Civil Rights*, 47–51, 91–93; Oldfield, "A High and Honorable Calling," 396–98.

15. "Hon. D. A. Straker Suggested as Mackey's Congressman Successor," *New York Globe*, March 8, 1884. On T. McCants Stewart, see Wynes, "T. McCants Stewart," 311–17.

16. Blight, *Frederick Douglass*, 635–42; *Washington Bee*, July 3, 1886.

17. "Hon. D. A. Straker Suggested as Mackey's Congressman Successor," *New York Globe*, March 8, 1884; March 13, 1884; "Gen Smalls' Walk-Over," *New York Globe*, March 29, 1884.

18. *Grit* (Washington, DC), April 12, 1884; "South Carolina Politics," *New York Globe*, April 5, 1884. On John Edward Bruce's Gilded Age journalism career, see Crowder, *John Edward Bruce*, chap. 3.

19. "Smalls Serenaded," *People's Advocate* (Washington, DC), April 5, 1884; "The Speakers for Emancipation Day," *Cleveland Gazette*, April 5, 1884; Billingsley, *Yearning to Breathe Free*, 109; "The Washington Cadets," *Washington Bee*, June 14, 1884; *Cleveland Gazette*, December 13, 1884; Muller, "Brief Note on Robert Smalls and Frederick Douglass."

20. "Charles Sumner Post G.A.R. to Erect a Monument to the Honored Soldiers and Sailors of the Race"; "The Republican State Convention," *Sumter (SC) Watchman and Southron*, April 22, 1884; *Morning Democrat* (Davenport, IA), June 5, 1884.

21. "A Colored Man's Complaints," *Charleston News and Courier*, August 7, 1883; "Negroes Seeking Redress," *Atlanta Constitution*, January 26, 1884; "A Letter from Congressman Smalls," *Washington Bee*, February 11, 1886.

22. *National Republican* (Washington, DC), March 6, 1886; *Cleveland Gazette*, August 21, 1886; *Indianapolis Freeman*, June 29, 1889; "Ten Greatest Negroes," *Indianapolis Freeman*, April 26, May 3, 7, 10, 17, and 24, June 7, 1890.

23. Stauffer, *Picturing Douglass*; Frisken, "'Song without Words.'" On the fight over race and image during the late nineteenth century, see Blight, *Frederick Douglass*; Gates, *Stony the Road*; Krauthamer and Willis, *Envisioning Emancipation*; and "Songs without Words," accessed June 28, 2025, http://songswithoutwords.org/about.

24. "Heroes of the Colored Race." On Black Americans' postbellum quest for a redemptive visual language, see Gates, *Stony the Road*, chap 4; Gonzalez, *Visualizing Equality*, chap. 7; and Lewis, *Unseen Truth*, chap 3.

25. "Heroes of the Colored Race."

26. "Heroes of the Colored Race."

27. For lithographic images of Robert Smalls, see *Cleveland Gazette*, August 21, 1886; *National Republican* (Washington, DC), March 6, 1886; *Indianapolis Freeman*, June 29, 1889; *Colored American* (Washington, DC), February 25, 1899; Gibson and Crogman, *Colored American*.

28. Simmons, *Men of Mark*, 164–66.

29. Hall, *Faithful Account of the Race*, chaps 4–5; McHenry, *Forgotten Readers*.

30. Cromwell, *History of the Bethel Literary and Historical Association*, 11–12. On the Bethel Literary and Historical Association, see McHenry, *Forgotten Readers*, 145–70; Hall, *Faithful Account of the Race*, 168, 186; and Gatewood, *Aristocrats of Color*, 220–21.

31. *People's Advocate* (Washington, DC), December 15, 1883.

32. Cromwell, *History of the Bethel Literary and Historical Association*, 15–17, 21–22.

33. "The Black District: Shall the Whites Interfere in Choosing a Congressman?," *Sumter (SC) Watchman and Southron*, June 10, 1884; Ambrose E. Gonzales to Emily Elliot, January 12, 1882, Elliott Family Papers, South Caroliniana Library, University of South Carolina, Columbia.

34. "The Seventh District," *Charleston News and Courier*, October 15, 1884; "Suffrage in the South: A Carolina Republican Convention in Washington," *San Francisco Bulletin*, April 24, 1884; "Is There a Free Ballot and a Fair Count?," *Palmetto Post* (Port Royal, SC), October 29, 1885.

35. "The Black District: Shall the Whites Interfere in Choosing a Congressman?," *Sumter (SC) Watchman and Southron*, June 10, 1884; *Charleston News and Courier*, October 10, 1884; "The Seventh District," *Charleston News and Courier*, October 15, 1884.

36. "South Carolina's Campaign," *New York Times*, October 22, 1884; "The Black District," *Columbia Register*, September 9, 1884; "An Incendiary Negro," *Atlanta Constitution*, August 14, 1884; "The Seventh District," *Charleston News and Courier*, November 20, 1884.

37. "What Is a Sauce for the Goose Is Sauce for the Gander," *Palmetto Post* (Port Royal, SC), April 30, 1885; "The Seventh Congressional District," *Palmetto Post* (Port Royal, SC), July 8, 1886; "Congressman Smalls's Canvass," *New York Times*, September 16, 1886; *Washington Bee*, May 31, 1884. On late nineteenth-century machine politics, see Summers, *Rum, Romanism, and Rebellion*.

38. Lockwood-Bergeson, *Race over Party*, 96–102; Du Bois, *Philadelphia Negro*, 372–84; "Stand by for Carson!," *Washington Post*, December 14, 1895.

39. Gelston, "Radical versus Straight-Out."

40. *Congressional Record*, 50th Cong., 2d Sess., 1788; US House of Representatives, Committee on Elections, *Robert Smalls vs. William Elliott*, 16; "A Misrepresentative," *Palmetto Post* (Port Royal, SC), October 28, 1886; *Congressional Record*, 50th Cong., 2d Sess., 1807.

41. Miller, *Gullah Statesman*, 153–56.

42. Miller, *Gullah Statesman*, 160; Crowder, *John Edward Bruce*, 102; Cowley, *Romance of History*; Ione, *Pride of Family*, 196.

43. US House of Representatives, Committee on Elections, *Robert Smalls vs. William Elliott*, 20.

44. US House of Representatives, Committee on Elections, *Robert Smalls vs. William Elliott*, 15, 20; *Congressional Record*, 50th Cong., 2d Sess., 1787. On "bloody shirt" politics in the post-Reconstruction era and Black engagement with violence, see Budiansky, *Bloody Shirt*, 219–54; Williams, *They Left Great Marks on Me*, 55–100; and Barkley Brown, "Negotiating and Transforming the Public Sphere."

45. US House of Representatives, Committee on Elections, *Robert Smalls vs. William Elliott*, 20, 35; "Shaking Off the Shackles," *Charleston News and Courier*, October 25, 1886.

46. "Rampant Radicalism," *Palmetto Post* (Port Royal, SC), August 24, 1882. On the Black men who represented Beaufort County in the South Carolina state legislature, see Wise et al., *Rebellion, Reconstruction, and Redemption*, chap. 19.

47. US House of Representatives, Committee on Elections, *Robert Smalls vs. William Elliott*, 16; "A Negro Paradise," *People's Advocate* (Washington, DC), August 11, 1883. On Beaufort's customshouse as a site of patronage politics, see Billingsley, *Yearning to Breathe Free*, 161–63, 166–67; Gelston, "Radical versus Straight-Out in Post-Reconstruction Beaufort County"; and White-Perry, "In Freedom's Shadow."

48. Smalls, *Contestant vs. William Elliott*, 13, 18, 16.

49. "War of the Tints," *New York Freeman*, November 20, 1886; *Star of Zion*, November 25, 1886, quoted in *New York Freeman*, November 27, 1886.

50. "More about the Battle of the Tints," *Springfield (MA) Republican*, November 14, 1886; "Educated Leadership Will Come," *New York Freeman*, December 4, 1886; "The Color Line: Interesting Letter from a South Carolina Negro," *Springfield (MA) Republican*, November 25, 1886.

51. "Wants to Know, You Know," *Boston Herald*, December 26, 1886; "Manufacturing Democratic Majorities," *Daily Inter Ocean*, November 22, 1886; Heersink, *Republican Party Politics*, 233, 290–91.

52. *Washington Bee*, March 19, 1887; "Exit Colored Congressmen," *New York Freeman*, November 13, 1886; "The Light Breaking," *Cleveland Gazette*, December 4, 1886.

Chapter 5

1. "Decoration Day Excursion," *Savannah Tribune*, May 7, 1892; "A Burlesque at Beaufort," *Charleston News and Courier*, May 31, 1890. On Decoration Day's Lowcountry roots, see Blight, *Race and Reunion*, 64–70. On railroad expansion in the New South, see Ayers, *Promise of the New South*, chap. 1.

2. "Decoration Day," *Palmetto Post* (Port Royal, SC), June 2, 1892. Later descriptions of early twentieth-century Decoration Day celebrations in the white Southern press often emphasized efforts of Beaufort County police to crack down on illegal alcohol sales. See

chap. 6 of this book. On the rise and fall of Black coastal communities as sites of leisure in the postbellum South, see Kahrl, *Land Was Ours*.

3. "Decoration Day," *Palmetto Post* (Port Royal, SC), June 5, 1890.

4. Ellery Brayton, "An Address Delivered on Decoration Day," May 30, 1890, Frederick Douglass Papers, Manuscripts Division, Library of Congress, Washington, DC.

5. "Decoration Day," *Palmetto Post* (Port Royal, SC), June 5, 1890; "More Good from Nazareth," *Washington Bee*, June 28, 1890.

6. *Robert Smalls, Contestant, vs. William Elliott, Contestee*, 8, 709.

7. Smalls, "Election Methods in the South."

8. *Congressional Record*, House, 51st Cong., 1st Sess. (26 June 1890), 6544; "Toward a 'Temporary Farewell,'" History, Art, and Archives: United States House of Representatives, accessed June 28, 2025, https://history.house.gov/Exhibitions-and-Publications/BAIC/Historical-Essays/Fifteenth-Amendment/Temporary-Farewell; *Charleston News and Courier*, November 9, 1888; "Mr. Smalls Not Snubbed," *Washington Post*, June 27, 1890.

9. Hampton, "What Negro Supremacy Means."

10. "Wade Hampton," *American Missionary* 42 (July 1888): 179–80; Niels Christensen, "Sea Islands and Negro Supremacy," Christensen Family Papers, South Caroliniana Library, University of South Carolina, Columbia.

11. "Bruce-Grit," *New York Age*, June 9, 1888; John E. Bruce, "Reply to Senator Wade Hampton's Article in *The Forum* for June on 'What Negro Supremacy Means'" (Washington, DC, 1888), John Edward Bruce Papers, Schomburg Library, New York.

12. "The Day We Celebrated," *Palmetto Post* (Port Royal, SC), July 2, 1891. On the role pensions played in postbellum Black Southern life, see Brimmer, *Claiming Union Widowhood*.

13. On fusionism, see Ayers, *Promise of the New South*, 42–43, 48; Gilmore, *Gender and Jim Crow*, 84–107; and Gelston, "Radical versus Straight-Out."

14. Gelston, "Radical versus Straight-Out," 235.

15. "South Carolina Politics: A Reply to the Card of Ex-Congressman Smalls," *Washington Post*, April 22, 1889; *Savannah Tribune*, February 16, 1889; "Why He Refused," *Washington Bee*, February 16, 1889; W. J. Whipper, *Fusionists and Fusionism: Robert Smalls' Arraignment by the New York World and Other Matters* (Beaufort, SC: Sea Island News Press, 1889), YA Pamphlet Collection, Rare Book and Special Collections Division, Library of Congress, Washington, DC. On the Gillisonville attack, see Laura Towne, entry for November 6, 1878, in Holland, *Letters and Diary of M. Laura Towne*, 285–88; and Dinnella-Borrego, *Risen Phoenix*, 1–3.

16. Petition by the Republicans of Beaufort County, South Carolina, n.d., United States Customs Records, Port of Beaufort, Department of Treasury, National Archives II, College Park, MD; Julius I. Washington to Secretary of Treasury William Windom, March 16, 1889, United States Customs Records, Port of Beaufort, Department of Treasury, National Archives II, College Park, MD; Thomas Wheeler to President Benjamin Harrison, April 16, 1889; Joseph Robinson to Secretary of Treasury William Windom, April 12, 1889.

17. John Sherman to President Benjamin Harrison; Rufus Saxton to President Benjamin Harrison, April 8, 1889; Richard Washington to President Benjamin Harrison, April 22, 1889, United States Customs Records, Port of Beaufort, Department of Treasury, National Archives II, College Park, MD.

18. S. J. Bampfield and George Reed to President Benjamin Harrison, March 25, 1889, United States Customs Records, Port of Beaufort, Department of Treasury, National Archives II, College Park, MD.

19. Republicans of Beaufort County to Benjamin Harrison, May 2, 1889, Beaufort Port of Customs Records, Department of Treasury, National Archives II, College Park, MD; Charleston *News and Courier*, November 4, 1888.

20. Robert Smalls to Benjamin Harrison, May 2, 1889; S. J. Bampfield and George Reed to President Benjamin Harrison, March 25, 1889.National Archives II, College Park, MD. On Black sexual politics during the Gilded Age, see Feimster, *Southern Horrors*, 87–124; and Mitchell, *Righteous Propagation*, 108–41. On temperance and sexual violence, see Murdoch, *Domesticating Drink*.

21. N.W. Ayer & Son's *Newspaper Annual*, 655; *Beaufort (SC) New South*, n.d., quoted in *Cleveland Gazette*, June 7, 1890.

22. *Beaufort (SC) New South*, September 15, 1890, quoted in *New York Age*, September 20, 1890; "Seven Reasons," *New York Age*, September 20, 1890.

23. National Colored Press Convention, 1880, Notable Kentucky African American Database, last modified June 17, 2024, https://nkaa.uky.edu/nkaa/items/show/1404; Penn, *Afro-American Press*, 114.

24. Penn, *Afro-American Press*, 429, 483.

25. *Cleveland Gazette*, August 18, 1894.

26. On the Colored Farmers' Alliance, see Ali, *In the Lion's Mouth*.

27. Ali, *In the Lion's Mouth*, 123, 126.

28. Marszalek, *Black Congressman*, 28–29; *Sumter (SC) Watchman and Southron*, December 7, 1892.

29. "Tillman in Beaufort," *Atlanta Constitution*, June 10, 1892; Kantrowitz, *Benjamin Tillman*, 204; *Charleston World*, May 12, 1890; Kantrowitz, *Benjamin Tillman*, 202.

30. Harris, "Sea Island Hurricanes." On the 1893 Sea Island hurricane, see Bland, "'Grim Memorial'"; and Grego, *Hurricane Jim Crow*.

31. Thomas Martin to editors of *Charleston News and Courier*, November 17, 1893, clipping in Clara Barton Papers, Manuscript Division, Library of Congress, Washington, DC.

32. "Cursing the Red Cross! Bitter Feeling against It in Beaufort County," *Columbia (SC) Daily Register*, May 25, 1894.

33. "Charleston's Sin," *The State* (Columbia, SC), December 14, 1893.

34. "To Test Election Laws," *The State* (Columbia, SC), May 16, 1894; G. W. Murray to McKinlay, April 25, 1894, in Carter G. Woodson Papers, Manuscript Division, Library of Congress, Washington, DC.

35. *Cleveland Gazette*, June 30, 1894.

36. "Decision in the Smalls-Murray Contest," *Washington Post*, August 18, 1894.

37. On the march toward disfranchisement, see Perman, *Struggle for Mastery*.

38. Tindall, *South Carolina Negroes*, 68–91.

39. Miller, *Suffrage Speeches*, 5–6; Miller, *Suffrage Speeches*, 6–7; *The State* (Columbia, SC), October 26, 1895.

40. "Brave and Many Were the Words of Gen. Whipper in Reply to Charges of Fraud," *Cleveland Gazette*, January 4, 1896.

41. Tindall, *South Carolina Negroes*, 78–82. "Colored Heroes," *Indianapolis Freeman*, December 21, 1895. The sixth Black delegate, Isaiah Reed, represented the Lowcountry's Georgetown County.

42. Miller, *Suffrage Speeches*, 2–3; Sarah V. Smalls, *Speeches at the Constitutional Convention* (Charleston, SC: Enquirer Press, 1896) in Daniel Murray Pamphlet Collection, Library of Congress, Washington, DC.

43. *Sumter (SC) Watchman and Southron* and Philadelphia church both quoted in Smalls, *Speeches*, 7–8.

44. Blight, *Frederick Douglass*, 745–64; "Apologizing for Wrongs," *Washington Bee*, October 26, 1895.

45. Perman, *Struggle for Mastery*; Kelley, *Right to Ride*; Zucchino, *Wilmington's Lie*.

46. Blight, *Race and Reunion*, 333–34; Wells, *Red Record*; Hopkins, *Contending Forces*; Bergeson-Lockwood, *Race over Party*, chap. 8. On the *Colored American Magazine*, see Brown, *Pauline Elizabeth Hopkins*, 284–317; and Wallinger, "Pauline E. Hopkins as Editor and Journalist."

47. "Hon. B. K. Bruce Dead," *Colored American* (Washington, DC), March 19, 1898; "Bethel's Spring Season," *Colored American* (Washington, DC), March 26, 1898; "Death of the Triumvirate," *Washington Bee*, March 26, 1898.

48. Taylor, *Original Black Elite*; Harris, "Daniel Murray."

49. Harris, "Daniel Murray"; Barkley Brown, "Negotiating and Transforming the Black Public Sphere"; Gatewood, "'Remarkable Misses Rollin.'"

50. Gatewood, "'Remarkable Misses Rollin'"; Lewis, "Frances Anne Rollin."

51. "Death of a Cultured Colored Woman," *The State* (Columbia, SC), October 19, 1901.

Chapter 6

1. "Antoinette Norwell's History Class," Photograph Album PA-3615/87, Penn School Papers, 1862–2005, Southern Historical Collection, Wilson Special Collections Library, University of North Carolina, Chapel Hill; 1900 US Census, Amherst County, Virginia. In the Penn School Papers' archive, as well as much of the Penn School programming material, Norvell's name is misspelled as "Norwell." In Hampton's records and the US Census records, she appears as Norvell.

2. Saperstein, "Out from behind the Mask."

3. Turner, *Soul Liberty*, chap. 5. On the Readjuster movement, see Dailey, *Before Jim Crow*.

4. On the Penn School and its twentieth-century transformation, see Holland, *Letters and Diary of Laura Towne*; Burton with Cross, *Penn Center*; and Cooley, *School Acres*.

5. Much of the classic and recent literature on Black teachers in the Jim Crow South emphasizes racial uplift, infrapolitics in the classroom, and the role that educators played in the long civil rights movement. See Fairclough, *Class of Their Own*; Givens, *Fugitive Pedagogy*; and Ramsey, *Reading, Writing, and Segregation*.

6. Anderson, *Education of Blacks in the South*, 37. On Armstrong and Hampton's relationship to civilizationist ideas, both in the Pacific and in the American South, see Mount, "Virginia in the Pacific."

7. Anderson, *Education of Blacks in the South*, 36.

8. Washington, *Up from Slavery*, 85–86.

9. Washington, *Up from Slavery*, 85, 87–88.

10. Taylor, *Embattled Freedom*; Manning, *Troubled Refuge*; Engs, *Freedom's First Generation*; Taylor, "Mary S. Peake."

11. P. W. Dawkins, "Work among a People," *Southern Workman*, July 1900, 397–400; Norrell, *Up from History*, 33, 44–45. On the impact of individual and generational trauma in Southern Black communities, see Williams, *I Saw Death Coming*.

12. Rowland and Wise, *Bridging the Sea Islands' Past and Present*, 89–110, 169–80.

13. Rowland and Wise, *Bridging the Sea Islands' Past and Present*, 100.

14. Rowland and Wise, *Bridging the Sea Islands' Past and Present*, 62; Anderson, *Education of Blacks in the South*, 151; Wertheimer, *Race and Slavery in South Carolina*, 145–48.

15. William Elliott Jr., "Reminisces," 1941, Elliott Family Papers, South Caroliniana Library, University of South Carolina, Columbia.

16. Muriel Washington Smalley, Adalee Brown Roberts, James N. Brown, and Gerhard Spieler, "Robert Smalls School History," Robert Smalls High School Reunion Pages, accessed June 28, 2025, https://resources.finalsite.net/images/v1676474571/beaufortk12scus/osgawlf2qxin2r8btn2a/RSHSReunionpages.pdf; Miller, *Gullah Statesman*, 238.

17. Crowder, *John Edward Bruce*, 68; Bruce, *Short Biographical Sketches*, 3.

18. Bruce, *Short Biographical Sketches*, 64–66.

19. Givens, *Fugitive Pedagogy*.

20. "General Robert Smalls Objects," *The State* (Columbia, SC), February 27, 1901. On the rise and fall of the Freedmen's Bank, see Edwards, *Savings and Trust*.

21. "Decoration Day," *Palmetto Post* (Port Royal, SC), May 31, 1906.

22. "Decoration Day Items," *Palmetto Post* (Port Royal, SC), June 7, 1906.

23. "Gen. Robert Smalls, Open Letter to Senator Cullom," *Colored American* (Washington, DC), December 1, 1900; "The Situation in South Carolina," *Colored American* (Washington, DC), March 21, 1903.

24. "The 'Lynching' at Port Royal," *Charleston News and Courier*, August 31, 1901; "Negroes Plot for Uprising," *Atlanta Journal*, August 8, 1901; "Negro Uprising Threatened," *The State* (Columbia, SC), January 21, 1907; "Armed Men at Beaufort," *Charlotte Observer*, January 21, 1907.

25. John S. Reynolds, "Reconstruction in South Carolina: Review and Reflections," *The State* (Columbia, SC), June 18, 1905.

26. "Gov D. H. Chamberlain on the Negro Question," *The State* (Columbia, SC), September 6, 1904.

27. Helen Lou James, "The Need for the Penn School on St. Helena Island," *Southern Workman*, February 1908, 90–92; Dawkins's views cited in Jacoway, *Yankee Missionaries*, 42, 62. On the world of Black teachers in Jim Crow–era industrial schools, see Fairclough, *Class of Their Own*, chap. 4.

28. Frissell to Helen Carnan Jenks, April 18, 1900, quoted in Jacoway, *Yankee Missionaries*, 26.

29. Henry Wilder Foote, "The Penn School on St. Helena Island," *Southern Workman*, May 1902, 266; Robert D. Jenks, "Confidential Statement of the Conditions at Penn School," n.d., Penn School Papers, Southern Historical Collection, Wilson Special Collections Library, University of North Carolina, Chapel Hill; Jenks and Frissell quoted in Jacoway, *Yankee Missionaries*, 30–32, 34.

30. J. E. Davis, "A Unique People's School," *Southern Workman*, April 1914, 217–30; Peabody, *Education for Life*, 260. On the politics of middle-class Black marriage during the Jim Crow era, see Hunter, *Bound in Wedlock*, chap. 8; and Mitchell, *Righteous Propagation*, chap. 3.

31. Jones, *Negro Education*, 479–85; Tetzlaff, *Cultivating a New South*, 165–66, 168; 1905 Port Royal Agricultural School pamphlet, 1905; and 1905 Port Royal Agricultural School pamphlet, 1905, both in Christensen Family Papers, South Caroliniana Library, University of South Carolina, Columbia. See also "Hampton Workers," *Southern Workman*, December 1916, 702. On early twentieth-century Black teachers' broader and more egalitarian vision of both industrial education and the politics of respectability, see Wolcott, "'Bible, Bath, and Broom.'"

32. Seaman Knapp to Rossa Cooley, May 25, 1909, Penn School Papers, Southern Historical Collection, Wilson Special Collections Library, University of North Carolina, Chapel Hill; Harlan, *Booker T. Washington*, 215; Kiser, *Sea Island to City*, 136.

33. Miller, *Gullah Statesman*, 239.

34. "Memorial Day at Beaufort," *New York Age*, June 11, 1908; "Memorial Day at Beaufort: Dr. Booker T. Washington Delivered a Practical Address to Thousands of People," *Savannah Tribune*, June 6, 1908; Norrell, *Up from History*, 318, 384. Spending several years without consistent employment, Fortune would later return to journalism and spend the final years of his career working for the New York *Amsterdam News* and the *Negro World* (New York). On Fortune's later journalism career, see Alexander, *T. Thomas Fortune*.

35. "Memorial Day at Beaufort"; "Memorial Day at Beaufort: Dr. Booker T. Washington Delivered a Practical Address to Thousands of People."

36. Grace House, "Unpublished Account of Penn School Fiftieth Anniversary," Penn School Papers, Southern Historical Collection, Wilson Special Collections Library, University of North Carolina, Chapel Hill; Grace House, "Fiftieth Anniversary of the Penn School," *Southern Workman*, May 1912, 317–22; "First School for Negroes Celebrates Its Fiftieth Anniversary on St. Helena Island," *New York Times*, April 21, 1912; "Penn School Celebrates Fiftieth Anniversary: Occasion of Joy for All—General Robert Smalls Speaks," *Baltimore (MD) Afro-American*, May 11, 1912.

37. Barbour and Carlos, "Honorable Hastings Gantt"; Johnson and Root, *Camera Man's Journey*, 24. Here, it is also useful to consider how power operated in the production of Black countermemory. Without the memory work of the Penn School teachers, Gantt's legacy would likely have been silenced. See Trouillot, *Silencing the Past*.

38. Barbour and Carlos, "Honorable Hastings Gantt"; Cooley, "Homes of the Free"; Hutchison, "Better Homes and Gullah," 102–10.

39. "Dr. Martin Luther King Jr at the Penn Center," January 2015, www.penncenter.com/news/emancipation-proclamation-pk7d6.

40. Fairclough, *Class of Their Own*, 221–62; *Southern Workman*, February 1914, 63; 1910 Census, Dorchester County, South Carolina; Charleston, South Carolina, City Directory, 1904; School Scrapbook, December 9, 1911; "Antoinette Norvell, Jeanes Teacher, Summerville, S.C.," December 9, 1911, Southern Educational Foundation Records, Robert Woodruff Library, Atlanta University Center, Atlanta; *Southern Workman*, October 1913, 576; 1920 Census, Macon County, AL; 1950 Census, Macon County, AL.

Chapter 7

1. Robert Smalls to Whitefield McKinlay, June 27, 1912, Carter G. Woodson Papers, Manuscript Division, Library of Congress, Washington, DC; "Displacing Negroes," *Washington Bee*, May 3, 1913; Miller, *Gullah Statesman*, 242–43; Billingsley, *Yearning to Breathe Free*, 220–21.

2. "Gen'l Robert Smalls of Steamer *Planter* Fame Passes Away," *Savannah Tribune*, February 27, 1915; "Last Tribute of Respect Paid General Smalls," *Savannah Tribune*, March 6, 1915.

3. "Robert Smalls of S.C., Dead," *New York Age*, March 4, 1915; "Hardstew Visits South Carolina," *Savannah Tribune*, April 29, 1916.

4. "The Week in Society," *Washington Bee*, July 6, 1907; "Ex-Gov. Chamberlain Dies in Virginia: Last Republican Governor of South Carolina Passes Away," *The State* (Columbia, SC), April 14, 1907; Rowland, *Bridging the Sea Islands' Past and Present*, 183; "Elliott, William:

1838–1907," Biographical Directory of the United States Congress, accessed June 28, 2025, https://bioguide.congress.gov/search/bio/E000129; Barbour and Carlos, "Honorable Hastings Gantt"; Miller, *Gullah Statesman*, 250.

5. *Washington Bee*, March 4, 1911; "Richard T. Greener Died May 9 in Chicago," *New York Age*, May 20, 1922; "Shadows of Light," *The Crisis*, August 2017, 181; "P. B. S. Pinchback."

6. Southern Poverty Law Center, *Whose Heritage?*; Best, "Confederate Statues Were Never Really about Preserving History."

7. On the UDC, *Birth of a Nation*, and the production of Lost Cause memory during the early twentieth century, see Cox, *Dixie's Daughters*, 107–8. On Woodrow Wilson and the Southern Democratic Party, see Yellin, *Racism in the Nation's Service*. On the place of *Birth of a Nation* in film history and American popular culture, see McEwan, *Birth of a Nation*.

8. "Decoration Day Quietly Observed," *Beaufort (SC) Gazette*, June 4, 1915; "UDC to Celebrate," *Beaufort (SC) Gazette*, January 15, 1914; *New York Age*, June 8, 1918; *Beaufort (SC) Gazette*, January 26, 1917; "Press Comments on Ku Klux Klan," *Beaufort (SC) Gazette*, September 23, 1921.

9. *Newberry (SC) Weekly Herald*, February 20, 1914; "Governor Attacks Senator Christensen," *Beaufort (SC) Gazette*, February 5, 1914; *Newberry (SC) Weekly Herald*, February 20, 1914; Tetzlaff, *Cultivating a New South*, 164. On Cole Blease, see Simon, "Appeal of Cole Blease"; and Simon, *Fabric of Defeat*, chap. 1.

10. *Beaufort (SC) Gazette*, April 16, 1915; "Colored Voters Held Meeting," *Beaufort (SC) Gazette*, September 24, 1915; "Take Part in S.C. Primary," *Baltimore (MD) Afro-American*, October 2, 1915.

11. Grego, *Hurricane Jim Crow*, 195, 199–206; Agbor-Taylor, "South Carolina's Black Majority."

12. Badger, *Why White Liberals Fail*; Link, *Paradox of Southern Progressivism*; "Visualizing the Great Migration," 2015, www.moma.org/interactives/exhibitions/2015/onewayticket.

13. Egerton, *Speak Now against the Day*.

14. Megginson, "Black South Carolinians in World War I"; "Beaufort County, South Carolina—World War I: The Official Roster of South Carolina Soldiers, Sailors, and Marines in the World War, 1917–1918," *Genealogy Trails*, accessed June 24, 2025, http://genealogytrails.com/scar/beaufort/wwi_dead.htm; "Drafted Men Entertained at Beaufort," *New York Age*, October 11, 1917; "Beaufort, S.C.," *New York Age*, January 18, 1919.

15. "Beaufort Negroes Ready to Serve," *Savannah Tribune*, April 14, 1917.

16. "Hold Patriotic Meetings in S. Carolina," *New York Age*, May 18, 1918; Joshua E. Blanton, "Men in the Making," *Southern Workman*, January 1919, 17, 20; *New York Age*, August 30, 1919; Blanton, "Men in the Making," 20. Williams, *Wounded World*.

17. "The Story of the Branches for 1918," *The Crisis*, April 1919, 281–84. On the rise of the NAACP, see Sullivan, *Lift Every Voice*. On the organization's rise in South Carolina during World War I, see Lau, *Democracy Rising*; NAACP Administrative File, Special Correspondences, William Pickens, 1917–1923; "Beaufort, S.C., News," *Savannah Tribune*, June 28, 1919.

18. Fultz, "Charleston, 1919–1920"; "Beaufort, S.C. News," *Savannah Tribune*, April 17, 1920; "Delinquent Branches," *The Crisis*, December 1920. On Du Bois's road to writing a history of Reconstruction, see Hinton, "Last Great Battle of the West."

19. Fultz, "Charleston, 1919–1920," 640.

20. Hahn, *Nation under Our Feet*, 469–72; Rolinson, *Grassroots Garveyism*, 89; "Beaufort, S.C.," *Negro World*, December 7, 1922.

21. Hill, *Marcus Garvey*, 106–10; "The New School Politician," *Negro World*, March 18, 1922.
22. Historical Census Browser. On the generation of Black politicians who emerged in the hubs of the first Great Migration, see Franklin and Meier, *Black Leaders*.
23. "Estill Citizens Stage a Protest," *Beaufort (SC) Gazette*, August 16, 1928; "Repeating the Great Crime," *Beaufort (SC) Gazette*, October 1, 1936.
24. Harris, *Sixteenth Annual Report*, 16; "Negroes Not Flocking to Harlem from St. Helena Island as Stated," *Beaufort (SC) Gazette*, January 5, 1933.
25. "Negroes Coming Back South," *Beaufort (SC) Gazette*, January 14, 1926; Dudley quoted in Cooley, *School Acres*, 129; Jacoway, *Yankee Missionaries*, 183–87.
26. On the South's interwar white liberals, see Badger, *Why White Liberals Fail*; Ellis, *Race Harmony and Black Progress*; Hall, *Revolt against Chivalry*; and Egerton, *Speak Now against the Day*.
27. "Proposed Social Survey of Bi-Racial Southern Counties Negro Survey—Coahoma County," May 5, 1925, General Education Board Folder, Laura Spelman Rockefeller Memorial records, Rockefeller Archive Center, Sleepy Hollow, NY; Proposed Study on Mound Bayou, Commission on Interracial Relations, 1923–1927 folder, Laura Spelman Rockefeller Memorial records, Rockefeller Archive Center, Sleepy Hollow, NY; Egerton, *Speak Now against the Day*; Kirby, *Rural Worlds Lost*; Noonan, *Strange Career of Porgy and Bess*; Yuhl, *Golden Haze of Memory*; Robeson, "Ambiguity of Julia Peterkin."
28. Ellis, *Race Harmony and Black Progress*, 63–66; Woofter, "Negro Migration."
29. Ellis, *Race Harmony and Black Progress*, 207–10, 212; T. J. Woofter Jr. to Leonard Outhwaite, January 18, 1929, Laura Spelman Rockefeller Memorial records, Rockefeller Archive Center, Sleepy Hollow, NY.
30. Woofter, *Black Yeomanry*; Johnson, *Folk Culture*; Kiser, *Sea Island to City*; Johnson, *Social History of the Sea Islands*. On the way the battle over folklore studies and Southern sociology unfolded in the Georgia Sea Islands, see Cooper, *Making Gullah*.
31. Kiser, *Sea Island to City*, 133, 135, 222.
32. "Life on St. Helena Island," *Hartford (CT) Courant*, September 14, 1930; Paul Green, "On Old St. Helena: Review of *Black Yeomanry*," *New York Herald-Tribune Books*, August 24, 1930; "Gullah Negroes," *New York Times*, November 30, 1930; Leo Favrot to Jackson Davis, August 14, 1930, Black Yeomanry Folder, Laura Spelman Rockefeller Memorial records, Rockefeller Archive Center, Sleepy Hollow, NY.
33. R. B. Eleazer, "The Book Shelf: Origin of the 'Gullah,'" *Chicago Defender*, October 18, 1930; W. E. B. Du Bois, "Reviewed Work: *Black Yeomanry, Life on St. Helena Island*, by T. J. Woofter Jr.," *The Crisis* (November 1930), 378; Woodson, review of *Black Yeomanry*.
34. Ellis, *Race Harmony and Black Progress*, 207; T. J. Woofter Jr. to Trevor Arnett, April 16, 1929, Black Yeomanry Folder, Laura Spelman Rockefeller Memorial records, Rockefeller Archive Center, Sleepy Hollow, NY; Ira De A. Reid (Chairman), J. Curtis Dixon, Alfonso Elder, Timothy W. Jones, Jane Ellen McAllister, and Fred G. Wale, "An Evaluation of the Facilities, Program, and Objectives of the Penn Normal, Industrial and Agricultural School," February 19, 1948, Penn School Papers folder, Laura Spelman Rockefeller Memorial records, Rockefeller Archive Center, Sleepy Hollow, NY. After the Civil Rights Movement, the Lowcountry would embody the crisis of Black land loss and epicenter of a movement to reverse this trend. On the Black land loss debates of the 1980s, see; Hickmott, "Black Land, Black Capital"; Clift, "Black Land Loss," 108–11; and Griggs, "How Blacks Lost 9,000,000 Acres of Land," *Ebony*, October 1974, 96–104.

35. Baldwin, *Chicago's New Negroes*, 121–35.

36. Holland, *Letters and Diary of Laura Towne*; Behrend, "Facts, Memories, and History"; Lewis, *W. E. B. Du Bois*, 357.

37. Baldwin, *Chicago's New Negroes*, 121–35.

38. Stokes-Hammond, "Pathbreakers: Oscar Stanton Depriest and Jessie L. Williams DePriest," Marszalek, *Black Congressman*; Behrend, "Facts, Memories, and History."

39. Work, "Some Negro Members"; Report on the Exploratory Effort to Collect Manuscript Materials among Negroes (n.d.), Laura Spelman Rockefeller Memorial records, Rockefeller Archive Center, Sleepy Hollow, NY.

40. Helen James Chisholm to Monroe Work, February 14, 1920, in Scurlock et al., "Additional Information and Correction."

41. Henry A. Wallace to Monroe N. Work, October 1917, in Work, "Some Negro Members," 93; R. C. Edmondson to Carter G. Woodson, May 9, 1920, in Work et al., "Letters on Reconstruction Records," 474–75.

42. Helen James Chisholm to Monroe Work, February 14, 1920, in Scurlock et al., "Additional Information and Correction." On Helen James Chisholm's work in the Black Pacific, see Mount, "Virginia in the Pacific"; John W. Cromwell to John Mitchell Jr., May 13, 1920, in Work et al., "Letters on Reconstruction Records."

43. Meier and Rudwick, *Black History and the Historical Profession*, 75–76; Baker, *What Reconstruction Meant*, 116; Augustus Granville Dill, "Negro History, Harvard Style," *The Crisis*, September 1925, 225–26.

44. "Annual Meeting of the Association for the Study of Negro Life and History," *Broad Ax* (Chicago), September 20, 1924; "Miller, Addresses Negro Pythians," *The State* (Columbia, SC), July 30, 1927; "6000 Honor Race Congressmen: DePriest, Lynch, Miller, Present," *Pittsburgh Courier*, February 22, 1930.

45. Lewis, *W. E. B. Du Bois*, 357–59; Du Bois, "Reconstruction of Freedom," 212.

46. Du Bois, "Reconstruction of Freedom," 190, 195, 219.

47. Du Bois, "Reconstruction of Freedom," 221–22.

48. 1895 speech by Thomas E. Miller, in Love, "Disfranchisement of the Negro," 11–13; Lewis, *W. E. B. Du Bois*, 367; Meier and Elliott, *Black History and the Historical Profession*, 101–2.

49. In the same essay, Hughes recounts a story of his great uncle John Mercer Langston encountering a wooden barrier meant to deter Black riders from passing through a well-to-do white neighborhood. Rather than reroute his journey home, Langston stopped at a hardware store, bought an axe, and proceeded to chop down the barrier while his coachmen held his gloves. Hughes, "Bright Chariots"; Dinnella-Borrego, "John Mercer Langston."

50. Henry A. Wallace to Monroe N. Work, March 1920, in Work et al., "Some Negro Members of Reconstruction Conventions and Legislatures," 110; "Leigh Whipper Scores on Broadway," *Pittsburgh Courier*, November 12, 1927.

51. On Harlem's interwar cultural and intellectual history, see Lewis, *When Harlem Was in Vogue*; Ransby, *Ella Baker and the Black Freedom Movement*, 64–104; and Hartman, *Wayward Lives*.

52. Dickerman, "Aaron Douglas."

53. Harlan Greene, "Get to Know the Charleston Man Who Opened a Hopping, Long-Running Harlem Jazz Club in the 1920s"; Gill, *Harlem*, 271.

54. On the falsification of Civil War–era memory, see Domby, *False Cause*. On Robert Smalls's complex familial network, see Billingsley, *Yearning to Breathe Free*, 185–226.

55. "Bethel Literary," *Washington Bee*, May 3, 1919. The last newspaper reference to a meeting of the Bethel Literary and Historical Association appeared November 14, 1931, in the *New York Age*. For a small sample of obituaries that mention Bethel leadership, see *New York Age*, September 15, 1945; and *New Pittsburgh Courier*, June 6, 1942, April 3, 1954.

Epilogue

1. "Singing by Robert Smalls Students Brings Controversy," *The State* (Columbia, SC), March 15, 1940; Mayme Eady Alston, "A Peep into the Past of W. Kent Alston and His Years at Robert Smalls High School," unpublished, 1987, Winifred Kent Alston Papers, Avery Research Center, College of Charleston, SC.

2. "Singing by Robert Smalls Students Brings Controversy."

3. "Beaufort, S.C. News," *Savannah Tribune*, April 17, 1920; "News from Beaufort," *New York Age*, September 12, 1925.

4. Anderson, *Education of Blacks in the South*, 141.

5. Driskell, *Schooling Jim Crow*.

6. "History of Booker T. Washington High School and Its Foundation, Booker T. Washington High School," Booker T. Washington High School Foundation, accessed June 28, 2025, https://bookertwashingtonfoundationsc.org/history/history-of-booker-t-washington-high-school-its-foundation; "A History of Booker T. Washington High School," Booker T. Washington High School, Norfolk Public Schools, 2025, www.npsk12.com/domain/358; Driskell, *Schooling Jim Crow*, chap. 5.

7. Zach Vance, "Tracing Langston High School's 100-Year History," *Johnson City (TN) Press*, December 16, 2017; Lawrence M. Clark, "A Brief History of the Education of African Americans in Danville, Virginia: From Dan's Hill to Langston High School," Virginia Center for Digital History, n.d., www.vcdh.virginia.edu/cslk/danville/media/pdfs/brief_history.pdf; Glaise, *From Danville to Destiny*; Central High School (Cardozo Senior High School), DC Historic Sites, 2025, https://historicsites.dcpreservation.org/items/show/77; "It's John R., not JR, Lynch Street," *Clarion-Ledger* (Jackson, MS), June 27, 1979.

8. Wright, *Black Boy*; Kenton Rambsy, "Richard Wright's Formal and Informal Networks," The Project on the History of Black Writing, May 10, 2011, https://projecthbw.ku.edu/uncategorized/richard-wrights-formal-and-informa; DC People & Places: Black History Spotlight—Cardozo Education Campus, DC Government, Department of General Services, 2025, https://dgs.dc.gov/page/dc-people-places-Black-history-spotlight-cardozo-education-campus; "James Mayo, Director Emeritus of Anacostia Museum Dies," *Washington Post*, July 16, 1995.

9. Muriel Washington Smalley, Adalee Brown Roberts, James N. Brown, and Gerhard Spieler, "Robert Smalls School History," Robert Smalls High School Reunion Pages, accessed June 28, 2025, https://resources.finalsite.net/images/v1676474571/beaufortk12scus/osgawlf2qxin2r8btn2a/RSHSReunionpages.pdf; "Rev. D. W. Bythewood of Beaufort Passes," *Palmetto Leader* (Columbia, SC), January 30, 1926; "Oyster Bowl Grid Games Set for January 1," *Beaufort (SC) Gazette*, December 10, 1948. On the rise of Jim Crow–era Black football, see White, *Blood, Sweat, and Tears*.

10. Mayme Eady Alston, *A Peep into the Past of W. Kent Alston and His Years at Robert Smalls High School* (1987), in Winfred Kent Alston Papers, Avery Research Center, College of Charleston, SC.

11. Freedmen and Southern Society Project, last revised February 2, 2025, www.freedmen.umd.edu; Connelly, "From Wheeler Hill to Capitol Hill"; Oral History Interview with Sara Dunlap Jackson, National Archives Oral History Project, July 5, 1982, National Archives and Records Administration, Washington, DC, www.archives.gov/files/about/history/sara-jackson.pdf; Berlin, "Remembering Sara Dunlap Jackson."

Bibliography

Primary Sources

MANUSCRIPT AND ARCHIVAL COLLECTIONS

Atlanta, GA
   Atlanta University Center, Robert F. Woodruff Library
      Southern Educational Foundation Records
Beaufort, SC
   Beaufort County Public Library, Beaufort District Collection
      Robert Smalls School Records
Chapel Hill, NC
   University of North Carolina, Wilson Special Collections Library
      Southern Historical Collection
         Penn School Papers
Charleston, SC
   Avery Research Center, College of Charleston
      Winifred Kent Alston Papers
College Park, MD
   National Archives II
      American Red Cross Papers
      Public Relations Photographs Relating to National Archives
         Personnel, Facilities, and Events, 1939–68
      Records of the United States Customs Service
Columbia, SC
   South Carolina Department of Archives and History
      Benjamin Tillman Papers
   University of South Carolina, South Caroliniana Library
      Christensen Family Papers
      Elliott Family Papers
      Federal Writers' Project Papers
Sleepy Hollow, NY
   Rockefeller Archive Center
      Laura Spelman Rockefeller Memorial records
Washington, DC
   Howard University, Moorland-Spingarn Research Center
      Leigh Whipper Papers
      Miscellaneous Newspaper Clippings
   Library of Congress
      Manuscript Division
         Clara Barton Papers

Frederick Douglass Papers
Mary Church Terrell Papers
Booker T. Washington Papers
Carter G. Woodson Papers
Rare Book and Special Collections Division
YA Pamphlet Collection

NEWSPAPERS AND PERIODICALS

African Repository and Colonial Journey
Afro-American Press
Anderson (SC) Intelligencer
Anglo-African
Atlanta Constitution
The Athenaeum
Atlanta Journal
Atlantic Monthly
Baltimore (MD) Afro-American
Beaufort (SC) Gazette
Beaufort (SC) New South
Beaufort (SC) Republican and Sea Island Chronicle
Beaufort (SC) Sea Island News
Beaufort (SC) Tribune and Port Royal Commercial
Black Enterprise
Boston Globe
Boston Herald
Broad Ax (Chicago)
Brooklyn Eagle
Charleston Daily Courier
Charleston Daily News
Charleston News and Courier
Charleston World
Charlotte Observer
Chicago Defender
Chicago Sun-Times
Chicago Tribune
Christian Recorder
Clarion-Ledger (Jackson, MS)
Cleveland Call and Post
Cleveland Gazette
Colored American (Washington, DC)
Columbia (SC) Daily Register
The Crescent (Beaufort, SC)
The Crisis
Daily Inter Ocean
Detroit Plaindealer
Ebony
Forum
Grit (Washington, DC)
Hartford (CT) Courant
Indianapolis Freeman
Johnson City (TN) Press
Juniata (PA) Sentinel and Republican
Lexington (NC) Dispatch
The Liberator
Los Angeles Sentinel
Macon (GA) Telegraph
Milwaukee Star
Morning Democrat (Davenport, IA)
Morning Republican (Little Rock, AR)
National Republican (Washington, DC)
Newberry (SC) Weekly Herald
New Era (Washington, DC)
New National Era
New York Age
New York Freeman
New York Globe
New York Herald
New York Herald-Tribune Books
New York Review of Books
New York Sun
New York Times
New York Tribune
Opportunity
Orangeburg (SC) Times and Democrat
Outlook
Palmetto Leader (Columbia, SC)
Palmetto Post (Port Royal, SC)
People's Advocate (Washington, DC)

Pittsburgh Courier
Pittsfield (MA) Sun
Pontotoc (MS) Press
Portland (ME) Daily Press
Port Royal (SC) Standard and Commercial
The Republican (Beaufort, SC)
Savannah Tribune
Scranton (PA) Tribune
Scribner's Monthly
Southern Workman
Springfield (MA) Republican

Star of Zion
The State (Columbia, SC)
Sumter (SC) Watchman and Southron
Survey
Survey Graphic
Union (SC) Times
Washington Bee
Washington Post
Weekly Louisianian (New Orleans)
Winnsboro (SC) News and Herald
Yorkville (SC) Enquirer

GOVERNMENT DOCUMENTS

Congressional Record

Harris, B. B. *Sixteenth Annual Report of the Commissioner of Agriculture, Commerce, and Industries of the State of South Carolina, 1919*. Columbia, SC: Gonzales and Bryan State Printers, 1920.

Jones, Thomas Jesse. *Negro Education: A Study of the Private and Public Education of Colored People in the United States*. Washington, DC: Government Printing Office, 1916.

"Population of South Carolina by Counties and Minor Civil Divisions. Table III—State of South Carolina." In *Ninth Census of the United States* (Washington, DC: Government Printing Office, 1870), 258–60.

Reports and Resolutions of the General Assembly of the State of South Carolina. Columbia, SC: Republican Printing, 1871.

Robert Smalls, Contestant, vs. William Elliott, Contestee. Contested-Election from the Seventh South Carolina District, before the House Committee on Elections, 50th Congress. Washington, DC: Rufus H. Darby, 1887.

South Carolina. *Journal of the Senate of the General Assembly of the State of South Carolina Being the Extra Session, Commencing Tuesday, June 27, 1882*. Columbia, SC: James Woodrow, 1882.

US House of Representatives. Committee on Elections. *Robert Smalls vs. William Elliott*. Rept. No. 3536, 50th Congress, 2nd Sess., December 7, 1888.

OTHER PUBLISHED PRIMARY SOURCES

An Address to the People of the United States Adopted at a Conference of Colored Citizens Held at Columbia, S.C., July 20 and July 21st, 1876. Columbia, SC: Republican Printing, 1876.

Allen, Walter. *Governor Chamberlain's Administration of South Carolina: A Chapter of Reconstruction in the Southern States*. New York: G. P. Putnam's Sons, 1888.

Bancroft, Frederic. *A Sketch of the Negro in Politics in South Carolina and Mississippi*. New York: J. F. Pearson, 1885.

Barton, Clara. *The Red Cross in Peace and War*. Washington, DC: American Historical, 1898.

Barton, Clara. *A Story of the Red Cross: Glimpses of Field Work*. New York: D. Appleton, 1928.

Billington, Ray, ed. *The Journal of Charlotte Forten*. New York: Dryden, 1953.

Bruce, John Edward, ed. *Short Biographical Sketches of Negro Men and Women in Europe and the United States: With Brief Extracts from Their Writings and Public Utterances*. Yonkers, NY: Gazette, 1910.

Campbell, Tunis. *Sufferings of Rev. T. G. Campbell and His Family, in Georgia*. Washington, DC: Enterprise Publishing, 1877.

Christensen, Niels, Jr. "Fifty Years of Freedom: Conditions in the Sea Coast Regions." *Annals of the American Academy of Political and Social Sciences* 49 (Fall 1913): 58–66.

Contested Election, G. D. Tillman vs. Robert Smalls, Fifth Congressional District of South Carolina: Brief for Contestant. Washington, DC: Gibson Bros., 1878.

Cooley, Rossa B. "America's Sea Islands." *Outlook* 131 (April 1919): 741.

Cooley, Rossa B. "The Homes of the Free: III. From Slave Hut to Home." *The Survey*, January 1, 1924, 343.

Cooley, Rossa B. *Homes of the Freed*. New York: New Republic, 1926.

Cooley, Rossa B. *School Acres*. New Haven, CT: Yale University Press, 1930.

Cooley, Rossa B. "Work among St. Helena Negroes." *Vassar Miscellany* (December 1914): 10–14.

Cowley, Charles. *Romance of History in "The Black County," and the Romance of War in the Career of Gen. Robert Smalls, "The Hero of the Planter."* Lowell, MA: self-published, 1882.

Cromwell, John W. *History of the Bethel Literary and Historical Association and Programme for the Year 1895–6*. Washington, DC: R. L. Pendelton, 1896.

Dixon, Thomas, Jr. *The Leopard's Spots*. New York: Doubleday, 1902.

Du Bois, W. E. B. *Black Reconstruction in America: An Essay toward a History of the Part Which Black Folk Played in the Attempt to Reconstruct Democracy in America, 1860–1880*. New York: Harcourt Brace, 1935.

Du Bois, W. E. B. *The Philadelphia Negro: A Social Study*. Philadelphia: University of Pennsylvania Press, 1899.

Du Bois, W. E. B. "The Reconstruction of Freedom." In *The Gift of Black Folk: The Negroes in the Making of America*. Boston: Stratford, 1924.

Du Bois, W. E. B. *Souls of Black Folk*. Chicago: A. G. McClurg, 1903.

Elkington, Joseph S. *Selections from the Diary and Correspondence of Joseph S. Elkington, 1830–1905*. Philadelphia: Leeds and Biddle, 1913.

Fortune, T. Thomas. *Black and White: Land, Labor, and Politics in the South*. New York: Fords, Howard and Hulbert, 1884.

Gibson, J. W., and W. H. Crogman. *The Colored American from Slavery to Honorable Citizenship*. Atlanta: J. L. Nichols, 1902.

Gonzales, Ambrose. *The Black Border: Gullah Stories of the Carolina Coast*. Columbia, SC: The State Printing Co., 1922.

Hampton, Wade. "What Negro Supremacy Means." *Forum* 5 (June 1888): 2.

Harris, B. B. *Sixteenth Annual Report of the Commissioner of Agriculture, Commerce, and Industries of the State of South Carolina, 1919*. Columbia, SC: Gonzales and Bryan State Printers, 1920.

Harris, Joel Chandler. "The Sea Island Hurricanes: The Devastation." *Scribner's*, March 1894, 246.

Heyward, DuBose. *Porgy*. New York: George H. Doran, 1925.

Higginson, Thomas Wentworth. *Army Life in a Black Regiment*. Boston: Lee and Shepard, 1869.

Holland, Rupert S., ed. *Letters and Diary of Laura M. Towne, Written from the Sea Islands of South Carolina, 1862–1884*. Boston: Riverside, 1912.

Hopkins, Pauline. *Contending Forces: A Romance Illustrative of Negro Life North and South*. Boston: Colored Co-operative, 1900.

Horton, McDavid. *St. Helena Island: A Negro Community*. Columbia, SC: The State Printing Company, 1924.

Hughes, Langston. "Bright Chariots." *Negro Digest* 9 (April 1951): 59–62.

Johnson, Guion Griffis. *A Social History of the Sea Islands, with Special Reference in St. Helena Island, South Carolina*. Chapel Hill: University of North Carolina Press, 1930.

Johnson, Guy B. *Folk Culture on St. Helena Island*. Chapel Hill: University of North Carolina Press, 1930.

Journal of the House of Representatives of the State of South Carolina, Regular Session of 1868. Columbia: John W. Denny, 1868.

King, Edward. *The Great South: A Record of Journeys in Louisiana, Texas, the Indian Territory, Missouri, Arkansas, Mississippi, Alabama, Georgia, Florida, South Carolina, North Carolina, Kentucky, Tennessee, Virginia, West Virginia, and Maryland*. Hartford, CT: American, 1875.

Kiser, Clyde. *Sea Island to City: A Study of St. Helena Islanders in Harlem and Other Urban Centers*. New York: Columbia University Press, 1932.

Love, John L. "The Disfranchisement of the Negro." *Occasional Papers of the Negro Academy*, no. 6 (1899).

Lynch, John R. *The Facts of Reconstruction*. New York: Neale, 1913.

Miller, Mary J., ed. *Suffrage Speeches by Negroes in the Constitutional Convention*. N.p., 1895.

N. W. Ayer & Son's Newspaper Annual: Containing a Catalogue of American Newspapers, a List of All Newspapers of the United States and Canada. Philadelphia: N.W. Ayers and Sons, 1890.

Parsons, Elsie Clews. *Folklore of the Sea Islands, South Carolina*. Cambridge, MA: American Folklore Society, 1929.

Peabody, Francis Greenwood. *Education for Life: The Story of Hampton Institute*. Garden City, NY: Doubleday, Page, 1922.

Pearson, Elizabeth Ware, ed. *Letters from Port Royal Written at the Time of the Civil War*. Boston: W. B. Clark, 1906.

Penn, Irvine Garland. *The Afro-American Press and Its Editors*. Springfield, MA: Willey, 1891.

Pierce, Edward Lillie. *The Negroes at Port Royal: Report of E. L. Pierce, Government Agent, to the Hon. Salmon P. Chase, Secretary of the Treasury*. London: Forgotten Books: [1862] 2000.

Pike, James S. *The Prostrate State: South Carolina under Negro Government*. New York: D. Appleton, 1873.

The Republican Campaign for 1882. Washington, DC: Republican Campaign Committee, 1882.

Reynolds, John S. *Reconstruction in South Carolina*. Columbia, SC: The State Printing Company, 1905.

Rollin, Frank (Frances) A. *Life and Public Services of Martin R. Delany*. Boston: Lee and Shepherd, 1868.

Satterthwait, Elisabeth. *Son of the Carolinas: A Story of the Hurricane upon the Sea Islands.* Philadelphia: Henry Altemus, 1898.

Simmons, William J. *Men of Mark: Eminent, Progressive, and Rising.* Cleveland: G. M. Rewell, 1887.

Smalls, Robert. *Contestant vs. William Elliott, Contestee: Contested Election from the Seventh South Carolina District before the House Committee on Elections—Brief for Contestant.* Washington, DC: Rufus H. Darby, 1887.

Smalls, Robert. "Election Methods in the South." *North American Review* 151 (November 1890): 593–600.

Stevenson, Brenda. *The Journals of Charlotte Forten Grimké.* Schomburg Library of Nineteenth-Century Black Women Writers. Oxford: Oxford University Press, 1988.

Taylor, Alrutheus Ambush. "Negro in South Carolina during the Reconstruction." *Journal of Negro History* 9 (October 1924): 383.

Taylor, Alrutheus Ambush. *The Negro in South Carolina during Reconstruction.* Washington, DC: Association for the Study of Negro Life and History, 1924.

"Wade Hampton." *American Missionary* 42 (July 1888): 179–80.

Washington, Booker T. *Up from Slavery: An Autobiography.* Garden City, NY: Doubleday, 1901.

Washington, Harold R. *Got Land Problems?* Frogmore, SC: Penn Community Services and Black Land Services, 1973.

Wells, Ida B. *The Red Record: Tabulated Statistics and Alleged Causes of Lynching in the United States.* Chicago: Donohue & Henneberry, 1894.

Woofter, Thomas Jackson, Jr. *Black Yeomanry: Life on St. Helena Island.* New York: Henry Holt, 1930.

Woofter, Thomas Jackson, Jr. "Negro Migration: Changes in Rural Organization and Population of the Cotton Belt." PhD diss., Columbia University, 1920.

Work, Monroe N. "Some Negro Members of Reconstruction Conventions and Legislatures and of Congress." *Journal of Negro History* 5 (January 1920): 63–119.

Wright, Richard. *Black Boy.* New York: HarperCollins, 1943.

Wright, Robert R., Jr. *Centennial Encyclopaedia of the African Methodist Episcopal Church, 1816–1916.* Philadelphia, 1916. https://archive.org/details/centennialencycloowrig.

ONLINE PRIMARY AND TERTIARY SOURCES

Beaufort County, South Carolina—World War I: The Official Roster of South Carolina Soldiers, Sailors, and Marines in the World War, 1917–1918, Genealogy Trails. March 1, 2006. http://genealogytrails.com/scar/beaufort/wwi_dead.htm.

Born in Slavery: Slave Narratives from the Federal Writers' Project, 1936–1938. American Memory, Library of Congress. www.loc.gov/collections/slave-narratives-from-the-federal-writers-project-1936-to-1938/about-this-collection.

"The Congressional Districts of South Carolina as 'Gerrymandered' by the Democracy in 1882." Library of Congress. www.loc.gov/item/2015588077.

Ex-Slave Narratives, 1936–1940. Mississippi Department of Archives and History. 2024. www.mdah.ms.gov/arrec/digital_archives.

Freedmen and Southern Society Project, University of Maryland, College Park. Last revised February 2, 2025. www.freedmen.umd.edu.

Gullah-Geechee Cultural Heritage Corridor. www.gullahgeecheecorridor.org.
Hergesheimer, Edwin. "1860 Map Showing the Distribution of the Slave Population of the Southern States of the United States." Library of Congress. https://lccn.loc.gov/99447026.
"Heroes of the Colored Race." Graphic Arts Collection Website, May 5, 2017. Special Collections, Firestone Library, Princeton University. https://graphicarts.princeton.edu/2017/05/04/heroes-of-the-colored-race.
Historical Census Browser. Geospatial and Statistical Data Center, University of Virginia. Accessed December 1, 2016. http://mapserver.lib.virginia.edu (site discontinued).
"P. B. S. Pinchback." *64 Parishes*, June 22, 2023. https://64parishes.org/entry/p-b-s-pinchback-adaptation.
"Visualizing the Great Migration." *One-Way Ticket: Jacob Lawrence's Migration Series*. Museum of Modern Art, April 3–September 7, 2015. www.moma.org/interactives/exhibitions/2015/onewayticket/visualizing-the-great-migration.

Secondary Sources

Abbott, Martin. *The Freedmen's Bureau in South Carolina, 1865–1872*. Chapel Hill: University of North Carolina Press, 1967.
Adeleke, Tunde. *Without Regard to Race: The Other Martin Robison Delany*. Jackson: University of Mississippi Press, 2009.
Agbor-Taylor, Phylisha. "South Carolina's Black Majority (1708–1920)." *Black Past*, January 24, 2022. www.blackpast.org/african-american-history/south-carolinas-black-majority-1708-1920.
Alexander, Elizabeth. *The Trayvon Generation*. New York: Grand Central, 2022.
Alexander, Shawn Leigh. "T. Thomas Fortune, Reconstruction, and Historical Memory." In *Remembering Reconstruction: Struggles over the Meaning of America's Most Turbulent Era*, edited by Carole Emberton and Bruce E. Baker. Baton Rouge: Louisiana State University Press, 2017.
Alexander, Shawn Leigh, ed. *T. Thomas Fortune: The Afro-American Agitator, 1880–1928*. Gainesville: University of Florida Press, 2010.
Ali, Omar H. *In the Lion's Mouth: Black Populism in the New South, 1886–1900*. Jackson: University Press of Mississippi, 2010.
Anderson, Benedict. *Imagined Communities: Reflections on the Origin and Spread of Nationalism*. Verso: New York, 1983.
Anderson, Eric. *Race and Politics in North Carolina, 1872–1901*. Baton Rouge: Louisiana State University Press, 1981.
Anderson, James D. *The Education of Blacks in the South, 1860–1935*. Chapel Hill: University of North Carolina Press, 1988.
Asch, Chris Myers, and George Derek Musgrove. *Chocolate City: A History of Race and Democracy in the Nation's Capital*. Chapel Hill: University of North Carolina Press, 2017.
Ayers, Edward L. *The Promise of the New South: Life after Reconstruction*. New York: Oxford University Press, 1992.

Ayers, Edward L. *Southern Journey: The Migrations of the American South, 1790–2020*. Baton Rouge: Louisiana State University Press, 2020.
Badger, Anthony. *Why White Liberals Fail*. Cambridge, MA: Harvard University Press, 2022.
Baker, Bruce E. *This Mob Will Surely Take My Life: Lynchings in the Carolinas, 1871–1947*. London: Bloomsbury, 2008.
Baker, Bruce E. *What Reconstruction Meant: Historical Memory in the American South*. Charlottesville: University of Virginia Press, 2007.
Baker, Bruce E., and Carole Emberton. *Remembering Reconstruction: Struggles over the Meaning of America's Most Turbulent Era*. Baton Rouge: Louisiana State University Press, 2017.
Baldwin, Davarian L. *Chicago's New Negroes: Modernity, the Great Migration, and Black Urban Life*. Chapel Hill: University of North Carolina Press, 2007.
Baradaran, Mehrsa. *The Color of Money: Black Banks and the Racial Wealth Gap*. Cambridge, MA: Harvard University Press, 2017.
Barbour, Urshula, and Paul Carlos. "The Honorable Hastings Gantt: 50 Acres and a School." 2022. https://static1.squarespace.com/static/60e4a8556e2d276622495974/t/6256da11b390ed11c9aa2050/1649859090890/Hastings+Gantt+Resource+Guide.pdf.
Barkley Brown, Elsa. "Negotiating and Transforming the Public Sphere: African American Political Life in the Transition from Slavery to Freedom." *Public Culture* 7 (Fall 1994): 107–46.
Barkley Brown, Elsa, and Gregg D. Kimball. "Mapping the Terrain of Black Richmond." *Journal of Urban History* 21 (March 1995): 295–346.
Barnes, Kenneth C. *Journey of Hope: The Back-to Africa Movement in Arkansas in the Late 1800s*. Chapel Hill: University of North Carolina Press, 2004.
Behrend, Justin. "Facts and Memories: John R. Lynch and the Revising of Reconstruction History in the Era of Jim Crow." *Journal of African American History* 97 (Fall 2012): 427–48.
Behrend, Justin. "Facts, Memories, and History: John R. Lynch and the Memory of Reconstruction in the Age of Jim Crow." In *Remembering Reconstruction: Struggles over the Meaning of America's Most Turbulent Era*, edited by Carole Emberton and Bruce E. Baker. Baton Rouge: Louisiana State University Press, 2017.
Behrend, Justin. *Reconstructing Democracy: Grassroots Black Politics in the Deep South after the Civil War*. Athens: University of Georgia Press, 2015.
Bergeson-Lockwood, Millington W. *Race over Party: Black Politics and Partisanship in Late Nineteenth-Century Boston*. Chapel Hill: University of North Carolina Press, 2018.
Berlin, Ira. *The Long Emancipation: The Demise of Slavery in the United States*. Cambridge, MA: Harvard University Press, 2018.
Berlin, Ira. *Many Thousands Gone: The First Two Centuries of Slavery in North America*. Cambridge, MA: Harvard University Press, 2000.
Berlin, Ira. "Remembering Sara Dunlap Jackson." *Black Past*, October 23, 2007. www.Blackpast.org/african-american-history/ira-berlin-remembering-sara-dunlap-jackson-1919-1991.
Berlin, Ira. *Slaves without Masters: The Free Negro in the Antebellum South*. New York: Pantheon, 1974.

Berlin, Ira, Barbara J. Fields, Thavolia Glymph, Joseph P. Reidy, and Leslie S. Rowland, eds. *The Destruction of Slavery.* Ser. 1, vol. 1 of *Freedom: A Documentary History of Emancipation, 1861–1867.* New York: Cambridge University Press, 1985.

Berlin, Ira, Barbara J. Fields, Steven F. Miller, Joseph P. Reidy, and Leslie S. Rowland. *Slaves No More: Three Essays on Emancipation and the Civil War.* Cambridge: Cambridge University Press, 1992.

Berlin, Ira, Thavolia Glymph, Steven F. Miller, Joseph P. Reidy, Leslie S. Rowland, and Julie Saville, eds. *The Wartime Genesis of Free Labor: The Lower South.* Ser. 1, vol. 3 of *Freedom: A Documentary History of Emancipation, 1861–1867.* New York: Cambridge University Press, 1990.

Berlin, Ira, Joseph P. Reidy, and Leslie S. Rowland, eds. *The Black Military Experience.* Ser. 2 of *Freedom: A Documentary History of Emancipation, 1861–1867.* New York: Cambridge University Press, 1982.

Best, Ryan. "Confederate Statues Were Never Really about Preserving History." *Five Thirty Eight,* July 8, 2020. https://Projects.Fivethirtyeight.com/confederate-statues.

Billingsley, Andrew. *Yearning to Breathe Free: Robert Smalls of South Carolina and His Families.* Columbia: University of South Carolina Press, 2007.

Blair, William A. *Cities of the Dead: Contesting the Memory of the Civil War in the South, 1865–1914.* Chapel Hill: University of North Carolina Press, 2015.

Blakely, Allison. "Richard T. Greener and the 'Talented Tenth's' Dilemma." *Journal of Negro History* 59 (October 1974): 305–21.

Bland, Robert D. "'A Grim Memorial of Its Thorough Work of Devastation and Desolation': Race and Memory in the Aftermath of the 1893 Sea Island Storm." *Journal of Gilded Age and Progressive Era* 17 (Spring 2018): 297–316.

Blassingame, John W. "Before the Ghetto: The Making of Black Savannah, Georgia, 1865–1880." *Journal of Social History* 6 (Summer 1973): 463–88.

Blight, David W. *Frederick Douglass: Prophet of Freedom.* New York: Simon and Schuster, 2018.

Blight, David W. *Race and Reunion: The Civil War in American Memory.* Cambridge, MA: Belknap Press of Harvard University Press, 2001.

Bodnar, John E. *Remaking America: Public Memory, Commemoration, and Patriotism in the Twentieth Century.* Princeton, NJ: Princeton University Press, 1991.

Bollinger, Heather K. "The North Comes South: Northern Methodists in Florida during Reconstruction." Master's thesis, University of Central Florida, 2011.

Bonner, Christopher James. *Remaking the Republic: Black Politics and the Creation of Citizenship.* Philadelphia: University of Pennsylvania Press, 2020.

Bonner, Christopher James. "Possessed: Understanding the Lives of Enslaved Americans." *Journal of Civil War Era* 14 (Spring 2024): 90–112.

Braungart, Richard G., and Margaret M. Braungart. "Life-Course and Generational Politics." *Annual Review of Sociology* 12 (1986): 205–31.

Brimmer, Brandi Clay. *Claiming Union Widowhood: Race, Respectability, and Poverty in the Post-Emancipation South.* Durham, NC: Duke University Press, 2020.

Brock, Euline W. "Thomas W. Cardozo: Fallible Black Reconstruction Leader." *Journal of Southern History* 47 (Summer 1981): 183–206.

Brown, Lois. *Pauline Elizabeth Hopkins: Black Daughter of the Revolution.* Chapel Hill: University of North Carolina Press, 2008.

Brundage, W. Fitzhugh. "Contentious and Collected: Memory's Future in Southern History." *Journal of Southern History* 75, no. 3 (August 2009): 751–66.
Brundage, W. Fitzhugh. *The Southern Past: A Clash of Race and Memory*. Cambridge, MA: Harvard University Press, 2005.
Brundage, W. Fitzhugh, ed. "Working in the 'Kingdom of Culture: African Americans and American Popular Culture.'" In *Beyond Blackface: African Americans and the Creation of American Popular Culture, 1890–1930*. Chapel Hill: University of North Carolina Press, 2011.
Budiansky, Stephen. *The Bloody Shirt: Terror after Appomattox*. New York: Penguin, 2008.
Burke, W. Lewis. *All for Civil Rights: African American Lawyers in South Carolina, 1868–1968*. Athens: University of Georgia Press, 2017.
Burton, Orville Vernon, with Wilbur Cross. *Penn Center: A History Preserved*. Athens: University of Georgia Press, 2014.
Camp, Stephanie M. H. *Closer to Freedom: Enslaved Women and Everyday Resistance in the Plantation South*. Chapel Hill: University of North Carolina Press, 2004.
Carney, Judith A. *Black Rice: The African Origins of Rice Cultivation in the Americas*. Cambridge, MA: Harvard University Press, 2001.
Cheek, William Francis, and Aimee Lee Cheek. *John Mercer Langston and the Fight for Black Freedom, 1829–65*. Urbana: University of Illinois Press, 1989.
Clark, Kathleen Ann. *Defining Moments: African American Commemoration and Political Culture in the South, 1863–1913*. Chapel Hill: University of North Carolina Press, 2005.
Clift, Eleanor. "Black Land Loss: 6,000,000 Acres and Fading Fast." *Southern Exposure* 2 (Fall 1974): 108–11.
Cohen, Deborah. *Last Call at the Hotel Imperial: The Reporters Who Took on a World at War*. New York: Random House, 2022.
Cohen, William. *At Freedom's Edge: Black Mobility and the Southern White Quest for Racial Control, 1861–1915*. Baton Rouge: Louisiana State University Press, 1991.
Connelly, Tom. "From Wheeler Hill to Capitol Hill." *State Magazine* (Columbia, SC), January 30, 1983.
Cooper, Abigail. "'Away I Goin' to Find My Mamma': Self-Emancipation, Migration, and Kinship in Refugee Camps in the Civil War Era." *Journal of African American History* 102 (Fall 2017): 444–67.
Cooper, William J., Jr. *The Conservative Regime: South Carolina, 1877–1890*. Baltimore: Johns Hopkins University Press, 1968.
Coulter, E. Merton. "Aaron Alpeoria Bradley: Georgia Negro Politician during Reconstruction Times, Part II." *Georgia Historical Quarterly* 51 (June 1967): 154–74.
Coulter, E. Merton. "Aaron Alpeoria Bradley: Georgia Negro Politician during Reconstruction Times, Part III." *Georgia Historical Quarterly* 51 (September 1967): 264–306.
Cox, Karen L. *Dixie's Daughters: The United Daughters of the Confederacy and the Preservation of Confederate Culture*. Gainesville: University of Florida Press, 2003.
Crowder, Ralph. *John Edward Bruce: Politician, Journalist, and Self-Trained Historian of the African Diaspora*. New York: New York University Press, 2004.
Dabbs, Edith M., ed. *Face of the Island: Leigh Richmond Miner's Photographs of St. Helena Island*. New York: Grossman, 1971.

Dailey, Jane. *Before Jim Crow: The Politics of Race in Postemancipation Virginia*. Chapel Hill: University of North Carolina Press, 2000.

Davidson, Christina Cecilia. *Dominican Crossroads: H. C. C. Astwood and the Moral Politics of Race-Making in the Age of Emancipation*. Durham, NC: Duke University Press, 2024.

Davis, John Martin, Jr. "Bankless in Beaufort: A Reexamination of 1873 Failure of Freedmans Savings Branch at Beaufort, South Carolina." *South Carolina Historical Magazine* 104 (January 2003): 25–55.

Davis, Thulani. *The Emancipation Circuit: Black Activism Forging a Culture of Freedom*. Durham, NC: Duke University Press, 2022.

Dawson, Michael C. *Behind the Mule: Race and Class in African-American Politics*. Princeton, NJ: Princeton University Press, 1995.

Dickerman, Leah. "Aaron Douglas and *Aspects of Negro Life*." *October* 174 (Fall 2020): 126–62.

Dickerson, Dennis C. *The African Methodist Episcopal Church: A History*. New York: Cambridge University Press, 2020.

Dinnella-Borrego, Luis-Alejandro. "John Mercer Langston (1829–1897)." *Encyclopedia Virginia*, Virginia Humanities, December 7, 2020.

Dinnella-Borrego, Luis-Alejandro. *The Risen Phoenix: Black Politics in the Post–Civil War South*. Charlottesville: University of Virginia Press, 2016.

Domby, Adam. *The False Cause: Fraud, Fabrication, and White Supremacy in Confederate Memory*. Charlottesville: University of Virginia Press, 2022.

Downs, Gregory P. *After Appomattox: Military Occupation and the Ends of War*. Cambridge, MA: Harvard University Press, 2019.

Downs, Gregory P., and Kate Masur, eds. *The World the Civil War Made*. Chapel Hill: University of North Carolina Press, 2015.

Driskell, Jay Winston, Jr. *Schooling Jim Crow: The Fight for Atlanta's Booker T. Washington High School and the Roots of Black Protest*. Charlottesville: University of Virginia Press, 2014.

Duncan, Russell. *Freedom's Shore: Tunis Campbell and the Georgia Freedmen*. Athens: University of Georgia Press, 1986.

Edelson, S. Max. *Plantation Enterprise in Colonial South Carolina*. Cambridge, MA: Harvard University Press, 2006.

Edwards, Justene Hill. *Savings and Trust: The Rise and Betrayal of the Freedman's Bank*. New York: W. W. Norton, 2024.

Edwards, Laura F. *A Legal History of the Civil War and Reconstruction: A Nation of Rights*. New York: Cambridge University Press, 2015.

Egerton, Douglas. "Terrorized African-Americans Found Their Champion in Civil War Hero Robert Smalls." *Smithsonian Magazine*, September 2018. www.smithsonianmag.com/history/terrorized-african-americans-champion-civil-war-hero-robert-smalls-180970031.

Egerton, John. *Speak Now against the Day: The Generation before the Civil Rights Movement in the South*. University of North Carolina Press, 1995.

Ellis, Mark. *Race Harmony and Black Progress: Jack Woofter and the Interracial Cooperation Movement*. Bloomington: Indiana University Press, 2013.

Emberton, Carole. *Beyond Redemption: Race, Violence, and the American South after the Civil War*. Chicago: University of Chicago Press, 2013.

Emberton, Carole. *To Walk About in Freedom: The Long Emancipation of Priscilla Joyner*. New York: Harper and Row, 2022.

Engs, Robert. *Freedom's First Generation: Black Hampton, Virginia, 1861–1890*. New York: Fordham University Press, 2004.

Fagan, Benjamin. *The Black Newspaper and the Chosen Nation*. Athens: University of Georgia Press, 2016.

Fairclough, Adam. *A Class of Their Own: Black Teachers in the Segregated South*. Cambridge, MA: Harvard University Press, 2007.

Faust, Drew Gilpin. *James Henry Hamond and the Old South: A Design for Mastery*. Baton Rouge: Louisiana State University Press, 1985.

Favors, Jelani M. *Shelter in a Time of Storm: How Black Colleges Fostered Generations of Leadership and Activism*. Chapel Hill: University of North Carolina Press, 2019.

Feimster, Crystal. *Southern Horrors: Women and the Politics of Rape and Lynching*. Cambridge, MA: Harvard University Press, 2009.

Field, Kendra Taira. *Growing up with the Country: Family, Race, and Nation after the Civil War*. New Haven, CT: Yale University Press, 2018.

Fields, Barbara Jeanne. *Slavery on the Middle Ground: Maryland during the Nineteenth Century*. New Haven, CT: Yale University Press, 1985.

Fields-Black, Edda L. *Combee: Harriet Tubman, the Combahee River Raid, and Black Freedom during the Civil War*. New York: Oxford University Press, 2024.

Foner, Eric. *Freedom's Lawmakers: A Directory of Black Officeholders during Reconstruction*. Baton Rouge: Louisiana State University Press, 1996.

Foner, Eric. *Free Soil, Free Labor, Free Men: The Ideology of the Republican Party before the Civil War*. New York: Oxford University Press, 1969.

Foner, Eric. *Nothing but Freedom: Emancipation and Its Legacy*. Baton Rouge: Louisiana State University Press, 1983.

Foner, Eric. *Reconstruction: America's Unfinished Revolution*. New York: Harper and Row, 1988.

Fordham, Damon L. *True Stories of Black South Carolina*. Charleston, SC: History Press, 2008.

Foreman, P. Gabrielle, ed. *The Colored Conventions Movement: Black Organizing in the Nineteenth Century*. Chapel Hill: University of North Carolina Press, 2021.

Foucault, Michel. "Nietzsche, Genealogy, History." In *Language, Counter-Memory, Practice: Selected Essays and Interviews*, edited by Donald F. Bouchard. Ithaca, NY: Cornell University Press, 1977.

Franklin, John Hope, and August Meier, eds., *Black Leaders of the Twentieth Century*. Urbana: University of Illinois Press, 1982.

Fraser, Walter J., Jr. *Charleston! Charleston! The History of a Southern City*. Columbia: University of South Carolina Press, 1992.

Fraser, Walter J., Jr. *Lowcountry Hurricanes: Three Centuries of Storms at Sea and Ashore*. Athens: University of Georgia Press, 2006.

Freeman, Joanne B. *The Field of Blood: Violence in Congress and the Road to the Civil War*. New York: Farrar, Straus, and Giroux, 2018.

Frisken, Amanda K. "'A Song without Words': Anti-Lynching Imagery in the African American Press, 1889–1898." *Journal of African American History* 97 (Summer 2012): 240–69.

Fultz, Michael. "Charleston, 1919–1920: The Final Battle in the Emergence of the South's Urban African American Teaching Corps." *Journal of Urban History* 27 (July 2001): 633–49.

Gaines, Kevin K. *Uplifting the Race: Black Leadership, Politics, and Culture in the Twentieth Century*. Chapel Hill: University of North Carolina Press, 1996.

Gallagher, Gary W. *Causes Won, Lost, and Forgotten: How Hollywood and Popular Art Shape What We Know about the Civil War*. Chapel Hill: University of North Carolina Press, 2008.

Gannon, Barbara. *The Won Cause: Black and White Comradeship in the Grand Army of the Republic*. Chapel Hill: University of North Carolina Press, 2011.

Gardner, Eric. *Black Print Unbound: The Christian Recorder, African American Literature, and Periodical Culture*. New York: Oxford University Press, 2015.

Gardner, Eric. "Remembered (Black) Readers: Subscribers to the 'Christian Recorder,' 1864–1865." *American Literary History* 23 (Summer 2011): 233.

Gates, Henry Louis, Jr. *Stony the Road: Reconstruction, White Supremacy, and the Rise of Jim Crow*. New York: Penguin, 2019.

Gatewood, Willard B., Jr. *Aristocrats of Color: The Black Elite, 1880–1920*. Fayetteville: University of Arkansas Press, 2000.

Gatewood, Willard B., Jr. "'The Remarkable Misses Rollin': Black Women in the Reconstruction South." *South Carolina Historical Magazine* 92 (Summer 1991): 172–88.

Gelston, Arthur Lewis. "Radical Versus Straight-Out in Post-Reconstruction Beaufort County." *South Carolina Historical Magazine* 75 (October 1974): 225–37.

Gill, Jonathan. *Harlem: The Four Hundred Year History from Dutch Village to Capital of Black America*. New York: Grove/Atlantic, 2011.

Gilmore, Glenda Elizabeth. *Defying Dixie: The Radical Roots of Civil Rights, 1919–1950*. New York: W. W. Norton, 2008.

Gilmore, Glenda Elizabeth. *Gender and Jim Crow: Women and the Politics of White Supremacy in North Carolina, 1896–1920*. Chapel Hill: University of North Carolina Press, 1996.

Givens, Jarvis. *Fugitive Pedagogy: Carter G. Woodson and the Art of Black Teaching*. Cambridge, MA: Harvard University Press, 2021.

Glaise, Joyce. *From Danville to Destiny: I Got Nerve*. Bloomington, IN: Trafford, 2016.

Glymph, Thavolia. "'Liberty Dearly Bought': The Making of Civil War Memory in Afro-American Communities in the South." In *Time Longer than Rope: A Century of African American Activism, 1850–1950*, edited by Charles M. Payne and Adam Green. New York: New York University Press, 2003.

Glymph, Thavolia. *Out of the House of Bondage: The Transformation of the Plantation Household*. New York: Cambridge University Press, 2008.

Gonzalez, Aston. *Visualizing Equality: African American Rights and Visual Culture in the Nineteenth Century*. Chapel Hill: University of North Carolina Press, 2020.

Gosse, Van. *The First Reconstruction: Black Politics in America from the Revolution to the Civil War*. Chapel Hill: University of North Carolina Press, 2021.

Green, Hilary N. *Unforgettable Sacrifice: How Black Communities Remembered the Civil War*. New York: Fordham University Press, 2025.

Greene, Harlan. "Get to Know the Charleston Man Who Opened a Hopping, Long-Running Harlem Jazz Club in the 1920s." *Charleston Magazine*, September 2021. https://charlestonmag.com/features/get_to_know_the_charleston_man_who_opened_a_hopping_long_running_harlem_jazz_club_in_the.

Greenidge, Kerri K. *The Grimkes: The Legacy of Slavery in an American Family*. New York: W. W. Norton, 2022.

Grego, Caroline E. *Hurricane Jim Crow: How the Great Sea Island Storm of 1893 Shaped the Lowcountry South*. Chapel Hill: University of North Carolina Press, 2022.

Griggs, Anthony. "How Blacks Lost 9,000,000 Acres of Land." *Ebony*, October 1974, 96–104.

Gronningsater, Sara L. H. *The Rising Generation: Gradual Abolition, Black Legal Culture, and the Making of National Freedom*. Philadelphia: University of Pennsylvania Press, 2024.

Grossman, James R. *Land of Hope: Chicago, Black Southerners, and the Great Migration*. Chicago: University of Chicago Press, 1989.

Guthrie, Patricia. *Catching Sense: African American Communities on a South Carolina Sea Island*. Westport, CT: Bergin and Garvey, 1996.

Gutman, Herbert. "Schools for Freedom: The Post-Emancipation Origins of Afro-American Education." In *Power and Culture: Essays on the American Working Class*, edited by Ira Berlin. New York: Pantheon, 1987.

Hahn, Steven. *A Nation under Our Feet: Black Political Struggles in the Rural South from Slavery to the Great Migration*. Cambridge, MA: Belknap Press of Harvard University Press, 2003.

Hahn, Steven. *The Roots of Southern Populism: Yeoman Farmers and the Transformation of the Georgia Upcountry, 1850–1890*. New York: Oxford University Press, 1983.

Hahn, Steven, Steven F. Miller, Susan E. O'Donovan, John C. Rodrigue, and Leslie S. Rowland, eds. *Land and Labor, 1865*. Ser. 3, vol. 1 of *Freedom: A Documentary History of Emancipation, 1861–1867*. Chapel Hill: University of North Carolina Press, 2008.

Halbwachs, Maurice. *On Collective Memory*. Chicago: University of Chicago Press, 1925.

Haley, Sarah. *No Mercy Here: Gender, Punishment, and the Making of Jim Crow Modernity*. Chapel Hill: University of North Carolina Press, 2016.

Hall, Jacquelyn Dowd. *Revolt against Chivalry: Jessie Daniel Ames and the Women's Campaign against Lynching*. New York: Columbia University Press, 1993.

Hall, Stephen G. *A Faithful Account of the Race: African American Historical Writing in the Nineteenth Century*. Chapel Hill: University of North Carolina Press, 2009.

Hall, Stuart, with John Clarke, Tony Jefferson, and Brian Roberts. "Subcultures, Cultures and Class: A Theoretical Overview." In *Resistance through Rituals: Youth Subcultures in Post-War Britain*, edited by Tony Jefferson. London: Routledge, 1976.

Harlan, Louis R. *Booker T. Washington: The Making of a Black Leader, 1856–1901*. New York: Oxford University Press, 1972.

Harlan, Louis R. *Booker T. Washington: The Wizard of Tuskegee, 1901–1915*. New York: Oxford University Press, 1983.

Harper, Frances. "The Democratic Return to Power—Its Effect." *African Methodist Episcopal Church Review* 1 (1884): 222–25.

Harris, John, updated by Beth Gniewek and Bradley Blankmeyer. "After Slavery: Hamburg Massacre." Lowcountry Digital History Initiative, College of Charleston. 2013–14. https://ldhi.library.cofc.edu/neatline/show/after-slavery-hamburg-massacre.
Harris, LaShawn. *Sex Workers, Psychics and Numbers Runners: Black Women in New York City's Underground Economy*. Urbana: University of Illinois Press, 2016.
Harris, Robert L., Jr. "Daniel Murray and the Encyclopedia of the Colored Race." *Phylon* 37 (Fall 1976): 270–82.
Hartman, Saidiya. *Wayward Lives, Beautiful Experiments: Intimate Histories of Social Upheaval*. New York: W. W. Norton, 2019.
Hayden, René, Anthony E. Kaye, Kate Masur, Steven F. Miller, Susan E. O'Donovan, Leslie S. Rowland, and Stephen A. West, eds. *Land and Labor, 1866–1867*. Ser. 3, vol. 2 of *Freedom: A Documentary History of Emancipation, 1861–1867*. Chapel Hill: University of North Carolina Press, 2013.
Heersink, Boris. *Republican Party Politics and the American South, 1865–1968*. Cambridge: Cambridge University Press, 2020.
Hickmott, Alec Fazackerley. "Black Land, Black Capital: Rural Development in the Shadow of the Sunbelt South, 1969-1976." *Journal of African American History* 101 (Fall 2016): 504–34.
Higginbotham, Evelyn Brooks. *Righteous Discontent: The Women's Movement in the Black Baptist Church, 1880–1920*. Cambridge, MA.: Harvard University Press, 1993.
Hild, Matthew. *Greenbackers, Knights of Labor, and Populists: Farmer-Labor Insurgency in the Late-Nineteenth-Century South*. Athens: University of Georgia Press, 2007.
Hill, Errol G., and James V. Hatch. *A History of African American Theater*. New York: Cambridge University Press, 2006.
Hill, Robert A., ed. *The Marcus Garvey and Universal Negro Improvement Association Papers*, vol. 2, August 1919–August 1920. Berkeley: University of California Press.
Hine, Darlene Clark, ed. *Black Women in America*. 2nd ed. New York: Oxford University Press, 2005.
Hinton, Elizabeth. "The Last Great Battle of the West." *American Historical Review* 127 (December 2022): 1909–15.
Hirshson, Stanley P. *Farewell to the Bloody Shirt: Northern Republicans and the Southern Negro, 1873–1893*. Bloomington: Indiana University Press, 1962.
Hobsbawm, Eric, and Terence Ranger, eds. *The Invention of Tradition*. Cambridge: Cambridge University Press, 1983.
Hoffman, Warren. *The Great White Way: Race and the Broadway Musical*. Piscataway, NJ: Rutgers University Press, 2014.
Holloway, Jonathan Scott. *Jim Crow Wisdom: Memory and Identity in Black America*. Chapel Hill: University of North Carolina Press, 2013.
Holloway, Vanessa. *In Search of Federal Enforcement: The Moral Authority of the Fifteenth Amendment and the Integrity of the Black Ballot, 1870–1965*. Lanham, MD: University Press of America, 2015.
Holt, Michael F. *By One Vote: The Disputed Presidential Election of 1876*. Lawrence: University of Kansas Press, 2008.
Holt, Thomas C. *Black over White: Negro Political Leadership in South Carolina during Reconstruction*. Urbana: University of Illinois Press, 1977.

Hunter, Tera W. *Bound in Wedlock: Slave and Free Black Marriage in the Nineteenth Century*. Cambridge, MA: Belknap Press of Harvard University Press, 2017.

Hunter, Tera W. *To 'Joy My Freedom: Southern Black Women's Lives and Labors after the Civil War*. Cambridge, MA: Harvard University Press, 1997.

Hutchison, Janet. "Better Homes and Gullah." *Agricultural History* 67 (Spring 1993): 102–18.

Ione, Carole. *Pride of Family: Four Generations of American Women of Color*. New York: Summit, 1991.

Jackson, Debra. "'A Cultural Stronghold': The Anglo-African Newspaper and the Black Community of New York." *New York History* 85 (Fall 2004): 331–57.

Jacobson, Matthew Frye. *Barbarian Virtues: The United States Encounters Foreign Peoples at Home and Abroad, 1876–1917*. New York: Hill and Wang, 2000.

Jacoway, Elizabeth. *Yankee Missionaries in the South: The Penn School Experiment*. Baton Rouge: Louisiana State University Press, 1980.

Janney, Caroline E. *Remembering the Civil War: Reunion and the Limits of Reconciliation*. Chapel Hill: University of North Carolina Press, 2013.

Jaynes, Gerald D. *Branches without Roots: Genesis of the Black Working Class in the American South, 1862–1882*. New York: Oxford University Press, 1986.

Johnson, Andre E. *No Future in This Country: The Prophetic Pessimism of Bishop Henry McNeal Turner*. Jackson: University of Mississippi Press, 2020.

Johnson, Kimberly S. *Reforming Jim Crow: Southern Politics and State in the Age before Brown*. New York: Oxford University Press, 2010.

Johnson, Rashauna. *Slavery's Metropolis: Unfree Labor in New Orleans during the Age of Revolutions*. New York: Cambridge University Press, 2016.

Johnson, Thomas, and Nina Root, eds. *Camera Man's Journey: Julian Dimock's South*. Athens: University of Georgia Press, 2002.

Jones, Marian Moser. *The Red Cross from Clara Barton to the New Deal*. Baltimore: Johns Hopkins University Press, 2013.

Jones, Martha S. *All Bound Up Together: The Woman Question in African American Public Culture, 1830–1900*. Chapel Hill: University of North Carolina Press, 2007.

Jones, Martha S. *Vanguard: How Black Women Broke Barriers, Won the Vote, and Insisted on Equality for All*. Basic Books, 2020.

Jones-Jackson, Patricia. *When Roots Die: Endangered Traditions on the Sea Islands*. Athens: University of Georgia Press, 1987.

Kachun, Mitch. *Festivals of Freedom: Memory and Meaning in African American Celebrations, 1808–1915*. Amherst: University of Massachusetts Press, 2003.

Kachun, Mitch. "Interrogating the Silences: Julia C. Collins, Nineteenth-Century Black Readers and Writers, and the 'Christian Recorder.'" *African American Review* 40, no. 4 (Winter 2006): 646–59.

Kahrl, Andrew. *The Land Was Ours: How Black Beaches Became White Wealth in the Coastal South*. Chapel Hill: University of North Carolina Press, 2012.

Kammen, Michael. *Mystic Chords of Memory: The Transformation of Tradition in American Culture*. New York: Alfred A. Knopf, 1991.

Kantrowitz, Stephen. *Benjamin Tillman and the Reconstruction of White Supremacy*. Chapel Hill: University of North Carolina Press, 2000.

Kantrowitz, Stephen. "One Man's Mob Is Another Man's Militia: Violence, Manhood, and Authority in Reconstruction South Carolina." In *Jumpin' Jim Crow: Southern Politics from the Civil War to Civil Rights*, edited by Jane Dailey, Glenda Elizabeth Gilmore, and Bryant Simon. Princeton, NJ: Princeton University Press, 2000.

Kantrowitz, Stephen. *More than Freedom: Fighting for Black Citizenship in a White Republic, 1829–1889*. New York: Penguin, 2012.

Katz, Michael. *In the Shadow of the Poorhouse: A Social History of Welfare in America*. New York: Basic Books, 1986.

Kaye, Anthony E. *Joining Places: Slave Neighborhoods in the Old South*. Chapel Hill: University of North Carolina Press, 2007.

Kelley, Blair L. M. *Right to Ride: Streetcar Boycotts and African American Citizenship in the Era of Plessy v. Ferguson*. Chapel Hill: University of North Carolina Press, 2010.

Kelley, Robin D. G. "Abolition Democracy's Forgotten Founder." *Boston Review*, April 19, 2022. www.bostonreview.net/articles/abolition-democracys-forgotten-founder.

Kelley, Robin D. G. "'We Are Not What We Seem': Rethinking Black Working-Class Opposition in the Jim Crow South." *Journal of American History* 80 (Summer 1993): 75–112.

Kelly, Brian. "Black Laborers, the Republican Party, and the Crisis of Reconstruction in Lowcountry South Carolina." *Journal of International Social History* 51 (December 2006): 375–414.

Keyssar, Alexander. *The Right to Vote: The Contested History of Democracy in the United States*. New York: Basic Books, 2000.

Kirby, Jack Temple. *Darkness at the Dawning: Race and Reform in the Progressive South*. New York: Lippincott, 1972.

Kirby, Jack Temple. *Rural Worlds Lost: The American South, 1920–1960*. Baton Rouge: Louisiana State University Press, 1986.

Kousser, J. Morgan. *Colorblind Injustice: Minority Voting Rights and the Undoing of the Second Reconstruction*. Chapel Hill: University of North Carolina Press, 1999.

Kousser, J. Morgan. *The Shaping of Southern Politics: Suffrage Restriction and the Establishment of the One-Party South, 1880–1910*. New Haven, CT: Yale University Press, 1974.

Kramer, Paul A. *The Blood of Government: Race, Empire, the United States, and the Philippines*. Chapel Hill: University of North Carolina Press, 2006.

Krauthamer, Barbara, and Deborah Willis. *Envisioning Emancipation: Black Americans and the End of Slavery*. Philadelphia: Temple University Press, 2012.

Kretz, Dale. *Administering Freedom: The State of Emancipation after the Freedmen's Bureau*. Chapel Hill: University of North Carolina Press, 2022.

Krugler, David F. *1919, The Year of Racial Violence: How African Americans Fought Back*. New York: Cambridge University Press, 2014.

Kytle, Ethan J., and Blain Roberts. *Denmark Vesey's Garden: Slavery and Memory in the Cradle of the Confederacy: A 150-Year Reckoning with America's Original Sin*. New York: New Press, 2018.

Lamothe, Daphne. *Inventing the New Negro: Narrative, Culture, and Ethnography*. Philadelphia: University of Pennsylvania Press, 2008.

Lamson, Peggy. *The Glorious Failure: Black Congressman Robert Brown Elliott and the Reconstruction in South Carolina*. New York: Norton, 1973.

Lande, Jonathan. "The Black Badge of Courage: The Politics of Recording Black Union Army Service and the Militarization of Black History in the Civil War's Aftermath." *Journal of American Ethnic History* 42 (Spring 2022): 5–42.

Lau, Peter F. *Democracy Rising: South Carolina and the Fight for Black Equality since 1865.* Lexington: University Press of Kentucky, 2006.

Levine, Robert Steven. *Martin Delany, Frederick Douglass, and the Politics of Representative Identity.* Chapel Hill: University of North Carolina Press, 1997.

Lewis, Andrew B. *The Shadows of Youth: The Remarkable Journey of the Civil Rights Generation.* New York: Hill and Wang.

Lewis, Carole Ione. "Frances Anne Rollin." In *Black Women Suffragists.* Part 2, edited by Thomas Dublin and Kathryn Kish Sklar. Alexandria, VA: Alexander Street Press, 2024.

Lewis, David Levering. *W. E. B. Du Bois: A Biography, 1868–1963.* New York: Henry Holt, 2009.

Lewis, David Levering. *When Harlem Was in Vogue.* New York: Alfred Knopf, 1981.

Lewis, Sarah Elizabeth. *The Unseen Truth: When Race Changed Sight in America.* Cambridge, MA: Havard University Press, 2024.

Link, William A. *The Paradox of Southern Progressivism, 1880–1930.* Chapel Hill: University of North Carolina Press, 1992.

Lipsitz, George. "History, Myth, and Counter-Memory: Narrative and Desire in Popular Novels." In Lipsitz, *Time Passages*.

Lipsitz, George. *Time Passages: Collective Memory and American Popular Culture.* Minneapolis: University of Minnesota Press, 1990.

Logan, Rayford W. *The Betrayal of the Negro: From Rutherford B. Hayes to Woodrow Wilson.* New York: Collier, 1965.

Lowe, Richard. "The Freedman's Bureau and Local Black Leadership." *Journal of American History* 80 (Fall 1993): 989–98.

Lowery, J. Vincent, and John David Smith, eds. *The Dunning School: Historians, Race, and the Meaning of Reconstruction.* Lexington: University of Kentucky Press, 2013.

Manigault-Bryant, LeRhonda S. *Talking to the Dead: Religion, Music and Lived Memory Among Gullah/Geechee Women.* Durham, NC: Duke University Press, 2014.

Manning, Chandra. *Troubled Refuge: Struggling for Freedom in the Civil War.* New York: Vintage, 2016.

Marszalek, John F. *A Black Congressman in the Age of Jim Crow: South Carolina's George Washington Murray.* Gainesville: University of Florida Press, 2006.

Masur, Kate. *An Example for All the Land: Emancipation and the Struggle over Equality in Washington, D.C.* Chapel Hill: University of North Carolina Press, 2010.

Masur, Kate. *Until Justice Be Done: America's First Civil Rights Movement from the Revolution to Reconstruction.* New York: W. W. Norton, 2021.

Matt, Susan J. *A Cultural History of the Emotions in the Age of Romanticism, Revolution, and Empire*, vol. 5. London: Bloomsbury, 2019.

McCurry, Stephanie. *Masters of Small Worlds: Yeoman Households, Gender Relations, and the Political Culture of the Antebellum South Carolina Low Country.* New York: Oxford University Press, 1995.

McEwan, Paul. *The Birth of a Nation.* London: British Film Institute, 2015.

McHenry, Elizabeth. *Forgotten Readers: Recovering the Lost History of African American Literary Societies*. Durham, NC: Duke University Press, 2002.

McKittrick, Katherine, and Clyde Woods, eds. *Black Geographies and the Politics of Place*. Boston: South End, 2007.

McKivigan, John R. "Stalwart Douglass: *Life and Times* as Political Manifesto." *Journal of African American History* 99 (Spring 2014): 46–55.

McMillen, Neil R. *Dark Journey: Black Mississippians in the Age of Jim Crow*. Urbana: University of Illinois Press, 1989.

McPherson, James M. *The Abolitionist Legacy: From Reconstruction to the NAACP*. Princeton, NJ: Princeton University Press, 1975.

McPherson, James M. *The Struggle for Equality: Abolitionists and the Negro in the Civil War and Reconstruction*. Princeton, NJ: Princeton University Press, 1964.

McWhirter, Cameron. *Red Summer: The Summer of 1919 and the Awakening of Black America*. New York: Henry Holt, 2011.

Megginson, W. J. "Black South Carolinians in World War I." *South Carolina Historical Magazine* 96 (April 1995): 162.

Meier, August. *Negro Thought in America: Racial Ideologies in the Age of Booker T. Washington, 1880–1915*. Ann Arbor: University of Michigan Press, 1963.

Meier, August, and Elliott Rudwick. *Black History and the Historical Profession, 1915–1980*. Urbana: University of Illinois Press, 1986.

Miller, Edward A. *Gullah Statesman: Robert Smalls from Slavery to Congress, 1839–1915*. Columbia: University of South Carolina Press, 1995.

Mitchell, Michele. *Righteous Propagation: African Americans and the Politics of Racial Destiny after Reconstruction*. Chapel Hill: University of North Carolina Press, 2004.

Morgan, Philip D. *Slave Counterpoint: Black Culture in the Eighteenth-Century Chesapeake and Lowcountry*. Chapel Hill: University of North Carolina Press, 1998.

Moses, Jeremiah Wilson. *Golden Age of Black Nationalism, 1850–1925*. Oxford: Oxford University Press, 1988.

Moten, Fred, and Stefano Harney. *The Undercommons: Fugitive Planning and Black Study*. Chico, CA: AK, 2013.

Mount, Guy Emerson. "Virginia in the Pacific: Slavery, Empire, and the Colonial Design of American Education." *Journal of African American History* 116 (December 2021): 601–25.

Muller, John. "A Brief Note on Robert Smalls and Frederick Douglass." *Lion of Anacostia*, February 24, 2024. https://thelionofanacostia.wordpress.com/2022/02/24/a-brief-note-on-robert-smalls-frederick-douglass.

Murdoch, Catherine Gilbert. *Domesticating Drink: Women, Men, and Alcohol in America, 1870–1940*. Baltimore: Johns Hopkins University, 1998.

Newby, I. A. *Black Carolinians: A History of Blacks in South Carolina from 1895 to 1968*. Columbia: University of South Carolina Press, 1973.

Noonan, Peggy. *The Strange Career of Porgy and Bess: Race, Culture, and America's Most Famous Opera*. Chapel Hill: University of North Carolina Press, 2012.

Nora, Pierre. "Between Memory and History: Les Lieux de Mémoire." *Representations* 26 (Spring 1989): 7–24.

Norrell, Robert J. *Up from History: The Life of Booker T. Washington*. Cambridge, MA: Belknap Press of Harvard University Press, 2009.

Oakes, James. *Freedom National: The Destruction of Slavery in the United States, 1861–1865*. New York: W. W. Norton, 2014.

O'Brien, Michael, and David Moltke-Hansen, eds. *Intellectual Life in Antebellum Charleston*. Knoxville: University of Tennessee Press, 1986.

Ochiai, Akiko. "The Port Royal Experiment Revisited: Northern Visions of Reconstruction and the Land Question." *New England Quarterly* 74 (Spring 2001): 94–117.

Oldfield, J. R. "A High and Honorable Calling: Black Lawyers in South Carolina, 1868–1915." *Journal of American Studies* (December 1989): 395–96.

Oswald, Emily. "Imagining Race: Illustrating the Poems of Paul Laurence Dunbar." *Book History* 9, no. 1 (2006): 213–30.

Paine, Albert B. *Thomas Nast, His Period and His Pictures*. New York: Macmillan, 1904.

Painter, Nell Irvin. *Exodusters: Black Migration to Kansas after Reconstruction*. New York: Alfred A. Knopf, 1976.

Painter, Nell Irvin. "Martin R. Delany: Elitism and Black Nationalism." In *I Just Keep Talking: A Life in Essays*. New York: Penguin, 2024.

Painter, Nell Irvin. "Soul Murder and Slavery: Toward a Fully Loaded Cost Accounting." In *Southern History Across the Color Line*. Chapel Hill: University of North Carolina Press, 2002.

Parry, Tyler D. "The Radical Experiment of South Carolina: The History and Legacy of a Reconstructed University." *Journal of African American History* 105 (Fall 2020): 539–66.

Parsons, Elaine Frantz. *Ku-Klux: The Birth of the Klan during Reconstruction*. Chapel Hill: University of North Carolina Press, 2015.

Parten, Bennett. *Somewhere toward Freedom: Sherman's March and the Story of America's Largest Emancipation*. New York: Simon and Schuster, 2025.

Patrick, Rembert W. *Reconstruction of the Nation*. New York: Oxford University Press, 1967.

Payne, Charles M. *I've Got the Light of Freedom: The Organizing Tradition and the Mississippi Freedom Struggle*. Berkeley: University of California Press, 1998.

Penningroth, Dylan. *Claims of Kinfolk: African American Property and Community in the Nineteenth-Century South*. Chapel Hill: University of North Carolina Press, 2003.

Perman, Michael. *Struggle for Mastery: Disfranchisement in the South, 1888–1908*. Chapel Hill: University of North Carolina Press, 2001.

Perry, Imani. *Black in Blues: How a Color Tells the Story of My People*. New York: HarperCollins, 2025.

Perry, Imani. *May We Forever Stand: A History of the Black National Anthem*. Chapel Hill: University of North Carolina Press, 2021.

Powers, Bernard E., Jr. *Black Charlestonians: A Social History, 1822–1885*. Fayetteville: University of Arkansas Press, 1994.

Pratt, Mary Louise. *Imperial Eyes: Travel Writing and Transculturation*. London: Routledge, 1992.

Prince, K. Stephen. *The Ballad of Robert Charles: Searching for the New Orleans Riot of 1900*. Chapel Hill: University of North Carolina Press, 2022.

Prince, K. Stephen. *Stories of the South: Race and the Reconstruction of Southern Identity, 1865–1915*. Chapel Hill: University of North Carolina Press, 2014.
Proctor, Bradley D. "'From the Cradle to the Grave': Jim Williams, Black Manhood, and Militia Activism in Reconstruction South Carolina." *American Nineteenth Century History* 19 (Fall 2018): 47–79.
Rael, Patrick. *Black Protest and Black Identity in the Antebellum North*. Chapel Hill: University of North Carolina Press, 2002.
Rambsy, Kenton. "Richard Wright's Formal and Informal Networks." Project on the History of Black Writing, May 11, 2011. https://hbw.ku.edu/blog/richard-wrights-formal-and-informal-networks.
Ramsey, Sonya. *Reading, Writing, and Segregation: A Century of Black Women Teachers in Nashville*. Urbana: University of Illinois Press, 2008.
Ransby, Barbara. *Ella Baker and the Black Freedom Movement: A Radical Democratic Vision*. Chapel Hill: University of North Carolina Press, 2003.
Rathbun, Betty Lou. *The Rise of the Modern American Negro Press, 1880–1914*. Buffalo: SUNY Kenton Press, 1979.
Reed, Adolph, Jr. *The South: Jim Crow and Its Afterlives*. New York: Verso, 2022.
Richardson, Heather Cox. *The Death of Reconstruction: Race, Labor, and Politics in the Post–Civil War North, 1865–1901*. Cambridge, MA: Harvard University Press, 2001.
Roane, J. T. "Plotting the Black Commons." *Souls* 20 (Fall 2018): 239–66.
Robeson, Elizabeth. "The Ambiguity of Julia Peterkin." *Journal of Southern History* 61 (November 1995): 761–86.
Roediger, David R. "And Die in Dixie: Funerals, Death, and Heaven in the Slave Community, 1700–1865." *Massachusetts Review* 22 (Spring 1981): 163–83.
Rolinson, Mary G. *Grassroots Garveyism: The Universal Negro Improvement Association in the Rural South, 1920–1927*. Chapel Hill: University of North Carolina Press, 2005.
Rose, Willie Lee. *Rehearsal for Reconstruction: The Port Royal Experiment*. Indianapolis: Bobbs-Merrill, 1964.
Rowland, Lawrence S., and Stephen R. Wise. *Bridging the Sea Islands' Past and Present, 1893–2006*. Vol. 3 of *The History of Beaufort County, South Carolina*, edited by Lawrence S. Rowland, Alexander Moore, and George C. Rogers Jr. Columbia: University of South Carolina Press, 2015.
Saperstein, Ray. "Picturing Dunbar's Lyrics." *African American Review* 41 (Summer 2007): 327–49.
Saperstein, Ray. "Out from behind the Mask." In *Pictures and Progress: Early Photography and the Making of African American Identity*, edited by Maurice Wallace and Shawn Michelle Smith. Durham, NC: Duke University Press, 2012.
Saville, Julie. *The Work of Reconstruction: From Slave to Wage Laborer in South Carolina 1860–1870*. New York: Cambridge University Press, 1996.
Schulten, Susan. *Mapping the Nation: History and Cartography in Nineteenth-Century America*. Chicago: University of Chicago Press, 2012.
Schwalm, Leslie A. *A Hard Fight for We: Women's Transition from Slavery to Freedom in South Carolina*. Urbana: University of Illinois Press, 1997.
Schwalm, Leslie A. "'Sweet Dreams of Freedom': Freedwomen's Reconstruction of Life and Labor in the Lowcountry South Carolina." *Journal of Women's History* 9 (Spring 1997): 9–32.

Schwarz, Frederic D. "The Reluctant Judge." *American Legacy* 10, no. 3 (Fall 2004).

Schweninger, Loren. *Black Property Owners in the South, 1790–1915*. Urbana: University of Illinois Press, 1990.

Scurlock, George C., N. H. Heard, Monroe N. Work, William H. Gray, George Freeman Bragg, E. W. Sherman, et al. "Additional Information and Correction in Reconstruction Records." *Journal of Negro History* 5 (April 1920): 247–78.

Sehat, David. "The Civilizing Mission of Booker T. Washington." *Journal of Southern History* 73 (Summer 2007): 323–62.

Sharma, Devika, and Frederick Tygstrup, eds. *Structures of Feeling: Affectivity and the Study of Culture*. Berlin: Walter de Gruyter, 2015.

Sharpe, Christina. *In the Wake: On Blackness and Being*. Durham, NC: Duke University Press, 2016.

Shaw, Stephanie J. *What a Woman Ought to Be and to Do: Black Professional Women Workers during the Jim Crow Era*. Chicago: University of Chicago Press, 1996.

Silber, Nina. "Reunion and Reconciliation, Reviewed and Reconsidered." *Journal of American History* 103 (June 2016): 59–83.

Silber, Nina. *The Romance of Reunion: Northerners and the South, 1865–1900*. Chapel Hill: University of North Carolina Press, 1993.

Simkins, Francis Butler. *Pitchfork Ben Tillman*. Baton Rouge: Louisiana State University Press, 1944.

Simkins, Francis Butler, and Robert L. Woody. *South Carolina during Reconstruction*. Chapel Hill: University of North Carolina Press, 1932.

Simon, Bryant. "The Appeal of Cole Blease of South Carolina: Race, Class, and Sex in the New South." *Journal of Southern History* 62 (February 1996): 57–86.

Simon, Bryant. *A Fabric of Defeat: The Politics of South Carolina Millhands, 1910–1948*. Chapel Hill: University of North Carolina Press, 1998.

Sinha, Manisha. *The Rise and Fall of the Second American Republic: Reconstruction, 1860–1920*. New York: Liveright, 2024.

Skocpol, Theda. *Protecting Soldiers and Mothers: The Political Origins of Social Policy in the United States*. Cambridge, MA: Belknap Press of Harvard University Press, 1992.

Southern Poverty Law Center. *Whose Heritage? Public Symbols of the Confederacy*, 3rd ed. 2022. www.splcenter.org/wp-content/uploads/files/whose-heritage-report-third-edition.pdf.

Spires, Derrick R. *The Practice of Citizenship: Black Politics and Print Culture in the Early United States*. Philadelphia: University of Pennsylvania Press, 2019.

Stauffer, John, ed. *Picturing Douglass: An Illustrated Biography of the Nineteenth Century's Most Photographed American*. New York: Liveright, 2015.

Stearns, Peter. *American Cool: Constructing a Twentieth-Century Emotional Style*. New York: New York University Press, 1994.

Stein, Luke C. D., and Constantine Yannelis. "Financial Inclusion, Human Capital, and Wealth Accumulation: Evidence from the Freedman's Savings Bank." *Review of Financial Studies*, February 10, 2020.

Sternhell, Yael. *Routes of War: The World of Movement in the Confederate South*. Cambridge, MA: Harvard University Press, 2012.

Stewart, Catherine A. *Long Past Slavery: Representing Race in the Federal Writers' Project*. Chapel Hill: University of North Carolina Press, 2016.

Strickland, Jeffrey G. *Unequal Freedoms: Ethnicity, Race, and White Supremacy in Civil War–Era Charleston*. Gainesville: University of Florida Press, 2015.

Stokes-Hammond, Shelley. "Pathbreakers: Oscar Stanton DePriest and Jessie L. Williams DePriest." White House Historical Association, June 9, 2015. https://web.archive.org/web/20150609045930/http://www.whitehousehistory.org/presentations/depriest-tea-incident/african-american-congress.html.

Suggs, Henry L. *The Black Press in the South, 1865–1970*. Westport, CT: Greenwood, 1983.

Sullivan, Patricia. *Lift Every Voice: The NAACP and the Making of the Civil Rights Movement*. New York: New Press, 2009.

Summers, Mark Wahlgren. *The Press Gang: Newspapers and Politics, 1865–1878*. Chapel Hill: University of North Carolina Press, 1994.

Summers, Mark Wahlgren. *Rum, Romanism, and Rebellion: The Making of a President, 1884*. Chapel Hill: University of North Carolina Press, 2000.

Táíwò, Olúfẹ́mi O. *Elite Capture: How the Powerful Took Over Identity Politics (And Everything Else)*. Chicago: Haymarket, 2022.

Taylor, Amy Murrell. *Embattled Freedom: Journey through the Civil War's Slave Refugee Camps*. Chapel Hill: University of North Carolina Press, 2018.

Taylor, Elizabeth Dowling. *The Original Black Elite: Daniel Murray and the Story of a Forgotten Era*. New York: Amistad, 2017.

Taylor, Kay Ann. "Mary S. Peake and Charlotte L. Forten: Black Teachers during the Civil War and Reconstruction." *Journal of Negro Education* 74 (Spring 2005): 124–87.

Tetzlaff, Monica Maria. *Cultivating a New South: Abbie Holmes Christensen and the Politics of Race and Gender, 1852–1938*. Columbia: University of South Carolina Press, 2002.

Tindall, George B. *South Carolina Negroes, 1877–1900*. Columbia: University of South Carolina Press, 1952.

Trelease, Allen W. *White Terror: The Ku Klux Klan Conspiracy and Southern Reconstruction*. New York: Harper and Row, 1971.

Trouillot, Michel-Rolph. *Silencing the Past: Power and the Production of History*. Boston: Beacon, 1995.

Turner, Nicole Myers. *Soul Liberty: The Evolution of Black Religious Politics in Postemancipation Virginia*. Chapel Hill: University of North Carolina Press, 2020.

Tuten, James H. *Lowcountry Time and Tide: The Fall of the South Carolina Rice Kingdom*. Columbia: University of South Carolina Press, 2010.

Underwood, James Lowell, and W. Lewis Burke Jr. *At Freedom's Door: African American Founding Fathers and Lawyers in Reconstruction South Carolina*. Columbia: University of South Carolina Press, 2005.

Uya, Okon Edet. *From Slavery to Public Service: Robert Smalls, 1839–1915*. New York: Oxford University Press, 1971.

Vogel, Todd, ed. *The Black Press: New Literary and Historical Essays*. New Brunswick, NJ: Rutgers University Press, 2001.

Walker, Clarence E. "The A.M.E. Church and Reconstruction." *Negro History Bulletin*, Spring 1985, 10–12.

Wallinger, Hannah. "Pauline E. Hopkins as Editor and Journalist: An African American Story of Success and Failure." In *Blue Pencils and Hidden Hands: Women Editing Periodicals, 1830–1910*, edited by Sharon M. Harris and Ellen Gruber Garvey. Boston: Northeastern University Press, 2004.

Waugh, Joan. *U.S. Grant: American Hero, American Myth*. Chapel Hill: University of North Carolina Press, 2009.

Wertheimer, John W. *Race and Slavery in South Carolina: From Slavery to Jim Crow*. Amherst, MA: Amherst College Press, 2023.

West, Stephen A. "Remembering Reconstruction in Its Twilight: Ulysses S. Grant and James G. Blaine on the Origins of Black Suffrage." *Journal of the Civil War Era* 10 (December 2020): 495–523.

White, Derrick E. *Blood, Sweat, and Tears: Jake Gaither, Florida A&M, and the History of Black College Football*. Chapel Hill: University of North Carolina Press, 2019.

White-Perry, Giselle. "In Freedom's Shadow: The Reconstruction Legacy of Renty Franklin Greaves of Beaufort County, South Carolina." *Prologue Magazine* 42 (Fall 2010). www.archives.gov/publications/prologue/2010/fall/greaves.html.

Williams, Chad. *The Wounded World: W. E. B. Du Bois and the First World War*. New York: Macmillan, 2023.

Williams, Heather Andrea. "'Clothing Themselves in Intelligence': The Freedpeople, Schooling, and Northern Teachers, 1861–1871." *Journal of African American History* 87 (Autumn 2002): 372–89.

Williams, Heather Andrea. *Help Me to Find My People: The African American Search for Family Lost in Slavery*. Chapel Hill: University of North Carolina Press, 2012.

Williams, Heather Andrea. *Self-Taught: African American Education in Slavery and Freedom*. Chapel Hill: University of North Carolina Press, 2005.

Williams, Kidada. *I Saw Death Coming: A History of Terror and Survival*. New York: Bloomsbury, 2023.

Williams, Kidada. *They Left Great Marks on Me: African American Testimonies of Racial Violence from Emancipation to World War I*. New York: New York University Press, 2012.

Williams, Lou Falkner. *The Great South Carolina Ku Klux Klan Trials, 1871–1872*. Athens: University of Georgia Press, 1996.

Williams, Raymond. *Marxism and Literature*. Oxford: Oxford University Press, 1977.

Williamson, Joel. *After Slavery: The Negro in South Carolina during Reconstruction, 1861–1877*. Chapel Hill: University of North Carolina Press, 1965.

Willis, Deborah. *The Black Civil War Soldier: A Visual History of Conflict and Citizenship*. New York: NHU Press, 2021.

Wise, Stephen R., and Lawrence S. Rowland, with Gerhard Spieler. *Rebellion, Reconstruction, and Redemption, 1861–1893*. Vol. 2 of *The History of Beaufort County, South Carolina*, edited by Lawrence S. Rowland, Alexander Moore, and George C. Rogers Jr. Columbia: University of South Carolina Press, 2015.

Wolcott, Victoria. "'Bible, Bath, and Broom': Nannie Helen Burroughs's National Training School and African-American Racial Uplift." *Journal of Women's History* 9 (Spring 1997): 88–110.

Wolfe, H. Scott. "The Idol of the Negroes: James D. Lynch: Galena Citizen, Mississippi Statesman." Galena History Museum, 1999. https://web.archive.org/web/20070928034150/http://www.galenahistorymuseum.org/lynch.htm.

Womac, Autumn. *The Matter of Black Living: The Aesthetic Experiment of Racial Data, 1880–1930*. Chicago: University of Chicago Press, 2022.

Wood, Peter H. *Black Majority: Negroes in South Carolina from 1670 through the Stono Rebellion*. New York: Alfred A. Knopf, 1974.

Woodman, Harold D. "Post–Civil War Southern Agriculture and the Law." *Agricultural History* 53 (January 1979): 319–37.

Woods, Clyde. *Development Arrested: The Blues and Plantation Power in the Mississippi Delta*. New York: Verso, 1998.

Woods, Michael E. *Emotional and Sectional Conflict in the Antebellum United States*. New York: Cambridge University Press, 2014.

Woodson, Carter G. "Review of *Black Yeomanry: Life on St. Helena Island*, by T. J. Woofter Jr." *Journal of Negro History* 16 (Spring 1931): 95–96.

Woodward, C. Vann. *Origins of the New South, 1877–1913*. Baton Rouge: Louisiana State University Press, 1951.

Work, Monroe N. "Some Negro Members of Reconstruction Conventions and Legislatures and of Congress." *Journal of Negro History* 5 (January 1920): 63–119.

Work, Monroe N., J. W. Cromwell, Mrs. M. E. Richardson, Henry A. Wallace, and R. C. Edmonson. "Letters on Reconstruction Records." *Journal of Negro History* 5 (October 1920): 467–75.

Wynes, Charles E. "T. McCants Stewart: Peripatetic Black South Carolinian." *South Carolina Historical Magazine* 80 (October 1979): 311–17.

Yellin, Eric S. *Racism in the Nation's Service: Government Workers and the Color Line in Woodrow Wilson's America*. Chapel Hill: University of North Carolina Press, 2013.

Yuhl, Stephanie E. *A Golden Haze of Memory: The Making of Historic Charleston*. Chapel Hill: University of North Carolina Press, 2005.

Zucchino, David. *Wilmington's Lie: The Murderous Coup of 1898 and the Rise of White Supremacy*. New York: Atlantic Monthly Press, 2020.

Zuczek, Richard. *State of Rebellion: Reconstruction in South Carolina*. Columbia: University of South Carolina Press, 1996.

Index

Abbeville County, SC, 43, 57, 59
African Methodist Episcopal Church, 1, 7, 32–33, 87, 95
African Methodist Episcopal Zion Church, 103
Aiken County, SC, 57, 59, 166
Alabama's Fourth Congressional District, 72
Allen, Macon B., Jr., 146
Allen, Macon B., Sr., 35
Allen University, 87
Alston, Winifred Kent, 183, 186–87
A.M.E. Church Revew, 7
American Historical Review, 176
American Missionary, 113
American Missionary Association, 30, 38, 141, 144
American Negro Academy, 8
American Red Cross, 122–23
Anderson, Marian, 183
Anglo-African (periodical), 30–31
antilynching legislation, 183
Armstrong, Samuel Chapman, 138–39, 141, 156
ASNLH, 8, 159, 173–74, 175, 176
Aspects of Negro Life (Douglas), 179
Association for the Study of Negro Life and History. *See* ASNLH
Atlanta Constitution (periodical), 97, 104–5
attorneys, Black, 35–36
Attucks, Crispus, 145
Avery School (Charleston, SC), 144

Bampfield, Elizabeth Smalls, 143, 180
Bampfield, Samuel Jones, 88, 103, 114, 116–19, 125
Bancroft, Frederic, 101
Barnwell, Benjamin, 168
Barnwell County, SC, 48, 58, 59, 61–62

Barton, Clara, 122
Battle of Fort Wagner, 27
Battle of Honey Hill, 27
Battle of Port Royal, 25, 27
Beaufort County, SC, 1, 11, 59, 32; Black public schools in, 143–46; during the antebellum period, 24–25; fusion political movement in, 114–17; in-migration during Civil War to, 26, 31–32; migration after Reconstruction to, 70, 78; and out-migration during Great Migration, 152, 163–64, 167–68, 170; Reconstruction-era political world of, 33–36, 53, 97–98, 101–5, 176; twentieth-century municipal politics in, 142–43, 162–63, 165
Beaufort Gazette, 168
Berkeley County, SC, 59, 99, 103
Berlin, Ira, 188
Bethel AME Church (Columbia, SC), 81
Bethel Literary and Historical Society, 9–10, 21, 100–104, 109; decline of, 181; at end of nineteenth century, 129–30; January 1883 meeting of, 1–2, 77, 140, 175; rise of, 94–96
Bethune, Mary McLeod, 186
Birth of a Nation, The (Griffith), 160–61, 162, 173
Black attorneys, 35–36
Black Belt (region), 13, 72, 107, 141, 156, 167–68
"Black Fourth District," 72
Black militias, 48–50, 52, 54, 56, 60, 137
Black Port Royal Experiment, 24, 30–33
Black public sphere, 8–10, 77, 84–86, 92, 109, 152, 160; at century's end, 128–31; gender politics of, 9, 84, 96, 194n18; and rise of postbellum Black press, 12–14, 32, 38, 117–19

Black Reconstruction (Du Bois), 177–78
Black schools. *See names of individual institutions*
"Black Second District," 86, 105
Black Yeomanry (Woofter), 169–71
Blaine, James G., 66
Blanton, Joshua, 150, 152, 165
Blease, Cole, 162–63
"blind tigers," 107, 146
Blue Shirts, 61
Board of Missions for the Freedmen of the Presbyterian Church, 144
Booker T. Washington High Schools, 184
Boston, MA, 22, 84, 99, 129
Boston Herald, 104
Bradford, William Rufus, 183
Bradley, Aaron Alpeoria, 36, 83
Brayton, Ellery, 99, 108–9
Bronzeville (Chicago neighborhood), 167
Brown Fellowship Society, 22
Bruce, Blanche K., 91, 95, 129, 140–41
Bruce, John Edward, 85, 88, 130, 145, 167; *Short Biographical Sketches of Eminent Negro Men and Women*, 145
bulldozing (political strategy), 56, 62
Bythewood, Daniel W., 185

Cain, Richard, 33
Campbell, Tunis, 49, 83
Cardozo, Francis, 37–38, 95, 144
Cardozo, Thomas, 38, 144
Cardozo Senior High School (Washington, DC), 185
Carson, Perry, 99
Catto, Octavius
Chamberlain, Daniel, 148–49
Charleston, SC, 11, 25, 31–32, 42, 50; antebellum free Black community in, 22, 31–32, 34; Black schools of, 143–44, 166; countermemory practices within, 146; postbellum Black political world of, 21, 29, 35, 38, 42, 45–46, 48–50, 54, 56, 75, 81, 83; and twentieth-century commemorative landscape, 211n27; white political elite in, 25, 47, 50, 75

Charleston County, SC, 59, 76
Charleston News and Courier, 70, 73–74, 96–97, 104, 107, 112, 122
Chase, Calvin, 99–100
Cheatham, Henry P., 129, 159
Chicago, IL, 42, 157, 167, 172–73, 175
Chicago Daily Tribune, 74
Chicago Defender, 173
Chisholm, Helen James, 1, 174
Christensen, Abbie, 151
Christensen, Niels, 113, 163
Christensen, Niels, Jr., 163
Christian Recorder, 30, 32–33, 37
Civil Rights Act of 1875, 81
Clara Ward Singers, 183
Clay, Henry, 71
Cleveland, Grover, 90, 98, 100, 105, 121
Cleveland Gazette, 105, 124–25
Clyde, William P., 152
Coahoma County, MS, 168
Colleton County, SC, 48, 53, 59, 67, 71
Colored American (Washington, DC), 129, 147–48
Colored American Magazine, 129
Colored Conventions Movement, 23, 33, 37
Colored Farmers Alliance, 120
Colored Normal, Industrial, Agricultural, and Mechanical College of South Carolina, 144
Columbia, SC, 46, 48, 54, 56, 97, 99, 107, 166; as center of Reconstruction-era Black political culture, 33–34, 63, 81, 174; as host of 1895 constitutional convention, 126
Columbia University, 101, 169–70, 183
Combahee River, 21, 27, 55, 68
Commission on Interracial Cooperation (CIC), 168
Confederate Memorial Day, 161. *See also* Decoration Day
Contending Forces (Hopkins), 129
Cooley, Rossa B., 150, 169
countermemory, definition of, 3–4, 6–10, 13
Cowley, Charles C., 101
Crisis, The, 160–61, 172, 175–76, 178

Cromwell, John W., 2, 21, 130, 175
Cuney, Norris Wright, 172

Daily Register (Columbia, SC), 123
David Hunter Post, 107, 114, 146, 152
Dawkins, Emma Jennie Fentress, 149
Dawkins, P. W., 149
Decoration Day, 107–10, 146, 161–62
Delany, Martin, 21–22, 31, 40, 48, 51, 83
Democratic Party, 82, 93, 97, 105, 108–12, 115, 120–23, 139, 143, 150, 160; disfranchisement efforts of, 56–58, 71–76, 111–12; divisions with South Carolina Party of, 66–67, 69, 78, 110, 123, 125–28; during Solid South era, 162–63, 167; in late nineteenth-century Lowcountry, 57–58, 60–62, 73, 77, 97, 101–3, 115, 121–22, 124; national party politics and leadership of, 47, 57, 66–67, 121, 143, 162; relationship to paramilitary violence of, 53, 58, 61–62. *See also* Red Shirts
De Priest, Oscar, 173
De Reid, Ira, 171
Dibble, Samuel, 71
Dimock, Julian, 147, 154
Dixon, Thomas, 175
Douglas, Aaron, 178; *Aspects of Negro Life*, 179
Douglass, Frederick, 7; in Black Washington's political culture, 88–89; death of, 128, 130; on Reconstruction's perceived defeats, 40, 66, 81; role of, in shaping of Gilded Age Black public sphere, 37, 91–92, 94; place of, in Black countermemory, 145
Douglass, Frederick, Jr., 89
Douglass, Sarah Mapps, 21
Du Bois, W. E. B, 171, 175, 181; *Black Reconstruction*, 177–78; *The Gift of Black Folks*, 176
Dunning, William Archibald, 148

Elliott, Robert Brown, 38–40, 81–84, 145, 188

Elliott, William (1838–1907), 97, 102, 111, 113, 122, 125, 160
Elliott, William (1872–1943), 144
Emancipation Day, 7, 44, 49–50, 64, 70, 89, 99
Emancipation Proclamation, 11, 25, 27, 32, 49, 153, 156
Encyclopedia of the Colored Race (Murray), 130

Facts of Reconstruction, The (Lynch), 172
federal election laws, 66, 71, 111–12
Federal Elections Bill of 1890, 111–12
Field Order Number 15, 28, 29, 176
First South Carolina Volunteers, 27, 48, 153
Florida Lowcountry, 11, 26, 86
Folk Culture on St. Helena Island (Johnson), 169
Forten, Charlotte, 21, 30
Forten, James, 30
Fort Monroe, Virginia, 141
Fortune, Thomas, 85–86, 88, 94, 103–4, 113, 118–19, 153
Frazier, Garrison, 28
Freedmen and Southern Society Project, 188
Freedmen's Bank, 40, 55–56, 146
Freedmen's Bureau, 9, 21–22, 25; Black attorneys and, 35, 37; emergence in the wartime Lowcountry, 28–31; leaders involved with postbellum Republican Party politics, 40, 42, 51, 99, 139
Freedom's Journal, 37
Frissell, Hollis B., 149

Gantt, Hastings, 153–55
Garfield, James, 66
Garrison, William Lloyd, 22
General Order Number 11, 26
Georgetown County, SC, 59, 67, 71, 114
Gerry, Elbridge, 71
gerrymandering, 71–76, 78, 87, 111, 123–24, 142
Gift of Black Folk, The (Du Bois), 176
Gillisonville, SC, 11, 58, 60–61, 115

Gleaves, Richard Howell, 33, 35, 37, 47–48, 52, 53, 56, 83, 159
Gonzales, Narciso, 96
Grand Army of the Republic, 7, 89, 100, 107, 114, 116, 137, 152, 157
Grant, Ulysses S., 34, 64–66, 131
Great Migration, 172–73, 177–78
Greenback-Labor Party, 66–68
Greener, Richard, 3, 22, 35, 38, 160
Griffith, D. W., 160; *The Birth of a Nation*, 160–61, 162, 173
Gullah Geechee, 12, 83, 104

Hamburg Massacre, 52–54, 129, 152
Hampton, Lionel, 183
Hampton, Wade, 58
Hampton County, SC, 48, 58–59, 150
Hampton-trained teachers, 135–36, 142, 149–51, 155–56
Hampton University (Hampton, VA), 136, 139, 140–42
Hancock, Winfield, 66
Hardstew, C. J., 158
Hare, Maud Cuney, 172
Harlem (New York neighborhood), 159, 166–67, 170, 177–80
Harlem Renaissance, 159, 177, 179
Harper, Frances Ellen Watkins, 7, 24, 129, 160
Harrison, Benjamin, 109, 115–17, 121
Hayes, Rutherford B., 56–57, 64–65
Hayne, Charles D., 46
Hayne, Henry E., 48, 174
Hayne, William A., 174
Heroes of the Colored Race (Hoover), 91–93, 179
Heyward, DuBose, 178; *Porgy*, 178, 197n34
Higginson, Thomas Wentworth, 22, 27
Hilton Head Island, 11, 21, 31, 152
Holland, Rupert, 172
Hoover, Joseph, 91–92; *Heroes of the Colored Race*, 91–93, 179
Hope, John, 153
Hopkins, Pauline, 129, 207n46; *Contending Forces*, 129

House, Grace, 150
Houston County, TX, 120
Howard, Oliver Otis, 37
Howard University, 38, 146
Howard University Law School, 3, 35, 37, 82, 87
Hughes, Langston, 177
Hunter, David, 16, 89, 100
Hurston, Zora Neale, 186

Indianapolis Freeman, 85, 91, 100, 127
industrial education, 128, 137–42, 149–53
Institute for Colored Youth, 21
Institute for Research in Social Science, 169
Izlar, J. F., 71

Jackson, Sara Dunlap, 186–88
James, Helen Lou, 149
Jenks, Helen Carnan, 149
Jim Hill Public School (Jackson, MS), 185
John Mercer Langston High School, 185
Johnson, Guion Griffis, 170; *A Social History of the Sea Islands*, 170
Johnson, Guy B., 169–70; *Folk Culture on St. Helena Island*, 169
Johnson, James Weldon, 175
Johnson, Mordecai, 186
Johnson, Solomon, 152
Johnson C. Smith University, 186
Journal of Negro History, 171, 174

King, Martin Luther, Jr., 156
Kirkland, Joseph, 60
Kiser, Clyde, 170; *Sea Island to City*, 170
Ku Klux Klan: during interwar era, 162; during Reconstruction era, 44, 45, 83, 89, 179

land loss, 211n34
landownership, 28, 169, 176, 196n16
Langston, John Mercer, 47, 95, 129–30, 136
Lauren Spelman Rockefeller Fund, 168
Lee, Robert E., 163
Lee, Samuel, 76–77
Life and Public Services of Martin R. Delaney (Rollin), 22

Lincoln, Abraham, 7, 26, 38, 100, 135
Lincoln University, PA, 103
Lost Cause, 5–7, 10, 36, 145, 159–63, 172, 181, 183
Louis, Joe, 186
Louverture, Toussaint, 145
Lowcountry, 1, 3–4, 11; as cultural geography, 10–13; demographic shifts, 31–32, 70, 163–64; during Civil War, 25–37; during Great Migration, 165–72; Reconstruction-era political world of, 48–51, 53–56, 70, 75–78; and rice strikes, 55, 68
Lynch, Jane, 30–31, 37
Lynch, John R., 91, 129, 185; *The Facts of Reconstruction*, 172
lynching, 1, 6, 63, 85; antilynching movement and legislation, 44, 183; Beaufort County's first report of, 148, 208n24; Lowcountry's longtime protection from, 142; postbellum Black press coverage of, 6, 85, 118–19, 127

MacDonald, John, 123
Mackey, Edmund William McGregor, 75–77
Macon County, Alabama, 156
Malden School (Washington, DC), 140
Martin, Thomas, 122–23
Mather, Rachel Crane, 150
Mayo, James E., 185
Mays, Benjamin, 186
McClane, J. Hendrix, 68, 78
McIntyre, George, 48
McKinlay, Whitefield, 124
Men of Mark (Simmons), 93, 145
Messenger, The (periodical), 178
Metropolitan AME Church (Washington, DC), 1, 94–95, 181
Micheaux, Oscar, 173; *Within our Gates*, 173
militias, Black. *See* Black militias
Miller, Mary J., 127, 177
Miller, Thomas E., 68, 70, 73, 103, 114–17, 126–27, 144, 166, 175–77
Miner, Leigh Richmond, 135–36

Miner Normal School (Washington, DC), 89
Mississippi Constitutional Convention of 1890, 125–26
Mississippi Delta, 13, 167
Mississippi's Sixth Congressional District, 173
Mitchell, John, Jr., 5, 119, 175
Morrison, Z. T., 60
Moses, Franklin, 47, 51–52, 83
Mother Emanuel AME Church (Charleston, SC), 32–33
Mound Bayou, Miss., 168
Murray, Daniel Payne, 130–31; *Encyclopedia of the Colored Race*, 130
Murray, Ellen, 149–50
Murray, George Washington, 173

NAACP, 160, 165–66, 172, 175, 184
Nash, Charles E., 91
National Archives, 187
National Association for the Advancement of Colored People. *See* NAACP
National Cemetery (Beaufort, SC), 107
National Colored Press Association, 5, 118
Negro Digest, 177
Negro in South Carolina during Reconstruction, The (Taylor), 175
Negro Society for Historical Research, 8
Negro supremacy idea, 112–13
Negro World (New York), 167, 178
Negro Yearbook (periodical), 173
New National Era (Washington, DC), 37–38, 40
New Orleans, LA, 13, 34, 81, 129, 160, 165, 176
New South (Beaufort, SC), 117–19, 125
New York Age, 85, 113, 118–19, 153, 157, 178
New York Freeman, 105
New York Globe, 87
New York Public Library, 135th Street Branch of, 178
North Carolina's Second Congressional District, 86, 105
North Star (periodical), 37
Norvell, Antoinette, 135–36, 150–51, 156

Odum, Howard, Jr., 169
Opportunity (periodical), 178
Orangeburg County, SC, 46, 59, 71, 143, 166, 186

Palmetto Post (Port Royal, SC), 77, 98
Paradise Valley (Detroit neighborhood), 167
Peake, Mary, 141
Penn, Irvine Garland, 86, 118
Penn School (Frogmore, SC), 27, 135–37, 143, 149–53, 55–56
Peterkin, Julia, 169
Phillips, Wendell, 22
Pike, James S., 39; *The Prostrate State*, 39, 112
Pinchback, P. B. S., 95, 129, 140–41, 160
Pope, John, 71
Porgy (Heyward), 178, 197n34
Port of Beaufort Customs House, 103, 157
Port of Charleston Customs House, 81
Port Royal Agricultural School (Beaufort, SC), 151
Port Royal Experiment, 26, 149, 155, 172
Port Royal Railway, 64
Prostrate State, The (Pike), 39, 112
public sphere, Black. *See* Black public sphere
Public Works Administration, 178
Purvis, Henry, 83
Purvis, Robert, 56

racial destiny: definition of, 8–9; during Civil War, 23–24, 27–28, 30; in national Black public sphere, 84–91, 93–94, 100, 103, 105, 109, 118–19, 124, 129; in postbellum Lowcountry, 31–33, 38, 48, 52, 55, 77, 82; in twentieth century, 145, 156, 159, 166, 177, 179, 181
Rainey, Joseph, 174
Rainey, Olive, 174
Rainey, Susan, 174
Randolph, Benjamin, 42–43, 45–46, 51, 63
Randolph Cemetery, 63
Raper, Arthur, 168
Rapier, James T., 173
Reconstruction generation: definition of, 4–6; emergence of, 24, 32–38, 40, 43, 45, 47, 55; in interwar North, 173, 176–77; major institutions of, 7–9, 94–96; passing of, 83, 129–30, 159–60, 181; production of countermemory by, 110, 128–31, 174, 176, 188
"Reconstruction in South Carolina" (Reynolds), 148
Red Cross, 122–23
Redemption movement, 44–45, 56–57, 61, 63, 70; afterlife of, 149, 150; erasure of, 135, 171; long movement of, 73, 122; twentieth-century Black politicians' relationship to, 173
Red Record, The (Wells), 129
Red Shirts, 15, 44, 53, 60–61, 63
Republican Party, 2–6, 12–13; conservative wing of, 36, 39–40, 47, 51–52, 148–49; coverage of, in Northern media, 38–39, 65, 73–74, 85–88, 111–13, 118–19, 124–28, 147; decline of, in post-Reconstruction South, 65, 72, 90, 105, 153–54, 162–63; national party politics and leadership of, 26, 34, 42, 62, 64–66, 72–73, 100, 125, 157; in postbellum Lowcountry, 31–34, 36–37, 44–49, 53–56, 58–61, 64–65, 70, 75–78, 98–99, 101–4, 107–9, 123–24, 142–43; in postbellum Upcountry, 43, 45; postbellum party politics of, in South Carolina, 34, 40, 42–43, 45, 56, 67–68, 82, 89, 108; tensions within, 51–52, 87–89, 114–17, 120–21
Revels, Hiram, 91
Reynolds, John S., 148
rice strikes, 55, 68
Richmond Planet, 5–6, 175
Rivers, J. R., 123–24
Rivers, Prince, 48, 52
Robert Smalls High School (Beaufort, SC), 183–87
Robeson, Paul, 183
Robinson, Joseph, 102–4

Rollin, Frances Anne, 21–23, 31, 34, 130–31; *Life and Public Services of Martin R. Delany*, 22
Rollin sisters, 34, 188, 195n1
Rosenwald Schools, 184

Savannah, GA, 11, 25, 28, 31, 56–57, 83, 96, 143, 146, 162, 166
Savannah News and Herald, 36
Savannah Tribune, 107, 152–53, 157
Saxton, Rufus, 27, 51, 116, 153
Schomberg, Arturo, 178
schools, Black. *See names of individual institutions*
Scott, Emmett, 152
Sea Island Hurricane of 1893, 110, 120–23
Sea Island to City (Kiser), 170
secession, 24–25
sectional reconciliation, 41, 96, 100–1, 108, 114, 160, 164, 171, 194n11
Sherman, John, 116
Sherman, William T., 28
Short Biographical Sketches of Eminent Negro Men and Women (Bruce), 145
Simmons, William J., 93; *Men of Mark*, 93, 145
Singleton, Benjamin, 70
Smalls, Annie Elizabeth (née Wigg), 128
Smalls, Edwin, 179–80
Smalls, Hannah, 28, 30
Smalls, Robert, 1, 3, 8–9, 27; career as customs house official of, 115–17; Civil War escape from slavery, 27–28, 91; death and funeral, 157–59; defense of voting rights, 65, 111–12, 147; escape from Gillisonville assault, 60–62, 115; in late nineteenth-century public sphere, 84–86, 91–94; nineteenth-century political career, 55, 58–63, 65–66, 75–77, 87–89, 96–105; relationship with northern Black press of, 33, 87–89; role of, in South Carolina state militia, 48–49; in twentieth-century Black memory, 148, 152
Smalls, Sarah, 89, 127, 157, 174

Smalls Paradise, 180
South Carolina Constitutional Conventions: of 1868, 1, 42, 51, 145; of 1895, 16, 110, 125–31, 164, 177
South Carolina National Guard, 44–46, 48–50
South Carolina's Seventh Congressional District, 71–78, 87, 89
South Carolina State University, 144
South Carolina stock law of 1882, 69–70
Southern Workman (periodical), 139
Springfield (MA) Republican, 104, 148
SS Robert Smalls, 167
Star of Zion, 103–4
State, The, 148
Stewart, T. McCants, 38, 81
St. Helena Island, SC, 11, 102, 136, 149–50, 152–53, 164–65, 169–72
Still, Mary, 21, 30
Still, William, 30, 94
Straker, Daniel, 77, 82, 87–88, 127
Sumter County, SC, 120–21, 166
Swails, Stephen, 45

Taft, William H., 157, 162
Taft, William N., 99
Taylor, Alrutheus Ambush, 14, 175–76, 177; *The Negro in South Carolina during Reconstruction*, 175
Teller Committee, 62
temperance movement, in the Lowcountry, 117
Thomas, Calhoun, 183
Thompson, W. H., 99
Tillman, Benjamin, 63, 100, 121–23, 125–26, 162–63, 183
Tillman, George, 58, 60, 62, 74
Towne, Laura, 27, 149
Tubman, Harriet, 21
Tuskegee Institute, 128, 147, 150–53, 152, 156
Tweed, William Macy, 52

Underground Railroad, 22, 24, 30
United Daughters of the Confederacy (UDC), 160–61

United States Colored Troops. *See* USCT
United States Department of Agriculture (USDA), 152
Universal Negro Improvement Association (UNIA), 166–67
University of North Carolina, 164, 168–69
University of South Carolina, 3
Upcountry (region of South Carolina), 12, 15; and regional hostility to Lowcountry, 83, 121–23, 162, 183; as site of anti-Black violence, 43, 45–46, 60; as site of Greenback Labor movement, 67, 70
Up from Slavery (Washington), 139–40
Urban League, 34
USCT, 1, 21, 32, 91, 147; Twenty-Sixth regiment, 42; Thirty-Third regiment, 27; Thirty-Fourth regiment, 99

Wallace, Henry, 174
Washington, Booker T., 117, 128, 147, 152; *Up from Slavery*, 139–40
Washington, DC: Anacostia neighborhood, 7, 213n8; and Black countermemory institutions, 94–96, 181, 185; Black elite of, 38, 89, 130, 140; Black political culture in, 89, 99; Black working class in, 99
Washington, Julius I., 115, 148, 153, 162, 166
Washington Bee, 77, 86, 98, 100, 105, 109, 128–29
Weaver, Elisha, 32
Wells, Ida B., 1, 5–7, 85, 119, 145, 193n9; *The Red Record*, 129
Whipper, Frances Anne. *See* Rollin, Frances Anne

Whipper, Leigh, 178
Whipper, William J. (1804–76), 30
Whipper, William J. (1834–1907): criticism of fusion politics by, 114–17; death of, 159; 1883 speech at Bethel Literary and Historical Society of, 1–3, 8, 77, 95; 1895 constitutional convention speech of, 126; influence on making of *Porgy*, 178; joining of Black Port Royal Experiment, 30, 33, 35; marriage to Frances Anne Rollin of, 1, 130–31; political activity during twentieth century of, 148; Reconstruction-era political career of, 46, 48–49, 51–52, 58, 76, 83, 149, 154
White, Walter, 175
Williams, George Washington, 94
Wilmington, NC, 11, 128
Wilson, Joseph T., 94
Wilson, Woodrow, 157
Within Our Gates (Micheaux), 173
Woman's American Baptist Home Mission Society, 150
Woodson, Carter G., 14, 171, 173–74, 176
Woofter, Thomas Jackson, Jr., 169, 170; *Black Yeomanry*, 169, 170–71
Work, Monroe, 152, 173–74
World War I, 158, 163, 164–65
Wright, Elizabeth, 150
Wright, Jonathan Japer, 30–31, 33, 35–38, 45, 47–48, 52, 83
Wright, Richard, 185

Yemassee Junction, 148
York County, 59, 183
Young Men's Christian Association (YMCA), 165, 172–73

www.ingramcontent.com/pod-product-compliance
Lightning Source LLC
Chambersburg PA
CBHW030537230426
43665CB00010B/924